William Hope Hodgson and the Rise of the Weird

Perspectives on Fantasy

Series Editors
Brian Attebery (Idaho State University, USA)
Dimitra Fimi (University of Glasgow, UK)
Matthew Sangster (University of Glasgow, UK)

The first academic series with an exclusive critical focus on Fantasy, *Perspectives on Fantasy* publishes cutting-edge research on literature and culture that brings sophisticated discussion to a broad community of debate, including scholars, students, and non-specialists.

Inspired by Fantasy's deep cultural roots, powerful aesthetic potential, and reach across a broad range of media—from literature, film and television to art, animation and gaming—*Perspectives on Fantasy* provides a forum for theorising and historicising Fantasy via rigorous and original critical and theoretical approaches. Works in the series will cover major creators, significant works, key modes and forms, histories and traditions, the genre's particular affordances, and the ways in which Fantasy's resources have been drawn on, expanded, and reconfigured by authors, readers, viewers, directors, designers, players, and artists. With a deliberately broad scope, the series aims to publish dynamic studies that embrace Fantasy as a global, diverse, and inclusive phenomenon while also addressing oversights and exclusions. Along with canonical Anglophone authors and texts, the series will provide a space to address Fantasy creators and works rooted in African, Asian, South American, Middle Eastern, and indigenous cultures, as well as translations and transnational mediations.

The series will be alive to Fantasy's flourishing fan cultures, studying how audiences engage critically and affectively and considering the ease with which participants in Fantasy communities move from being readers and watchers to players, writers, and artists.

Editorial Board Members
Catherine Butler (Cardiff University, UK)
Pawel Frelik, (University of Warsaw, Poland)
Rachel Haywood Ferreira (Iowa State University, USA)
Robert Maslen (University of Glasgow, UK)
Ebony Elizabeth Thomas (University of Pennsylvania, USA)
Anna Vaninskaya (University of Edinburgh, UK)
Rhys Williams (University of Glasgow, UK)
Helen Young (Deakin University, Australia)

Titles in this Series

Queering Faith in Fantasy Literature: Fantastic Incarnations and the Deconstruction of Theology, Taylor Driggers
Imagining the Celtic Past in Modern Fantasy edited by Dimitra Fimi and Alistair J. P. Sims

Forthcoming Titles

Mapping Middle Earth: Environmental and Political Narratives in J. R. R. Tolkien's Cartographies, Anahit Behrooz
Justice and the Power of Wonder in 21st-Century Fairy Tales, Cristina Bacchilega and Pauline Greenhill
Femslash Fanfiction: Analysing Queer Time in Swan Queen Fan Narratives, Alice Kelly
Reading Tolkien in Chinese: Religion, Fantasy and Translation, Eric Reinders

William Hope Hodgson and the Rise of the Weird

Possibilities of the Dark

Timothy S. Murphy

BLOOMSBURY ACADEMIC
LONDON • NEW YORK • OXFORD • NEW DELHI • SYDNEY

BLOOMSBURY ACADEMIC
Bloomsbury Publishing Plc
50 Bedford Square, London, WC1B 3DP, UK
1385 Broadway, New York, NY 10018, USA
29 Earlsfort Terrace, Dublin 2, Ireland

BLOOMSBURY, BLOOMSBURY ACADEMIC and the Diana logo
are trademarks of Bloomsbury Publishing Plc

First published in Great Britain 2023
Paperback edition published 2025

Copyright © Timothy S. Murphy, 2023

Timothy S. Murphy has asserted his right under the Copyright,
Designs and Patents Act, 1988, to be identified as Author of this work.

For legal purposes the Acknowledgments on p. xii constitute
an extension of this copyright page.

Series design by Rebecca Heselton
Cover illustration: Rebecca Heselton

All rights reserved. No part of this publication may be reproduced or transmitted
in any form or by any means, electronic or mechanical, including photocopying,
recording, or any information storage or retrieval system, without prior permission
in writing from the publishers.

Bloomsbury Publishing Plc does not have any control over, or responsibility for,
any third-party websites referred to or in this book. All internet addresses given in
this book were correct at the time of going to press. The author and publisher regret
any inconvenience caused if addresses have changed or sites have ceased to exist,
but can accept no responsibility for any such changes.

A catalogue record for this book is available from the British Library.

Library of Congress Cataloging-in-Publication Data
Names: Murphy, Timothy S., 1964-, author.
Title: William Hope Hodgson and the rise of the weird: possibilities of
the dark / Timothy S. Murphy.
Description: London ; New York : Bloomsbury Academic, 2023. |
Series: Perspectives on fantasy | Includes bibliographical references and index.
Identifiers: LCCN 2022055798 (print) | LCCN 2022055799 (ebook) |
ISBN 9781350365698 (hardback) | ISBN 9781350365735 (paperback) |
ISBN 9781350365704 (pdf) | ISBN 9781350365711 (epub)
Subjects: LCSH: Hodgson, William Hope, 1877–1918–Criticism and
interpretation. | LCGFT: Literary criticism.
Classification: LCC PR6015.O253 Z77 2023 (print) | LCC PR6015.O253 (ebook) |
DDC 823/.912–dc23/eng/20221219
LC record available at https://lccn.loc.gov/2022055798
LC ebook record available at https://lccn.loc.gov/2022055799

ISBN:	HB:	978-1-3503-6569-8
	PB:	978-1-3503-6573-5
	ePDF:	978-1-3503-6570-4
	eBook:	978-1-3503-6571-1

Series: Perspectives on Fantasy

Typeset by Integra Software Services Pvt. Ltd.

To find out more about our authors and books visit www.bloomsbury.com
and sign up for our newsletters.

To friends lost

They leaned over the port rail and held their lamps out into the mist and unknown darkness beyond the ship's side. I remember how the lamps made just two yellow glares in the mist, ineffectual, yet serving somehow to make extraordinarily plain the vastitude of the night and the possibilities of the dark.
  William Hope Hodgson, "The Thing in the Weeds" (1912)

Contents

Acknowledgments	xii
List of Abbreviations	xiii
Preface: Weird before the Weird	xiv
Introduction: Decognition and the Labor of the Weird	1
Decognitive Estrangement	3
Weird Materialisms	18
Part One Hope in Space and Time	
1 The Larger English	35
2 Spoken to My Own Brother	51
3 Teach Him to Know a Man	64
Part Two Hope Out of Place	
4 The Sea Is All the God There Is	89
5 A Cemetery of Lost Ships and Wrack and Forgotten Things	96
6 Familiar Land of Strangeness	110
Part Three Hope Out of Time	
7 The Time That Is Left Us	129
8 That Song Past Human Tongue to Sing	144
9 Beautiful Things Hid in the Abyss of the Years	157
Envoi: Hope's Legacy	170
References	181
Index	189

Acknowledgments

Sections of the Introduction and Chapter One originally appeared as "Labor of the Weird: William Hope Hodgson's Fantastic Materialism" in *Science Fiction Studies* 138, vol. 46, part 2 (July 2019), and sections of Chapters Seven and Nine originally appeared as "It Might Have Been a Million Years Later: Abyssal Time in William Hope Hodgson's Weird Fiction" in *Studies in the Fantastic* 9 (summer/fall 2020), a special issue on Weird Temporalities. Thanks to these journals and their editors for permission to include revisions of these articles in the present work, and thanks also to the referees for their helpful comments and suggestions.

Mark Payne, Cody Jones, and the 2019–20 participants in the University of Chicago Speculative Fiction/Nonhuman Theory Workshop graciously let me try out some ideas on them, as did many colleagues at the International Conferences on the Fantastic in the Arts and the Science Fiction Research Association conferences since 2016. Their engagement encouraged me to complete this project despite the discouragements of the pandemic and global politics. I'm grateful to Emily Alder, whom I've never met, for her pioneering scholarship on Hodgson's cultural milieu. Although this project wasn't inspired by China Miéville's passionate advocacy of Hodgson (I've been a Hodgson fan since I first discovered the Sphere paperback reissues of his novels forty years ago), his description of Hodgson's "nihilist humanism" crystalized the interpretive framework that allowed me to complete it, so I owe him a debt as well.

Linda Austin, Jeff Menne, Graig Uhlin, Martin Wallen, and Lindsay Wilhelm, friends and colleagues at Oklahoma State, provided me with references, sage counsel, and beverage opportunities, even when pandemic lockdowns limited our contacts. My advisor on all things fantastika, Ben Robertson, has heard more rehearsals of this project than anyone else, but he's also given me more useful advice than anyone else; he's the ideal reader I imagined for this book. My friend Dan Cottom, who passed away as I was finishing this project, will always be the model teacher, scholar, and colleague I strive to emulate, and his reaction to this book is the one I will miss the most.

My wife Julie and our little ones—Daisy, Emma, Sylvie, and Charlotte—made my hermitage comfortable most of the time, and coaxed me out of it the rest of the time.

Abbreviations

Hodgson's writings are cited from the following sources:

BGC   *The Boats of the "Glen Carrig"* (1907). London: Holden & Hardingham, 1920.

CF 1–5   *The Collected Fiction of William Hope Hodgson*, volumes 1 to 5. Volumes 1 to 4 edited by Jeremy Lassen; volume 5 edited by Douglas A. Anderson. San Francisco: Night Shade Books, 2003–9. Reprinted by special arrangement with Skyhorse Publishing.

GP   *The Ghost Pirates*. London: Stanley Paul & Co., 1909.

HB   *The House on the Borderland*. London: Chapman & Hall, 1908.

LP   *The Lost Poetry of William Hope Hodgson*. Edited by Jane Frank. Hornsea, East Yorkshire: Tartarus Press, 2005.

NL   *The Night Land: A Love Tale*. London: Eveleigh Nash, 1912.

U   *The Uncollected William Hope Hodgson* volume 1, *Non-Fiction*. Edited by Sam Gafford. Bristol, RI: Hobgoblin Press, 1995.

VO   *The Voice of the Ocean*. London: Selwyn & Blount, 1921.

WS   *The Wandering Soul: Glimpses of a Life—A Compendium of Rare and Unpublished Works by William Hope Hodgson*. Edited by Jane Frank. Hornsea, East Yorkshire: Tartarus Press, 2005.

Biographical information is cited from the following sources:

E   R. Alain Everts, *William Hope Hodgson, Night Pirate* vol.2: *Some Facts in the Case of William Hope Hodgson, Master of Phantasy* (Toronto: Soft Books, 1987).

M1   Sam Moskowitz, "William Hope Hodgson" (biographical sketch) in Moskowitz, ed., *Out of the Storm: Uncollected Fantasies* by William Hope Hodgson (West Kingston, RI: Donald M. Grant, 1975), 9–117.

M2   Sam Moskowitz, "The Posthumous Acceptance of William Hope Hodgson 1918–1943" in Moskowitz, ed., *The Haunted "Pampero": Uncollected Fantasies and Mysteries* by William Hope Hodgson (Hampton Falls, NH: Donald M. Grant, 1991), 11–76.

Preface: Weird before the Weird

William Hope Hodgson, author of *The House on the Borderland* (1908) and *The Night Land* (1912), is an anomaly who presents a challenge to both literary and intellectual history. A self-educated former sailor, photographer, and bodybuilder, he somehow invents new forms and themes for fantastic narration that explicitly and implicitly respond to the new scientific and philosophical conceptions of the late nineteenth and early twentieth centuries, anticipating the later development of science fiction, horror, fantasy, and especially weird fiction. Writers as antithetical in their views as the Decadent aesthete Clark Ashton Smith and the Christian allegorist C.S. Lewis laud his achievements, the former praising his "realism of the unreal" (Berrutti, Joshi, and Gafford 2014: 36) while the latter classes "the unforgettable sombre splendour of the images [his work] presents" alongside the achievements of Thomas Malory, Samuel Taylor Coleridge, and J.R.R. Tolkien (Lewis 1966: 71). Critically praised but not popular with contemporaneous readers, his works went out of print and his reputation went into eclipse following his early death on the front lines in the First World War, and neither experienced a revival for a generation. Since no critical or autobiographical reflections and only a handful of letters and essays by him survive, anyone who seeks to contextualize, understand, and evaluate his work faces a daunting task. The only way to proceed is through close reading, historicization, and comparison with other writers, which necessarily leads to conclusions based largely on extrapolation and speculation. Readers should be aware that this is what follows, after the brief detour of this preface.

Although today Hodgson is considered an innovator of weird fiction, he almost certainly did not think of himself that way. The simplest and most obvious reason for this is the fact that, as Emily Alder notes, the phrases "weird tale" and "weird story" were already circulating through the British literary world of the 1880s as descriptors for works by Mary Elizabeth Braddon, Charlotte Riddell, E.T.A. Hoffman, Sheridan Le Fanu, and Stuart Cumberland, among others, but they were "being used to describe a diverse range of very different texts—ghost stories like those of Riddell, sensation mysteries like Braddon's novel, uncanny horror tales like Hoffman's 'Der Sandmann,' occult romances like [Cumberland's] *A Fatal Affinity*" (Alder 2020: 9)—that did not constitute a recognizably unified proto-genre. Conversely, the writers credited with inventing the particular combination of fantastic traits that we today call the weird, such as Robert W. Chambers, Arthur Machen, and M.P. Shiel, did not adopt or privilege the term in their own work. At the same time, pastiche medieval romances such as George Macdonald's *Phantastes* (1858) and William Morris's *The Well at the World's End* (1896) were laying the foundations for what would later be labelled epic fantasy, while the scientific romances of Jules Verne, who began to produce his immensely popular *Voyages Extraordinaires* in the 1860s, and H.G. Wells, who published *The Time Machine* in 1895, were establishing the generic conventions for what would later become science fiction. Meanwhile, the Gothic tale was being updated for a new era of horror by writers such as Bram Stoker, Robert Louis Stevenson, and M.R. James. While Hodgson was no doubt attracted by the seemingly unlimited possibilities opened up for non-realist writers at the end of the nineteenth and the start of the twentieth century, there is no evidence that he set out to privilege any of these coalescing but still fuzzy sets, or to restrict himself to any emerging set of proto-generic constraints.

My decision to label Hodgson a weird writer is a retrospective, a posteriori construction based upon present usage of the term "weird fiction," itself derived from the legendary pulp magazine *Weird Tales*, which began publication in 1923 and in which many of the genre's acknowledged innovators such as H.P. Lovecraft, Clark Ashton Smith, Robert E. Howard, Catherine L. Moore, and Robert Bloch appeared during the 1920s, 1930s, and 1940s. *Weird Tales,* which ceased publication in 1954, carried the subtitle "The Unique Magazine," but its stated editorial policy did not define the genre of storytelling it sought to showcase beyond the claim to emphasize fiction that was *sui generis*. Lovecraft would ultimately provide the most influential definition for a genre that had essentially emerged from the circle of his correspondents, a definition that was initially addressed to and ultimately disseminated by them as well. I will analyze Lovecraft's definition, and its limits, in detail in the Introduction; for now, I will simply quote the best-known capsule definition from his writings, which appears in the introduction to his influential essay *Supernatural Horror in Literature* (1927–35):

> The true weird tale has something more than secret murder, bloody bones, or a sheeted form clanking chains according to rule. A certain atmosphere of breathless and unexplainable dread of outer, unknown forces must be present; and there must be a hint, expressed with a seriousness and portentousness becoming its subject, of that most terrible conception of the human brain—a malign and particular suspension or defeat of those fixed laws of Nature which are our only safeguard against the assaults of chaos and the daemons of unplumbed space.
> (Lovecraft 2000: 22–3)

More concisely, weird fiction is the *"non-supernatural cosmic art"* that Lovecraft demanded in a 1931 letter to his protégé Frank Belknap Long (Lovecraft 1971: 296). In the same sense that Alfred North Whitehead called the history of Western philosophy "a series of footnotes to Plato" (Whitehead 1978: 39), we can assert that virtually every subsequent attempt to define the weird has been little more than a footnote to these passages from Lovecraft.

The figures whom Lovecraft identified in his letters and essays, especially *Supernatural Horror in Literature*, as the primary models for his own fictional practice are Edgar Allan Poe, Ambrose Bierce, Arthur Machen, M.R. James, Walter de la Mare, M.P. Shiel, Algernon Blackwood, and Lord Dunsany; at one point or another in *Supernatural Horror*, each is lauded as a major contributor to the development of a literature of "cosmic fear." As Lovecraft refined and extended his conception of the weird through his own storytelling, however, he came to find most of these predecessors lacking. By late 1930, the list had been whittled down considerably, as Lovecraft admitted to Clark Ashton Smith: "In literature we can easily see the cosmic quality in Poe, Maturin, Dunsany, de la Mare, & Blackwood, but I profoundly suspect the cosmicism of Bierce, James, & even Machen. It is not every macabre writer who feels poignantly & almost intolerably the pressure of cryptic & unbounded outer space" (Lovecraft and Smith 2017: 248). Near the end of his life, in late 1936, his original pantheon of precursors had dwindled almost to nothing, as he complained in a letter to Fritz Leiber: "What I miss in Machen, James, Dunsany, de la Mare, Shiel, & even Blackwood & Poe, is a sense of the *cosmic*. Dunsany—though he seldom adopts the darker & more serious approach—is the most cosmic of them all, but he gets only a little way" (Lovecraft 2017: 266). Here Lovecraft's formerly extensive list has shrunk to a single figure, his disappointment in his former idols is tangible, and this perhaps helps to explain the surprise and enthusiasm with which he responded to his first reading of Hodgson's fiction at around the same period.

In 1934 Lovecraft received a package of Hodgson's books from his correspondent H.C. Koenig as part of a round-robin reading group that also included Smith, Moore, and Leiber. As he explained to Smith soon after,

> I duly received the Hodgson books—& when I came to read them I was veritably knocked cold! Aedopol, what splendid stuff! Suggestions of unknown presences & conditions …. sieges by hellish things from the abyss …..& the magnificently expansive cosmic vistas in "The House on the Borderland"! This bird knows how to evoke atmosphere of the most authentic sort—just what to say & what not to say. […] This stuff certainly requires major mention in my history of weird literature. Curious I didn't ever strike Hodgson before—but it's a pleasure to discover totally new things late in life.
>
> (Lovecraft and Smith 2017: 565–6)

Lovecraft's pleasure, slightly tempered by the disappointment Hodgson's "clumsy [, …] grotesque and absurd" attempts at archaic diction caused him, took him so much by surprise that he repeats his assessment in letters to several other correspondents, including Moore, Leiber, Bloch, and August Derleth. Only three weeks later he confesses, "Well—as you see, I surely have become a premier Hodgson fan! […] All told, I believe that nobody but Blackwood can equal or surpass him in capturing the exact shades of the cosmic horror mood in all their actual details" (Lovecraft and Smith 2017: 573). The ringing endorsement of Hodgson that Lovecraft inserted into the final version of his "history of weird literature," *Supernatural Horror in Literature*, is unquestionably the single most important cause of the former's revival.

Lovecraft's reaction to the belated discovery of Hodgson bears a perhaps surprising resemblance to Friedrich Nietzsche's reaction to his own discovery of Spinoza half a century earlier: "I am amazed, really delighted! I have a precursor, and *what* a precursor! I hardly knew Spinoza: what brought me to him now was the guidance of instinct … *In summa*: my solitariness which, as on very high mountains, has often, often made me gasp for breath and lose blood, is now at least a solitude for two. Strange!" (Nietzsche 1969: 177). In each case, a writer who considered himself intellectually isolated and artistically unappreciated in his lifetime as a consequence of his unsettling ideas takes solace from the discovery of a precursor who persevered despite comparable experiences of solitude and incomprehension. Our access to these moments of recognition in personal letters highlights another aspect of Hodgson's anomalous situation: whereas both Lovecraft and Nietzsche were the central nodes in large networks of sympathetic correspondents that constituted genuine epistolary communities, Hodgson seems to have been much more thoroughly isolated. Although he joined the British Society of Authors as soon as his first writings began to appear in periodicals, and devotedly followed the Society's monthly magazine *The Author* (M1: 28, 37–8) which published several of his letters and short essays, he does not seem to have become a member of any literary circles, notable or otherwise. This is all the more remarkable in light of the extent to which the other major proponents of weird fiction developed the field through communal effort. The extent and significance of the Lovecraft Circle in this regard have already been noted, but a similar pattern holds for most of their precursors as well. Among the first British generation of weird writers, Arthur Machen and M.P. Shiel shared an awkward and intermittent friendship, memorialized by the latter in his most famous work, *The Purple Cloud* (1901), when he makes Machen's Cornwall cottage the site where Shiel's protagonist Adam Jeffson begins to write his memoir of humanity's extinction (Shiel 2012: xvii–xix, 116–17). Algernon Blackwood, born into a prosperous but narrow-minded Victorian family against which he rebelled, could always fall back on its wealth and social connections when his forays into the Hermetic Order of the Golden Dawn (of which Machen was already a member) became onerous, and in fact lived long enough to become a radio celebrity as well as a popular writer of horror fiction. The importance of such friendships among like-minded authors reveals weird fiction's reliance upon community for its development, particularly during its earliest and least popular periods.

In the twenty-first century, of course, weird fiction not only is popular but makes money, at least if book jackets are to be believed. For example, China Miéville's and Jeff VanderMeer's books are regularly emblazoned with the marketing slogan "*New York Times* Bestselling Author." Their work also wins lots of awards, which often lead to increased sales: between them they have eleven Locus awards, four World Fantasy Awards, three British Fantasy Awards, three Arthur C. Clarke Awards, two British Science Fiction Awards, one Nebula Award, one Hugo Award, and one Shirley Jackson Award. Nineteenth- and early twentieth-century weird fiction, on the other hand, won no awards—there were no specialist awards to win, and the very few mainstream ones were totally out of reach[1]—and likewise it made very little money for its creators. Indeed, it was a literature of metaphysical excess that emerged from experiences of material poverty. Today, the success of HBO's series *Lovecraft Country* has brought the racial politics of "Old Weird" fiction into the broader discussion of race, and especially anti-Black racism, currently taking place in the United States. To a lesser degree, it has also posed questions about misogyny and gender inequality in the genre's history. Both these issues have been acknowledged and engaged in recent scholarship on weird fiction as well. Despite this attention to hierarchy and exclusion at the origin of the

---

[1] The closest any Old Weird writer seems to have come to a literary award is Lovecraft's inclusion in several lists of best short stories compiled by Edward J. O'Brien and by the O. Henry Prize committee during the late 1920s (Joshi 2010: 693–4).

weird, however, critics have shown much less interest in the correlation between its writers' class positions and the historical development of weird fiction. Writing is, after all, a form of labor, most often an unwaged form, and almost all the innovators of weird fiction experienced economic distress during youth or adolescence, were denied access to higher education, and spent much or even all of their active writing careers in poverty.

This correlation first emerges in the case of the weird's most influential precursor, Edgar Allan Poe, who was effectively orphaned in infancy and taken in by a wealthy foster family. Poe later quarreled with his foster father over gambling debts and was disowned shortly after his twenty-first birthday; as one of the first American writers to attempt to live by writing alone during an era in which copyrights were not enforced, he spent the remaining twenty years of his life drifting from one unreliable and underpaid editorial job to another. In an unsigned essay, "Some Secrets of the Magazine Prison-House," published in 1845, he addressed the market constraints that entrapped him:

> The want of an International Copy-Right Law, by rendering it nearly impossible to obtain anything from the booksellers in the way of remuneration for literary labor, has had the effect of forcing many of our very best writers into the service of the Magazines and Reviews, which with a pertinacity that does them credit, keep up in a certain or uncertain degree the good old saying, that even in the thankless field of Letters the laborer is worthy of his hire ... hence we have Magazine publishers ... who, under certain conditions of good conduct, occasional puffs, and decent subserviency at all times, make it a point of conscience to encourage the poor devil author with a dollar or two, more or less as he behaves himself properly and abstains from the indecent habit of turning up his nose.
>
> (Poe 1984b: 1036–7)

The situation herein described would remain the situation of most weird writers, including Hodgson, for the next century or more, even after international copyrights began to be enforced first by the Berne Convention (1886) and later by the Buenos Aires Convention (1910). Hodgson's shrewd practice of publishing short pamphlet versions of his novels in the United States in order to gain some degree of international copyright protection indicates he was well aware of this danger (see Berruti, Joshi, and Gafford 2014: 209–12).

The correlation between weird fiction and poverty applies equally well to the British first generation and the American second generation of weird writers who followed in Poe's wake. Like Arthur Machen's, Hodgson's father was a provincial minister of little means. Hodgson was born in Essex in 1877 to the Anglican Rev. Samuel Hodgson and his wife Lissie Brown Hodgson, but Samuel's outspoken "differences with the church ... caused him to be shifted from place to place serving 11 parishes in 21 years ... As a result, the family frequently lived on the thin edge of poverty" (M1: 15). After Samuel's death in 1892, "the rest of the still-sizable family ... had to throw themselves [on] the mercy of a church in which Samuel Hodgson had not been too popular .... The family subsisted on hand-outs and hand-me-downs from co-religionists until the older sons were able to contribute more substantially.

The mother received small sums from the church for bringing aid to the 'poor'" (M1: 16–17). Hope, as his family and friends called him, was apprenticed to the merchant navy in 1891, shortly before his fourteenth birthday, and the only formal schooling he had after that was the two-year training course for a mate's certificate that he took in 1895–7. After leaving the merchant navy for good in 1899, he tried several careers, including "physical culture" (bodybuilding or personal training), photography, and public lecturing, without conspicuous success before the acceptance of the story "The Goddess of Death" for publication in *Royal Magazine* in 1904 drew him into the writer's trade. Fittingly for one used to manual labor, Hodgson treated writing as a job like any other, keeping meticulous records of his story submissions, sales, and rejections, carefully husbanding publication rights, and writing essays aimed at opening up new markets for creative writers, for example, as epitaph writers for tombstones ("The Poet vs. the Stonemason," published in *The Author* in 1906 [WS: 159–61]). Although his novels were praised by reviewers, they failed to find a paying audience during his lifetime; as he wrote his brother Frank in 1914, "I've not made one single penny piece out of my last books (*The Night Land* and *Carnacki the Ghost Finder*) – just a lot of quite genuine admiration; but no cash at all, &, ye ken, admiration's no great filler of an empty tummy!" (M1: 111). When he was blown to bits at the battle of Ypres in April 1918, he was no closer to financial success than he had been when his first story appeared fourteen years earlier.[2]

The pervasive poverty, informal education, and limited publication opportunities faced by writers of the weird like Hodgson stand in sharp contrast to the bourgeois origins, university educations, and resulting economic security of the writers associated with nascent fantasy (George Macdonald, William Morris, Lord Dunsany, Hope Mirrlees, J.R.R. Tolkien, C.S. Lewis) and nascent science fiction (Jules Verne, Sir Arthur Conan Doyle, H.G. Wells, Olaf Stapledon) who were their contemporaries. From a critical sociological perspective informed by Pierre Bourdieu's conception of the space of cultural practices (Bourdieu 1984: chapters 2 to 6), we might say that the writers who founded fantasy and science fiction as genres succeeded in reproducing their own bourgeois familial dispositions in a cultural field that they themselves helped to expand, gaining thereby both a high degree of symbolic capital from their artistic and intellectual activities and life-long sources of financial support in the form of royalties (though Morris and Stapledon, both committed socialists, were conflicted by this). They positioned themselves within the dominated fraction of the dominant class. The weird writers, on the other hand, who were for the most part children of professional bourgeois ideologists or the petit bourgeoisie rather than of the owners of the means of production, rejected their own familial dispositions but then failed either to find new positions of similar financial security or to resituate themselves at the artistic pole of symbolic capital. They effectively fall into the dominated fraction of the dominated class, despite the intellectuality of their labor.

More importantly, the weird writers' doubly subordinate class positions did not necessarily produce similar forms of class consciousness in them: Machen became

---

[2] Similar circumstances of poverty and interrupted formal education also mark the careers of Machen, Shiel, Lovecraft, Clark Ashton Smith, and Robert E. Howard.

an anti-materialist, anti-scientific mystic focused on the spiritual world, as did Blackwood, while Shiel flirted briefly with Bolshevism before retiring to a country cottage purchased for him by his longsuffering wife; Lovecraft and Smith coped with poverty through a conscious renunciation of material wealth that was ascetic as well as aesthetic. Although Lovecraft belatedly embraced New Deal social democracy and the critique of classical market liberalism, only Howard and Hodgson consciously considered themselves members of what a Marxist might call classes engaged in struggle. In a paradigm case of ideological mystification, however, Howard saw the fundamental human historical conflict as one that pitted the decadent hierarchies of urban civilization against the egalitarian vigor of frontier barbarism, a notion that underpins his most successful fantastic fiction and which he defended at length in his correspondence with Lovecraft. Only Hodgson's view of writing as one form of labor among others, along with his sense of solidarity with common sailors and other exploited workers as expressed in his essays[3] and a few poems,[4] corresponds to any meaningful degree with the conventional definition of working-class consciousness. Like the other weird writers, Hodgson expressed through his fiction a fundamental distrust of liberal capitalism's market-based value system, scientific division of labor, and institutional bureaucracy, even though he did not develop a fully coherent critical analysis of it or embrace a viable political alternative to it.

But this is to characterize the ideas of Hodgson and his compatriots negatively, in conformity with theories of radical subjectivity and revolutionary organization that view the weird's defining claims as mere metaphysics, or in other words as ideology. A more affirmative—and thereby polemical—characterization might suggest that at least some of these versions of weirdness, with their epistemological and ontological assumptions regarding the unknowable excess of the real over any representation or attempt to instrumentalize it, constitute a displaced or alternative class consciousness, especially insofar as each version generates its own specific phenomenology of weird experience. At the most immediate level, this simply means that the economic insecurity and existential inconsequentiality produced in the literary marketplace by the course of capitalist development give rise, in cases like Hodgson's, to conceptions of cosmic inconsequentiality and/or ontological insecurity, but also, correlatively, that the metaphysical inflation of the unknown and the inversion of anthropocentrism that accompany such insecurity can affirmatively express the search for non-capitalist terms for valorizing both writing and life itself. In the autonomist tradition of Marxism, this process is called self-valorization, while Nietzsche advocated something similar with his notion of the nonmoral will to power, and the forms of both are multiple. In the case of the Old Weird under discussion here, these forms range from the visionary expectancy of transcendent revelation we find in Machen and Blackwood to Smith's macabre ironies combining desire with decomposition,

---

[3] "Is the Merchantile Navy Worth Joining? Certainly Not" (originally published in *The Grand Magazine*, 1905), "The Trade in Sea Apprentices" (originally published in *Nautical Magazine*, 1906), and "The Peril of the Mine" (originally published in *Westminster Gazette*, 1910), all now in WS 155–8, 163–76.

[4] "Pillars of the Empire" and "Gun Drill," posthumously published in WS 217–21.

and from Lovecraft's contemplative materialism that topples the pretensions of reason to Howard's exuberantly athletic atheology and, most importantly for this study, Hodgson's nihilist humanism of the resistant laboring body.

***

The second son of the Reverend Samuel Hodgson and Lissie Brown Hodgson, William Hope Hodgson was named for Samuel's father William, a tailor whose business success allowed him to become a gentleman and who outlived his argumentative and improvident son by eight years. Grandfather William's importance to the family may have been one consideration that led them to address his namesake as "Hope," though R. Alain Everts notes that several of the other Hodgson children were also addressed by their middle names (E: 1–2). In any case, this practice would later be taken up by the younger man's friends (Gafford 2013a: 15) and even by his wife Bessie Farnsworth Hodgson (M2: 11), a fact that is confirmed by a few surviving inscribed copies of his books that are signed "Hope" (WS: 42–3). We have no way of knowing for certain whether the verbal paradox that is apparent to us—a man named Hope who is best known for purveying cosmic fear—was equally apparent to his contemporaries. We do know that Hodgson's major works are suffused as much by hope as by fear. *The Boats of the "Glen Carrig"* (1907) begins not with the titular shipwreck, but rather at the precise moment when the "beginning of hope within our hearts" is kindled by the survivors' first sighting of the Land of Lonesomeness (Boats of the Glen Carrig: 11). *The House on the Borderland* (1908) pivots around the Recluse's refusal to leave his besieged house because only there is it possible for him to meet again his long-lost beloved, whom he seeks "in a very agony of remembrance, of terror, and of hope" (HB: 166). Most significant in this regard is *The Night Land* (1912), the main narrative of which begins in chapter two, "The Last Redoubt," when the narrator, formerly despairing over the death of his wife Mirdath, writes that "of late a wondrous hope has grown in me, in that I have, at night in my sleep, waked into the future of this world, and seen strange things and utter marvels, and known once more the gladness of life" (NL: 33). In two of Hodgson's novels—*The House on the Borderland* and *The Ghost Pirates* (1909)—hope is brutally disappointed, but in the other two—*The Boats of the "Glen Carrig"* and *The Night Land*—hope is fulfilled, though only after long, intense physical and mental struggle.

In several important ways, the link between hope and fear that Hodgson's fiction continually enacts, like the balance he establishes between hope fulfilled and hope disappointed, looks forward to Ernst Bloch's philosophy of hope, which is expressed most extensively in his encyclopedic, three-volume work *The Principle of Hope* (1959) and most succinctly in his inaugural address at the University of Tübingen, "Can Hope Be Disappointed?" (1961). In the introduction to the former, Bloch asserts that "Expectation, hope, intention towards possibility that has still not become: this is not only a basic feature of human consciousness, but, concretely corrected and grasped, a basic determination within objective reality as a whole," and on that basis he concludes that "*Philosophy will have conscience of tomorrow, commitment to the future, knowledge of hope, or it will have no more knowledge*" (Bloch 1959: 7). But this does not mean that such hope will necessarily be fulfilled; on the contrary, in the Tübingen address Bloch argues that "hope must be unconditionally disappointable," for two reasons. First, "because it is open in a forward direction, in a future-oriented direction; it does not address itself to that which already exists," which means that it is "committed to change rather than repetition, and what is more, incorporates the element of chance, without which there can be nothing new. Through this portion of chance … openness is at the same time also *kept open*." Second, because hope "can never be mediated by solid facts," which are "merely subjectively reified moments or objectively reified stoppages within a historical course of events" that is itself "both historical and processual, precisely because nothing has been settled yet as an irrevocable fact, completed in its becoming." The conclusion to his argument is worth quoting in full as a prelude to this study of Hodgson:

> Consequently, not only hope's affect (with its pendant, fear) but, even more so, hope's methodology (with its pendant, memory) dwells in the region of the not-yet, a place where entrance and, above all, final content are marked by an enduring indeterminacy. In other words, referring directly to disappointability: hope holds *eo ipso* the condition of defeat precariously within itself: it is not confidence. It stands too close to the indeterminacy of the historical process, of the world-process that, indeed, has not yet been defeated, but likewise has not yet won.
> (Bloch 1961: 341)

Fredric Jameson interprets this essential indeterminacy to mean that, for Bloch, "hope is *always* thwarted, the future is always something *other* than what we sought to find there, something ontologically excessive and necessarily unexpected." In this process, "the negative is reabsorbed back into the positive, not as facile consolation, but as … an enlargement of our anticipations to include and find satisfaction in their own negations as well" (Jameson 1971: 137). Only such an enlargement of our anticipations can serve as an effective basis for the paradoxical nihilist humanism that is expressed in Hodgson's major fictions as an ongoing engagement with what he calls the "possibilities of the dark" (CF 1: 193).

For hope is the key that most readily unlocks the apparent contradiction between humanism and nihilism that marks Hodgson's best work. If hope is, as Bloch states, both a "basic feature of human consciousness" and a "basic determination within objective reality," then it follows that hope so conceived has a solid ontological status as a material force comparable to matter or energy, and therefore must somehow be conserved just as energy is conserved, despite being subject to phase transitions and other transformations that can alter its characteristics beyond recognition. Indeed, Bloch assures us that, "if hope could be annihilated, that is, if it could be literally *made nihilistic*, it would never have proved so intractable to those despots who represent its opposite" (Bloch 1961: 344). As such, hope serves as the mediating force between the affirmative, constructivist humanism based in labor that we find throughout Hodgson's writings on the one hand, and on the other, the disenchanted nihilism of ultimate meanings and ends that forms the inescapable cosmic context of all human striving. Bloch could just as well be referring to Hope (Hodgson) as to hope (the principle) when he writes, "Above all, hope knows—by its own definition, so to speak—not only that danger implies salvation, but that wherever salvation exists, danger increases. Hope knows, too, that defeat pervades the world as a function of nothingness; and that futility is latent in objective-real possibility, which carries both redemption and perdition, unreconciled, within itself" (Bloch 1961: 345). Hope is what enables humanism to both acknowledge and survive, though certainly not overcome, the nothingness that pervades the world.

Once we recognize this fundamental convergence of Hodgson's and Bloch's approaches to hope, we can identify further elements of similarity among the details of their conceptions. Perhaps the simplest of these is the athletic development of the body, which Hodgson first embraced while working as a sailor to defend himself against shipboard abuse and later tried unsuccessfully to transform into a business opportunity with the School of Physical Culture he operated in Blackburn between 1899 and 1904 (E:7–12, M1 20–6)[5]. In his 1903 essay "Health from Scientific Exercise," which first appeared in *Cassell's Magazine* and is illustrated with demonstration photographs of Hodgson he himself took, he insists that "exercise, properly carried out, develops the whole frame, and imparts new life not to the body only, but to the brain itself" (WS: 65). Bloch's account, from *The Principle of Hope*, is more expansive along the same lines:

> Even athletic exercise remains wishful, hopeful. It does not merely seek to gain control over the body so that there is no fat on it and every movement is pleasantly uninhibited. It also seeks to be able to do more, to be more with the body than this body seemed to promise at birth ... [to produce] a return to health which does not presuppose any illness at all, but is rather the verb, the action of health itself, a healing precisely without an illness.
>
> (1986: 452–3)

Thus bodybuilding or physical culture itself can be seen as a modality of hope, one that Bloch argues should help the human physique "shed the distortions and disfigurements which an alienating society based on the division of labour has inflicted on it" (1986: 453). Hodgson concurs, noting in a newspaper interview about his School of Physical Culture that, "If the weavers and other operatives of Lancashire would go in for a course of physical training they would not suffer nearly so much from the conditions they have to work under" ("Physical Culture: A Talk with an Expert," originally published in the *Blackburn Evening Telegraph*, 1901, now in WS: 57). His protagonists, whether explicitly described as students of physical culture or not, likewise gain much of their diegetic agency through their bodily empowerment, which includes not merely physical strength but also dexterity, endurance, and a range of acquired physical skills.

In Bloch's classification of sea-voyage narratives in search of an earthly paradise as examples of "geographical utopias" (1986: 746–94), he briefly discusses the "bad

---

[5] These dates are as uncertain as anything else we know about Hodgson's life: Everts claims that the School operated from 1901 to 1904, while Moskowitz asserts that it was in business from 1899 to 1901.

Atlantic" that blocked European exploration of the western hemisphere for centuries before Columbus, noting that "There were fields of seaweed west of the Azores in fact, Columbus noticed them, but for Plato, Aristotle, and Theophrastus the entire Atlantic became a sea of mud, governed by perpetual night" (1986: 757). While it is tempting to link these "fields of seaweed" and "sea of mud" with the muddy Land of Lonesomeness and the Sargasso Sea in *The Boats of the "Glen Carrig*," as well as Hodgson's other maritime settings, we must not lose sight of the fact that for Hodgson, the perils of the sea were most often obstacles to the mariner's safe return home or the reunion of lovers, and only rarely part of "*the cordon full of terrors [which] lies around Eden*" that Bloch saw in them (1986: 759). A more productive connection would proceed instead by utilizing Bloch's remarkable pre-Anthropocenic insight that

> With and through the changes made by human beings, the Pleistocene and Holocene epochs, and the Quaternary period of our planet can still be followed by the Quintenary period, with a better attained fund of what the earth, no geological antiquarium, still potentially contains. The earth as a whole, in its latency, is the *unfinished setting of a scene in a play which has by no means been written as yet in our previous history.*
>
> (1986: 791)

Like Bloch, Hodgson imagined unprecedented possibilities for the earth's future as a setting for dramatic action, though most are dark rather than utopian for the human species. As we will see in Part Two, Hodgson's attention to landscapes, seascapes, and other geographical spaces constitutes an intentional construction of space for narrative purposes, but not in the form of the utopian "wishful landscape" that Bloch traces through the history of European painting, opera, literature, and philosophy (1986: 794–885).

The limits of the two writers' convergence can perhaps be summed up by saying that while Hodgson's reliance on an unstable balance between hope and fear and between fulfilment and disappointment—which cannot be synthesized dialectically, as Bloch (as well as Jameson) insists they must be—clearly manifests a kind of utopian longing, his resistance to any sort of final or total(izing) overcoming or transcendence of fear, defeat, and suffering makes his work much more difficult to incorporate into the wider logic of rational utopia that Bloch theorizes and that Jameson, along with Darko Suvin and Carl Freedman, has identified as the root of science fiction. Although Jameson's gloss on Blochian negativity—that "horror and the black emotions are infinitely precious insofar as they also constitute forms of that elemental ontological astonishment which is our most concrete mode of awareness of the future latent in ourselves and in things" (Jameson 1971: 133)—illuminates the darkness of Hodgson's authorial practice equally well, we cannot say of him what Jameson writes at the end of his analysis of Bloch: his system, Jameson prophesizes,

> stands as a solution to problems of a universal culture and a universal hermeneutic which have not yet come into being. It lies before us, enigmatic and enormous,

like an aerolite fallen from space, covered with mysterious hieroglyphs that radiate a peculiar inner warmth and power, spells and the keys to spells, themselves patiently waiting for their own ultimate moment of decipherment.

(Jameson 1971: 159)

In Hodgson's work we are given no solutions, even future ones, and the signs we encounter yield meaning to no hermeneutic; instead, like his distant heir M. John Harrison, he leads us to, and leaves us with, "the mystery which preserves itself and which is seen to be more important than its solution" (Harrison 2003: 435).

More relevant to Hodgson are two modest aspects of hope that Bloch introduces early in his compendium of hope's manifestations. First, he notes that "The emotion of hope goes out of itself, makes people broad instead of confining them ... The work of this emotion requires people who throw themselves actively into what is becoming, to which they themselves belong" (Bloch 1986: 3). By this standard, Hodgson the sailor, bodybuilder, photographer, author, and soldier is undoubtedly a figure of hope, as are the formidably energetic protagonists of his fictions, even those whose hopes are thwarted just as their creator's were. Second, Bloch reminds us that

every great work of art, besides its manifest essence, is also carried towards a *latency of its coming side*, that is: towards the contents of a future which had not yet appeared in its time, in fact ultimately towards the contents of an as yet unknown final state. For this reason alone, great works of every age have something to say, and indeed something new that the previous age had not yet noticed in them.

(1986: 98)

Nietzsche expressed this notion of latency toward the unknown future more elegantly when he described his own writings as "untimely—that is to say, acting counter to our time and thereby acting on our time and, let us hope, for the benefit of a time to come" (Nietzsche 1983: 60). This latency or untimeliness is the power that allows Hodgson's fictions not merely to express ideas current in his lifetime, but to address the future in ways that continually astonish and provoke later readers, including us, despite his flaws, his limitations, and the constitutive darkness of the possibilities he presents. Such perennial untimeliness is perhaps the most important aspect of the anomaly that is William Hope Hodgson.

In a series of brief essays published in the magazine *The Author* in 1906, before his first novel appeared, Hodgson proposed that authors should adopt a simple visual sign, an icon or "totem whereby they might become distinguishable from others of the same name" by displaying their unique totems on the covers, spines, and title pages of their books, and he looked forward hopefully to selecting a totem of his own: "Yes, I intend to have one, though perhaps it is early times. Yet, I would have you to know that, like many people with the maternal instinct, I am 'on the way'" (U: 22–3). No evidence exists that he ever chose one, but what better totem could he have than a visual schema of hope, perhaps in the form of an outward opening door, a dark shadow silhouetted against the light from a space beyond that may hold threat as well as reward? After all, hope too is a possibility of the dark. In any case, as we proceed through this study, we must always keep in mind the fact that Hope is a verb and a noun, but also a force and a name.

***

Some readers may consider this study to have an idiosyncratic structure. It begins conventionally enough with an introduction, "Decognition and the Labor of the Weird," that provides a theoretical definition of weird fiction, and Hodgson's version of the weird in particular, as a (counter-) genre situated in the space between science fiction, fantasy, and horror, and as an aspect of the broader critique of scientific positivism, universalism, and anthropocentrism that marked the end of nineteenth-century certainties and the start of twentieth-century uncertainties. Weird fiction's primary aim is to identify the limits of human cognition and the techno-scientific mastery of nature that cognition grounds through a process of logical, affective, and embodied destructuring that I call decognition. As a corollary to this deflation of cognition, weird fiction calls into question all transcendent, universalizing moral orders and reveals their limitations as well. This profound metaphysical challenge, articulated from a liminal genre position, constitutes weird fiction's most significant contribution to emergent modernism and its sequels. Indeed, it allows us to situate weird fiction as one of modernism's shadows. Hodgson's fictions present the weird as a form of physical labor that both characters and readers must perform in the course of his narratives, an approach that contrasts sharply and productively with the contemplative, intellectualized emphasis of most other weird pioneers as a means of carrying out the weird's decognitive program.

The introduction is followed by three parts consisting of three chapters each that treat Hodgson's work along lines that are simultaneously thematic and formal, and it is here that idiosyncrasy may be suspected. Let me try to forestall that suspicion here. I decided to organize my analysis neither chronologically nor book by book, as most studies of this sort are organized, mainly because the absence of manuscripts, letters, journals, and other archival materials makes it impossible to establish Hodgson's writing chronology. This fact, combined with the high degree of thematic overlap and variation among his writings, means that choosing any single book as a starting or ending point for this project would have been arbitrary. By organizing my chapters around thematic and formal issues that cut across individual stories and novels, I intend to make the case for Hodgson as a profound though untrained, non-professional thinker who nevertheless engaged with major philosophical, scientific, and social issues of his day, and as a careful, self-conscious literary craftsman exploring difficult and ambitious techniques of expression even as he seeks to earn a precarious living in the marketplace of popular fiction. Part of my aim was to counter the notion, still widespread, that he was a sort of literary idiot savant who somehow generated brilliant ideas that he was utterly incapable of expressing in well-written narratives. In order to understand both the strengths and the weaknesses of his most important texts, we need to situate them in the context of his full body of work.

Part One, "Hope in Space and Time," constitutes a tripartite examination of Hodgson's engagements with the historical events, conceptions, and values of his own lifetime as manifested primarily in his realist fiction, but also in his weird fiction. This analysis of his "timeliness" is subdivided into the following chapters: Chapter One, "The Larger English," analyzes Hodgson's formal experiments in code-switching, vernacular invention, and the representation of contemporary dialects related to class, nationality, and ethnicity, all of which provide interpretive context for his most ambitious linguistic innovation, the artificially archaic language of *The Night Land*. Chapter Two, "Spoken to My Own Brother," evaluates Hodgson's depictions, in both his weird and his realist fiction, of ethnic or racial differences and the conflicts that arise from them, in the global context of British imperialism at the beginning of its historical decline in the early twentieth century. Chapter Three, "Teach Him to Know a Man," examines Hodgson's diverse, eccentric, and controversial representations of gender and sexuality as differential forms of power and performance operating in the Edwardian era as well as at the end of time.

Part Two, "Hope out of Place," maps the ways that space and place function in Hodgson's fiction both to expand the possibilities of narration and to unground and destructure knowledge and mastery. His work does this through processes of what I call decognitive mapping that contest both the cognitive mapping of new knowledge characteristic of science fiction and the ethical mapping that redeems a threatened social order, which is the kind of mapping upon which fantasy relies. This elaboration of Hodgson's spatial imagination begins to address what I called his "untimeliness" a few paragraphs back, and it also occupies three chapters: Chapter Four, "The Sea Is All the God There Is," discusses the ways Hodgson adapted his shipboard experiences in order to transform realist maritime environments into new spaces for both fantastic and non-fantastic storytelling. Chapter Five, "A Cemetery of Lost Ships and Wrack and Forgotten Things," shows how Hodgson extrapolates new fantastic settings from unexplored and legendary aspects of the sea, especially the "weed landscapes" of the Sargasso Sea where his breakthrough stories and first-published novel *The Boats of the "Glen Carrig"* (1907) were set. Chapter Six, "Familiar Land of Strangeness," explicates the methods by which Hodgson's most important fiction radically undermines the stability, intelligibility, and possibility for control of both specific places and space in general, focused on the unmappable geographies of *The House on the Borderland* and *The Night Land*.

My analysis of Hodgson's "untimeliness" comes to completion in Part Three, "Hope out of Time," which likewise offers a three-stage study of Hodgson's characteristic uses of abyssal time, defined as a decognitive temporality or timescale too vast for human experience or measurement, as a means of extracting his visions from historical time so as to pose fundamental questions of both ethics and cosmology in his most ambitious weird fictions, *The House on the Borderlands* and *The Night Land*. The first stage is Chapter Seven, "The Time That Is Left Us," an interpretation of abyssal time in *The House on the Borderland* and *The Night Land* as an example of messianic time, philosopher Giorgio Agamben's notion of the irresistible and inhuman time that time takes to come to an end, which stands in contrast and challenge to H.G. Wells's rational humanist effort to measure and master evolutionary time in *The Time*

Machine, an effort which set the pattern for the rationalist utopianism of conventional science fiction. The second stage is Chapter Eight, "That Song Past Human Tongue to Sing," an excursus investigating Hodgson's weird long poem *The Voice of the Ocean* as a formal and thematic resource for the conceptual challenges of abyssal time as well as its relationship to and effects on subjectivity, both human and nonhuman. The third and final stage is Chapter Nine, "Beautiful Things Hid in the Abyss of the Years," an investigation of the unique combination of mutable humanism (often stigmatized as sentimentalism) and unflinching nihilism that Hodgson synthesizes into a paradoxical source of measured affirmation for a cosmically insignificant humanity facing its own inevitable passing.

The book concludes with an Envoi or sendoff, "Hope's Legacy," that surveys Hodgson's influence on fantastic writing since his early death, with special emphasis on his contemporary status as a posthumanist visionary whose innovations have spawned many pastiches but whose more significant legacy can be seen reflected in tales by Catherine L. Moore and Henry Kuttner, M. John Harrison, China Miéville, Jeff VanderMeer, Greg Bear, and Charlie Jane Anders, as well as graphic novels, film, and television. If, in the course of my arguments, I manage to encourage others to engage seriously with the anomaly that is William Hope Hodgson's contribution to literature, in full or in part, then I will be well rewarded for my own labor.

Introduction: Decognition and the Labor of the Weird

Weird fiction is a tradition—or perhaps, given its unstable liminal position at the intersection of science fiction, fantasy, and horror, "counter-tradition" is a more accurate term—that, ever since its inception in the late nineteenth century, has been riven by conflicts between idealism and materialism. Although many of the weird's innovators, including Arthur Machen and Algernon Blackwood, were avowedly mystical and anti-materialist writers,[1] the tradition's central figure, H.P. Lovecraft, consistently advocated an atheistic and anti-idealist philosophy that he called variously "mechanistic materialism" and "cosmic indifferentism" throughout his life, in his letters and essays as well as his fiction. Unsurprisingly, given what Lovecraft considered to be his "aristocratic" heritage as well as the conservative political views and genteel work habits that he derived from that heritage, his materialism is essentially contemplative and theoretical, focused on intellectual investigations of and philosophical reflections on various manifestations of the weird. This approach is fundamentally scientific or scientistic, but as China Miéville notes, it is "a scientific methodology presiding over the collapse of its own predicates," a collapse that often drives Lovecraft's narrators and protagonists to madness (Miéville 2005: xiii). The well-known opening paragraph of "The Call of Cthulhu" (1928) sums up this paradox:

> The sciences, each straining in its own direction, have hitherto harmed us little; but some day the piecing together of dissociated knowledge will open up such terrifying vistas of reality, and of our frightful position therein, that we shall either go mad from the revelation or flee from the deadly light into the peace and safety of a new dark age.
>
> (Lovecraft 2015a vol.2: 21–2)

Lovecraft's most important predecessor in this regard, the English writer William Hope Hodgson, introduced a different kind of materialism into weird fiction: a materialism not of aristocratic contemplation, scientific experimentation, and resulting madness but of manual labor, physical struggle, and psychological resistance. Since no records of his intellectual development survive, it is impossible to trace the specific historical

---

[1] See Joshi 1990, chapters one and three.

sources of Hodgson's materialism, but we can deduce that, like H.G. Wells's, it was largely inspired by the revolutionary scientific discourses of the late Victorian period, especially the materialist account of biological development that emerged from Darwinian evolutionary theory and the conception of cosmological historicity that emerged from the confluence of astronomy, geology, and thermodynamics in the work of Charles Lyell and Lord Kelvin. Abstract philosophical discussions of materialism are infrequent in Hodgson's work; instead, his protagonists, and through them his readers, most often encounter the apparent disruptions of natural law that define the weirdness of his vision through the concrete forms of labor which define the characters' lives, and those encounters reveal the weird itself to entail a kind of labor that subtends, encompasses, and exceeds human activity. In fact, the labor of the weird and the resistance to it often (but not always) transform the human subject who undergoes them, and those transformations are materially reflected in the language of Hodgson's tales, imposing a labor of the weird on the reader as well as on the characters. This attention to labor, to its psychological effects, and to its textual representation makes Hodgson's materialism, which I will call weird materialism in order to emphasize both its indefinable provenance and its unique literary application, particularly relevant to contemporary debates over the controversial aesthetics and politics of the weird.

Over the past two decades weird fiction has experienced a revival that is simultaneously a celebration and a critique of the tradition's original innovators, so a brief discussion of the conception of the weird at stake in this investigation, as well as its relation to science fiction, fantasy, and horror, may be helpful at the outset.[2] In essays such as *Supernatural Horror in Literature* and "Notes on Writing Weird Fiction," Lovecraft formulated the first and still the most influential definition of weird fiction's aim, which is

> to achieve, momentarily, the illusion of some strange suspension or violation of the galling limitations of time, space, and natural law which for ever imprison us and frustrate our curiosity about the infinite cosmic spaces beyond the radius of our sight and analysis. These stories frequently emphasize the element of horror because fear is our deepest and strongest emotion, and the one which best lends itself to the creation of nature-defying illusions. Horror and the unknown or the strange are always closely connected, so that it is hard to create a convincing picture of shattered natural law or cosmic alienage or "outsideness" without laying stress on the emotion of fear.
>
> (Lovecraft 2004b: 176)

This defiance of rational limits is the aspect of weird fiction that Carl Freedman has described as inflationary in its intent "to suggest reality to be richer, larger, stranger, more complex, more surprising—and indeed, 'weirder'—than common sense would suppose" (Freedman 2013: 14).

---

[2] For a brief history and periodization of weird fiction, see Noys and Murphy 2016.

In his letters, Lovecraft positions weird fiction more precisely at the border between knowledge and ignorance, between rationality and superstition, which is where such illusions of violation or suspension most often appear:

> Reason as we may, we cannot destroy a normal perception of the highly limited & fragmentary nature of our visible world of perception & experience as scaled against the outside abyss of unthinkable galaxies & unplumbed dimensions ... Superadded to this simple curiosity is the galling sense of *intolerable restraint* which all sensitive people ... feel as they survey their natural limitations in time & space as scaled against the freedoms & expansions & comprehensions & adventurous expectancies which the mind can formulate as abstract conceptions.
> (Lovecraft 1971: 294–5)

This combination of horror and expectancy, of aesthetic pain and pleasure, leads Miéville to define the "awe" characteristic of the weird as the anti-theological obverse of Kant's sublime (Miéville 2009a: 510–1). From this it follows that the literature that would strive to represent such an awe-inspiring violation or suspension of natural law cannot ground itself on the supernatural assumption of divine or malign interference with the physical laws and ethical norms we tentatively attribute to the cosmos; as Lovecraft insists, "The time has come when the normal revolt against time, space, & matter must assume a form not overtly incompatible with what is known of reality—when it must be gratified by images forming *supplements* rather than *contradictions* of the visible & mensurable universe." Lovecraft presents his challenge in the form of a rhetorical question, but its provocation is clear: "And what, if not a form of *non-supernatural cosmic art*, is to pacify this sense of revolt—as well as gratify the cognate sense of curiosity?" (Lovecraft 1971: 295–6). Weird fiction is precisely the non-supernatural cosmic art for which Lovecraft calls.

Decognitive Estrangement

Lovecraft's notion of supplements to the visible and mensurable universe is the key to weird fiction, and also key to the fraught relationship it has with the adjacent genres of science fiction, fantasy, and horror. If these supplements could be cognized, incorporated into the immanent growth of human knowledge, and their social consequences articulated, then they would function like the "novum" at the center of Darko Suvin's well-known Marxist conception of science fiction, and consequently weird fiction would fit into Suvin's definition of science fiction as the literature of cognitive estrangement from and critical reflection upon the author's (and reader's) empirical reality (Suvin 1979: chapters 1–4). Suvin himself categorically rules this out: "Even less congenial to SF [than the folktale] is the *fantasy* (ghost, horror, Gothic, weird) tale, a genre committed to the interposition of anti-cognitive laws into the empirical environment. Where the folktale is indifferent, the fantasy is inimical to the empirical world and its laws," which means that its deviation from that world does not constitute a novum, and hence its irrationalism is ultimately ideological and reactionary (Suvin 1979: 8–9).³ Leaving aside for a moment Suvin's inaccurate and misleading assimilation of weird fiction to Gothic horror and subsumption of both under the heading of fantasy, let us delve deeper into the conflict noted here between the weird and science fiction. I will return to fantasy and horror later in this Introduction.

Miéville agrees with Suvin that weird fiction does not fit the latter's definition of science fiction, and presents it instead "as the bad conscience of the Gernsback/Campbell sf paradigm, and as a rebuke to much theorizing that takes that paradigm's implicit self-conception as its starting point" (Miéville 2009a: 510). In his afterword to the collection *Red Planets: Marxism and Science Fiction*, Miéville argues that non-science fiction fantastika, including the variety known as weird fiction, "in its form as well as its many contents, is no less an ideological product that SF is. However, nor is it more so" (Miéville 2009b: 243). This conclusion emerges not only from a consideration of the ambiguous formal operation of cognition within SF theory but also from a recognition of the deeply ambivalent historical role that scientific cognition has played over the past century:

> In the aftermaths of two world wars and a holocaust which saw "hard" *and* social science harnessed to mass industrial slaughter—an epoch which unsurprisingly shattered the bourgeois reformist daydreams of ineluctable progress-through-rationality—and following the aesthetic upheavals of the radical modernisms (including their pulp-fantastic wings) that were born out of a repudiation of that species of capitalist-comprador rationalism that was all that had been officially on offer, one might expect Marxist theory, which has for several generations drawn out these connections, to exhibit a certain caution about claims of the self-evident progressiveness of self-styled rationalism. One might consider ... that the model of a "scientific rationality" that is "progressive" in opposition to "reactionary" "irrationalism" is, generously, roughly nine decades out of date—a bad joke after World War I, let alone after the death camps. Yet this model is at the heart of the *Grundnorm* of the mainstream Marxist theory of SF.
>
> (Miéville 2009b: 241)

The critical conception of weird fiction used in this study, which builds on Miéville, defines it not as anti-cognitive (and therefore irrationalist, ideological, and reactionary in Suvin's terms) narration but rather as decognitive narration, that is, narrative that takes the logical universalism and normative subjectivity implied by triumphalist scientific rationality as objects of suspicion, evasion, and disruption.

Decognition should not be confused with discognition as articulated in Steven Shaviro's book with that title. Shaviro argues that

---

³ In *Critical Theory and Science Fiction*, Carl Freedman shifts the emphasis from cognition per se to the fictive "cognition effect" produced by science-fiction narration, but otherwise follows Suvin in his condemnation of weird fiction; see Freedman 2000: 16–19.

We ought to resist the all-too-common equation of sentience with cognition. We often find this assumption taken for granted in contemporary philosophy of mind, as well as in neurobiological research. But mental functioning and subjective experience need not themselves be cognitive—even though cognition seems impossible without them. Sentience, whether in human beings, in animals, in other sorts of organisms, or in artificial entities, is less a matter of cognition than it is one of what I have ventured to call *discognition*. I use this neologism to designate something that disrupts cognition, exceeds the limits of cognition, but also subtends cognition.

(Shaviro 2015: 10–1)

Shaviro follows up this claim with seven case studies in the modes of non-universal, non-normative, nonhuman "thinking," most of which he finds depicted in recent science fiction texts, that sketch but do not exhaust the variety of alternative cognitive forms made imaginatively accessible to us through the process of speculative extrapolation that science shares with fiction. Whereas discognition emphasizes the plurality of cognitive modes that both contemporary cognitive science and contemporary science fiction investigate and dramatize, decognition attempts to map the resistance to totalizing or universalizing models of cognition that is widespread in early twentieth-century culture, especially weird fiction. In other words, the process of decognition is one of the historical preconditions that allows us to think the diverse forms of discognition Shaviro maps.

The hypothesis that guides this investigation of decognition can be stated concisely as follows: if science fiction proper is not possible prior to the establishment of modern science, then weird fiction proper is not possible prior to the recognition that the absolutist and universalist pretensions of that science, of which philosophical positivism is the most extreme manifestation, run up against inescapable limits that prevent science from completing its project of mastery over nature. This hypothesis finds support in Emily Alder's argument that

> weird fiction emerged because of, and could not have emerged without, the particular state of late nineteenth-century biology, physics, psychology, and the scientific discourses constructed around the occult revival ... Weird fiction and science belong to the same, widespread cultural conversation taking place at this time about new knowledge and between competing versions of what valid knowledge is. Weird tales not only take part in that conversation but contribute their own versions of knowledge.
>
> (Alder 2020: 26–7)

The process of decognition, of which weird fiction is an important locus and symptom, does not necessarily involve the blanket rejection of scientific reason we find in Machen and Blackwood, but rather the critique of its claims to universalism, the identification of its limits, and the investigation of alternative forms of rationality and relationships other than objectification and mastery; as such it shares concerns and methods with the so-called "irrationalism" or "immoralism" of Arthur Schopenhauer, Søren

Kierkegaard, Friedrich Nietzsche, and Henri Bergson and looks forward to the radical philosophical pluralisms of Gilles Deleuze, Félix Guattari, and Paul Feyerabend.

This approach explains why weird fiction emerges at the cusp of the nineteenth and twentieth centuries, and how its practitioners differentiate their work from that of their contemporaries in the more straightforward genre of science fiction that emerges at roughly the same time. Hodgson's work, like Lovecraft's later, spans the conceptual transition from the nineteenth to the twentieth centuries, which is also the transition from an orderly, absolute, deterministic world to a chaotic, relative, indeterminate world. His fictions both reflect upon and intervene into the transition from order to chaos, from determinism to indeterminacy, and from moral universalism to ethical relativism, particularly as it manifests itself in the conception of science that dominates this period. Broadly speaking, at this time the physical sciences shift, more or less rapidly, from a positivist conception of empirical inquiry and scientific cognition to a problematic or negative conception of such enquiry and cognition. However, most early science fiction—from the pioneering scientific romances of Jules Verne and H.G. Wells to the so-called Pulp and Golden Ages—evades, resists, or represses the most significant consequences of this transition, as can be seen in the careers of the genre's two most important early editors and publishers, Hugo Gernsback and John W. Campbell, who maintain an implicit commitment to scientific positivism that their purported role models in laboratories largely abandon (see Ashley and Lowndes 2004 and Nevala-Lee 2018). I find a degree of corroboration for this claim in Suvin's observation that "something changed radically in the North American 'reception aesthetics' around 1910, roughly with the advent of E.R. Burroughs. That not yet properly investigated 'something' amounts to an absorption of bourgeois ideology into SF" (Suvin 1988: 57). One form of that ideology was undoubtedly positivism. Andrew Milner concurs: "Verne and Wells had generally written from within a self-confidently optimistic positivism, often bordering on the utopian … Positivistic SF would be resumed in inter-war America—but in a different register, nonetheless—as an escapist response to the Great Depression rather than the easy celebration of scientific triumphalism" (Milner 2009: 226-7). Both Hodgson and Lovecraft reject the arrogance and narcissism implicit in positivism without rejecting the value of materialist scientific inquiry that underlies it.

In his brief but lucid critique of positivist thought, Leszek Kolakowski lays out the four rules that define it across the half-century of its historical development. The relevance of these rules for an understanding of both Hodgson's and Lovecraft's fiction will be evident to readers familiar with their work. The first rule is *phenomenalism*: "According to positivism, the distinction between essence and phenomenon should be eliminated from science on the ground that it is misleading. We are entitled to record only that which is actually manifested in experience; opinions concerning occult entities of which experienced things are supposedly the manifestations are untrustworthy" (Kolakowski 1968: 3). The second is *nominalism*, which follows from the first: "every abstract science is a method of ordering, a quantitative recording of experiences, and has no independent cognitive function in the sense that, via its abstractions, it opens access to empirically inaccessible domains of reality" such as deities, Platonic Forms, or mathematical entities (Kolalowski 1968: 7). These rules are correlative in the sense that they deny validity to all claims that go beyond empirical observation, whether these are metaphysical, theological, or conceptual. The third rule is the *denial of the cognitive value of value judgments and normative statements*:

> We are not to assume that any value assertion that we recognize as true "in itself," rather than in relation to something else, can be justified by experience ... we are entitled to express value judgments on the human world, but we are not entitled to assume that our grounds for making them are scientific [when] the only grounds for making them are our own arbitrary choices.
>
> (Kolakowski 1968: 8)

This rule echoes Nietzsche's ethical perspectivism, with its assertion that value judgments of good and bad relative to specific forms of life cannot logically or legitimately be universalized into moral judgments of Good and Evil except through a pure exercise of despotic power; we will examine this later while investigating the differences between weird fiction and fantasy. The fourth and final rule is the *unity of the scientific method*: "the belief that the methods for acquiring valid knowledge, and the main stages in elaborating experience through theoretical reflection, are essentially the same in all spheres of experience" (Kolakowski 1968: 8–9). These methods are those of the empirical physical sciences, with which all other claims to knowledge or judgment must conform. This final rule is the primary source of positivism's reductivist arrogance.

Positivism takes its name from the major works of its founder, Auguste Comte: *Course in Positive Philosophy* (6 volumes, 1830–42) and *System of Positive Polity, or Treatise on Sociology instituting the Religion of Humanity* (4 volumes, 1851–4). Looking back to the classical Greek geometers, but more systemically to Francis Bacon and Galileo (Comte 1975: 76), Comte sought to unify all human knowledge under a single method, the experimental method of the physical sciences, and all human society under a single mode of organization derived from that method. In his view, the developmental sequence of the physical sciences corresponds to the logical hierarchy of those sciences, which grows from the most simple, abstract, and general to the more specific and complex: first mathematics, in ancient Greece, then astronomy during the Renaissance, physics and chemistry in the seventeenth and eighteenth centuries, and physiology in the nineteenth century (Comte 1975: 93–101). This sequence, simultaneously logical and historical, implies a culminating point that Comte himself claims to invent: "Now that the human mind has grasped celestial and terrestrial physics—mechanical and chemical; organic physics, both vegetable and animal—there remains one science, to fill up the series of sciences of observation: social physics" (Comet 1975: 76–7), which he will later call sociology. Gertrud Lenzer paraphrases the aim of Comte's system as follows:

> The claim that social phenomena can and must be studied by the same positive methods used in the natural sciences completes natural philosophy. It is a philosophy of science—and its first major formulation at that—in its assumption that one form of reasoning is applicable to the entire realm of natural and social

phenomena and in its strivings toward greater generality not only in the different disciplines but also in its aim of setting itself up as a superordinated discipline that will impel such generalizations to ever higher abstractions. In Comte's view, this is the only major goal of all science and the only true source of scientific progress.

(Lenzer 1975: xlix)

Once his "social physics" is established as the science of society, Comte's unification of the sciences would be theoretically complete and the final state of the system of human knowledge would be imminent. With the initial support of John Stuart Mill and Herbert Spencer, Comte's conception was taken up by both philosophers and scientists (including such key figures of modernity as Marx and Freud[4]) to the point that positivism became the dominant philosophical system in the Anglo-European world by the late nineteenth century.

Evidence of this dominance can be found not only in the socio-political ideologies of European imperialism and social Darwinism but also in the conceptions of science held by working scientists. For example, in 1896 Albert Michelson, head of the University of Chicago Physics Department and the first American Nobel laureate in the physical sciences, proclaimed,

While it is never safe to affirm that the future of Physical Science has no marvels in store even more astonishing than those of the past, it seems probable that most of the grand underlying principles have been firmly established and that further advances are to be sought chiefly in the rigorous application of these principles to all the phenomena which come under our notice. It is here that the science of measurement shows its importance—where quantitative results are more to be desired than qualitative work. An eminent physicist has remarked that the future truths of Physical Science are to be looked for in the sixth place of decimals.

(Michelson 1896: 159)

Artists and writers as well as scientists adopted this positivist spirit. For the purposes of this argument regarding the emergent incompatibility between positivist science fiction and decognitive weird fiction, the most important of those are Verne and Wells, the direct forerunners of genre science fiction. Although there is no evidence that Verne read Comte, his elder by a generation, Michel Serres insists, near the beginning of his structuralist study *Jouvences sur Jules Verne*, that "ultimately, the *Extraordinary Voyages* are the *Course in Positive Philosophy* for the use of everyone" (Serres 1974: 13, my trans.). And in studies focused on the didacticism of Verne's writing, Arthur B. Evans candidly labels the period of Verne's career that produced his most famous works, such as *Journey to the Center of the Earth, From the Earth to the Moon, Around the World in Eighty Days,* and *20,000 Leagues Under the Seas,* the "positivist period" (Evans 1998; see also Evans 1988: 37–57). Presumably Verne absorbed the main

---

[4] On Marx, see Wellmer 1971; on Freud, see Tauber 2009. The influence of positivism on these figures central to the development of cultural modernism helps to explain why the critique of positivism is not fully congruent with the rise of modernism, although the two events overlap both chronologically and logically.

elements of a positivist attitude from his immediate intellectual environment, and Evans describes his longtime publisher Pierre-Jules Hetzel, who set the terms under which Verne's works were accepted for publication, as "an innovative Positivist" (Evans 1988: 14). In his publisher's preface to the *Extraordinary Voyages* Hetzel approvingly cites the fact that "in the newspapers, art and theatre columns are making way for articles on the proceedings of the Academy of Science" as demonstration that "Art for Art's Sake is no longer enough for our era. The time has come for Science to take its place in the realm of literature" (cited in Evans 1988: 30).

Wells's case is more complicated in that not only did he know the works of both Comte and Spencer, but he also specifically criticized both relatively early in his career. In the essay "The So-Called Science of Sociology" (1907), Wells castigates positivism for submerging the unique, self-reflective human individual beneath the weight of abstractly uniform aggregation of units that marks the foundational sciences of physics and chemistry, and advises sociologists to eschew the pursuit of such abstraction in the study of society. Instead, anticipating Suvin and Jameson, he redefines "the proper and distinctive method of sociology" as "the creation of Utopias—and their exhaustive criticism" (Wells 1907: 367). Indeed, he sees the outline of such a scientific utopia as the one valuable contribution Comte's work made to the world, in effect re-orienting sociology—and therefore positivism—around the investigation of how to perfect human society (Wells 1907: 367–8). Of course, that investigation constitutes the central labor of Wells's own career from beginning to end, which has left an ineradicable mark on later science fiction. Consider the Time Traveler's discovery of future human degeneration into the clades called Eloi and Morlocks, which is profoundly tragic and dystopian; nevertheless, his scientific method of discovering it is implicitly intended to be utopian, allowing us to change our ways rationally in order to avoid that future, as the narrator exhorts us to recall: "If that is so, it remains for us to live as though it were not so" (Wells 1934: 66). Forty years later, in *The Shape of Things to Come*, Wells still considered science and technology as keys to the construction of utopia, now labeled "technocracy" (Wells 2005: 277–80) and accomplished by the establishment of an "Air Dictatorship" of scientists, engineers, technicians, and skilled machine operators (Wells 2005: 336–7, 367–71). Although Wells would undoubtedly deny that this utopian vision of science running through all his work is evidence of a continuing commitment to positivism, it would be very difficult to completely disentangle his utopian project from that of Comte and his disciples. Wells' influence on subsequent science fiction consists, at least in part, of that vision's further development, as the work of Suvin, Jameson, Freedman, and their heirs reveals.

Michelson's positivist notion that the rapid pace of scientific discovery in the eighteenth and nineteenth centuries would soon culminate in a final universal theory was widespread though not ubiquitous at century's end; the more thoughtful participants in the discussion cautiously hedged their bets. For example, in an address to the British Royal Society in 1900, the physicist Lord Kelvin drew attention to what many considered the last remaining obstacles in the way of a final physical theory:

The beauty and clearness of the dynamical theory, which asserts heat and light to be modes of motion, is at present obscured by two clouds. I. The first came into existence with the undulatory theory of light, and ... it involved the question, How could the earth move through an elastic solid, such as essentially is the luminiferous ether? II. The second is the Maxwell-Boltzmann doctrine regarding the partition of energy.

(Kelvin 1902: 363)

Those two "clouds," of course, turned out to be more substantial than Kelvin's metaphor implied: the wave theory of light and the problem of the ether soon led to Einstein's relativity theory, while the "partition" or quantization of energy later led to the formulation of quantum theory. These "clouds" didn't simply slow the finalization of a universal physical theory based in Euclidean geometry and Newtonian mechanics, they fatally undermined its grounds, as well as the positivist assumptions of its adherents (including Michelson, whose interferometric attempts to detect the motion of matter through the ether, carried out in collaboration with Edward Morley, produced null results that ultimately led Einstein to formulate the special theory of relativity in 1905).

The theory of relativity, in both its special and its general form, was the first major blow to the consensus in physics that had persisted from Newton's day until the end of the nineteenth century, and its significance for the ultimate defeat of positivism lies in its elimination of any uniquely privileged frame of reference for measurement, which it replaced with a formal method for achieving deterministic results regardless of the frame chosen. In other words, although relativity remained deterministic and thus could be readily assimilated to the universalism of scientific cognition, its elimination of any absolute reference frame or viewpoint implicitly undermined the methodological absolutism underlying positivism. Quantum theory, on the other hand, could not be so assimilated to universalizing cognition, as its architects Niels Bohr and Werner Heisenberg emphasized. Whereas in classical physics, Bohr writes, a single experimental arrangement can be used to investigate several of an object's properties and the results of those investigations can be combined into a consistent picture that can be utilized to predict future states of the object,

> In quantum physics ... evidence about atomic objects obtained by different experimental arrangements exhibits a novel kind of complementary relationship. Indeed, it must be recognized that such evidence which appears contradictory when combination into a single picture is attempted, exhausts all conceivable knowledge about the object. Far from restricting our efforts to put questions to nature in the form of experiments, the notion of *complementarity* simply characterizes the answers we can receive by such inquiry, whenever the interaction between the measuring instruments and the objects forms an integral part of the phenomena.
>
> (Bohr 1963: 4)

In other words, the results of experiments at the quantum level depend upon the choice of experimental arrangements, which form an undecomposable whole with the objects investigated. Results of experiments using different arrangements to investigate similar objects cannot be combined to form a single consistent picture, but permit only juxtaposition, leaving an unbridgeable gap between them. Such gaps appear whenever physicists investigate the wave-particle dualism of light or the kinematic and dynamic variables of atomic and subatomic motion, among other sets of conjugate variables. The complementarity of kinetics and dynamics gave rise to the uncertainty principle, first articulated by Heisenberg in 1927, which demonstrates that either the position or the velocity of a subatomic particle can be measured, but not both, since the measurement process itself will perturb the particle in an unpredictable way (see Heisenberg 1927). Even more troubling to the aim of positivism than this revelation that physical knowledge is not logically cumulative is the fact that these gaps between complementary measurements are not epistemological effects that could in principle be overcome through better measurement technology, but inescapable ontological features of the quantum universe, which demands, in Bohr's words, "the irrevocable abandonment of the ideal of determinism" (Bohr 1963: 5).

Relativity and quantum theory represent only the first major steps in the decognitive critique of positivism, but they are the only ones that had reached a meaningful level of acceptance by the time Hodgson died in 1918, and thus they are the only ones to which his work might reasonably be argued to respond. Nevertheless, the project of decognition continued to expand in the interwar period, which saw Kurt Gödel's 1931 proof of the logical incompleteness of axiomatic mathematics (see Nagel and Newman 1958) and Karl Popper's demonstration (Popper 1959) that empirical knowledge derived from experiment could never be positively verified but only negatively corroborated by attempts to falsify it. The first of these developments showed that valid mathematical demonstrations have no common or universal structure or content, so no universal physical theory can be logically founded upon them as positivists hope to do, while the second defines scientific knowledge not as positive but as tentative, a form of temporary local information and not timeless universal wisdom, the result of a negative method which can only disprove theoretical claims but never prove them. This demonstration effectively eliminates the logical ground of positivism, that is, the conception of positive inductive science from which it took its name (Kolakowski's fourth rule).

At roughly the same time when Gödel and Popper were writing, Frankfurt School critics T.W. Adorno and Max Horkheimer began to articulate their own sociological account of positivist science, which turned Comte's new discipline back upon its own sources. In a 1932 essay Horkheimer claimed that

> Science ... shows a double contradiction. First, science accepts as a principle that its every step has a critical basis, yet the most important step of all, the setting of tasks, lacks a theoretical grounding and seems to be taken arbitrarily. Second, science has to do with a knowledge of comprehensive relationships; yet, it has no realistic grasp of that comprehensive relationship upon which its own existence and the direction of its work depend, namely, society.
>
> (Horkheimer 1972: 8)

This is one of the earliest formulations of Kolakowski's third rule of positivism, the refusal of science to interrogate and establish social values and norms, leaving it at the mercy of the existing order of things. Horkheimer and Adorno would further develop this critique in their most influential work, *Dialectic of Enlightenment* (1944), which Lenzer echoes in her assertion that Comte's positivism explicitly demanded that

> Philosophy ... shed its metaphysical, speculative, and critical ambitions and constitute itself solely as philosophy of science .... This reduction of philosophy was explicitly directed against the metaphysical and critical role of reason, a role that was to be banned from the realm of proper conscious activity. Instead the sole function allowed to reason was for it to become an instrument of computation and logic in the service of the existing order, an instrument continually enhancing its powers while at the same time relinquishing for itself any power that would transcend the 'nature of things,' social as well as natural.
>
> (Lenzer 1975: xlix)

As Miéville recognizes, far from constituting a critical and therefore progressive form, then, narrative mobilized around the ongoing cognitive transformation of human mastery over the material world, whether fictional or nonfictional, occupies a profoundly ambivalent position in relation to the alienation and inequality that characterize capitalist exploitation.

Important events *external* to the development and critique of Western physical science also played an important role in decognitive critique, such as the anthropological study of the epistemologies, cosmologies, and ontologies of non-European indigenous peoples, which developed in an uneasy partnership with the extension of European imperialism during Hodgson's lifetime. As this complex of concepts is both vast and resistant to synthesis or summary, I will simply cite Jacques Derrida's assertion that "ethnology could have been born as a science only at the moment when a decentering had come about: at the moment when European culture—and, in consequence, the history of metaphysics and of its concepts [*including science and positivism*]—had been *dislocated*, driven from its locus, and forced to stop considering itself as the culture of reference" (Derrida 1978: 282). Among the earliest and most influential scientists defending the intellectual rigor of indigenous cultures were the linguistic anthropologists Edward Sapir and Benjamin Lee Whorf. Sapir first articulated a version of the hypothesis that bears both their names in 1929, arguing that "No two languages are ever sufficiently similar to be considered as representing the same social reality. The worlds in which different societies live are distinct worlds, not merely the same world with different labels attached" (Sapir 1968: 162). This multiplicity of worlds necessarily interferes with the project of totalizing and completing scientific knowledge. Sapir's student Whorf put the claim much more forcefully, and his version remains controversial to this day:

> We dissect nature along lines laid down by our native languages. The categories and types that we isolate from the world of phenomena we do not find there because they stare every observer in the face; on the contrary, the world is presented in a kaleidoscopic flux of impressions which has to be organized by our minds—and this means largely by the linguistic systems in our minds.
>
> (Whorf 1956: 212–3)

If the Western scientific method and the mode of cognition specific to it are in any way consequences of the common structure of Indo-European languages, then they can neither claim logical universality nor serve as the model for all other cognitive approaches to the world, and thus the positivist project must scale itself back or reveal itself to be nothing more than an ideological cover for imperialism.

Thus far we have focused our attention on decognitive critiques of Western physical science's universalizing ambitions as embodied in the positivist movement, since that is the framework that provides us with tools for grasping weird fiction's differences from nascent science fiction. In order to assess how the weird distinguishes itself from fantasy and Gothic horror, we must shift our attention from epistemological questions to ethical ones, because fantasy and Gothic focus less on the true and false of cognitive judgment than on the right and wrong of value judgment. Nevertheless, our approach will remain consistent in its attention to the critique of and escape from universalizing anthropocentric conceptions. Whereas Gothic horror, with its reliance on the return of the (familial or collective) repressed past, has been effectively theorized using a combination of psychoanalytic and historical materialist tools, fantasy scholarship has never really developed a theoretical model that has achieved consensus the way that Suvin's notion of cognitive estrangement has been adopted by science fiction critics. Indeed, Suvin's own view of fantasy in all its varieties (including horror) as no more than reactionary ideology—a perspective shared by other critics such as Fredric Jameson and Rosemary Jackson (see Gifford 2018: 16–39)—effectively rules out any more affirmative critical account of it, and despite the determinedly formalist efforts of Farah Mendlesohn and Brian Attebery, most fantasy scholarship focuses on thematic issues of conflict among collective values and the terms of its resolution, which is justifiable because much of the fiction itself focuses on such matters.

The fantasy genre's historical roots in medieval European romances account for much of this emphasis on the conflict of values, which has two basic modalities that Gilles Deleuze's account of Spinoza will help me to define. The first, oldest, and most popular modality of fantasy is the moral, and as Deleuze reminds us, morality "always refers existence to transcendent values. Morality is the judgment of God, the *system of judgment*" (Deleuze 1988: 23). As such it is absolute, total, and universal in its range of application, and conceives disagreement or conflict in terms of an opposition that can only be equally absolute, total, and universal, which is to say polar. The Grail quest of Arthurian legend and the Christian allegory of Edmund Spenser's *Faerie Queene* narrativize the pursuit of absolute morality, and the techniques they pioneer are essentially modernized in J.R.R. Tolkien's influential conception of secondary world "subcreation" as an imperfect but faithful analog of God's creation of the primary world. Just as believers living in the primary world can look forward to divine redemption as the climax of time's monological narrative, the characters in a well-made secondary world can expect a similar happy ending or redemptive "eucatastrophe" at the climax of a conventional fantasy (see Tolkien 1966). The legions of dark lords, battalions of prophesied heroes, and catalogs of apocalyptic battles filling the pages of fantasy trilogy after fantasy trilogy constitute overwhelming evidence of Tolkien's transcendent-idealist moral legacy.

The only significant alternative to this modality within fantasy fiction is the ethical, which Deleuze defines as "a typology of immanent modes of existence [which] overthrows the system of judgment" central to morality (Deleuze 1988, 23). Ethical fantasy revolves around values that are socially constructed and hence historically variable rather than uniform, supernaturally imposed ones, and finds one of its earliest expressions in William Morris's late Victorian romances *The Well at the World's End* (1896) and *The Water of the Wondrous Isles* (1897), which eschew the universalizing logic of Christian morality in favor of relational values defined by socio-cultural particularities. Morris's dark lords are not demons but simply human tyrants, his heroes and heroines are not born to any inescapable destiny that they don't produce through their own efforts, and his battles are motivated by demands for political and social emancipation rather than the eschatology of spiritual redemption. As I have argued at length elsewhere (see Murphy 2019), Morris's heirs are less numerous than Tolkien's, but they are far more significant in the innovations they have brought to fantasy fiction: Ursula K. Le Guin, Michael Moorcock, Samuel R. Delany, China Miéville, and our subject here, Hodgson. Deleuze sums up the opposition between these modes using Nietzschean terms: "Life is poisoned by the categories of Good and Evil, of blame and merit, of sin and redemption," so when we shift from moral fantasy to ethical fantasy, "The opposition of values (Good-Evil) is supplanted by the qualitative difference of modes of existence (good-bad)" (Deleuze 1988: 26, 23).

How does this genealogy of fantasy fiction's metaphysics help us to define the interstitial status of the weird? By giving us the tools to extend the decognitive critique of rationalist universalism to what I will call an *anethical* critique of moral universalism. Just as decognition is not opposed to cognition but only to its totalizing extension, anethical critique is not the reversal of absolute morality into immorality or amorality but rather its pluralization into many situated and incommensurable ethical systems. This argument may be easier to follow if we first map its progress through philosophy rather than literature. If, as Deleuze demonstrates, Spinoza is among the first European philosophers to criticize abstract, transcendent moral universalism, he is not the most widely influential such critic, both because of the difficulty of his works and because their contents lead him to be marginalized—and even excommunicated—as an atheist or pantheist. Writing for a popular audience, on the other hand, Karl Marx and Friedrich Engels, in the *Communist Manifesto* (1848), lucidly assert the historical variability of morality:

> When the ancient world was in its last throes, the ancient religions were overcome by Christianity. When Christian ideas succumbed in the eighteenth century to rationalist ideas, feudal society fought its death battle with the then revolutionary bourgeoisie. The ideas of religious liberty and freedom of conscience merely gave expression to the sway of free competition within the domain of knowledge.
> (Marx & Engels in Marx 1973: 85)

Despite their over-optimistic claim that Christianity had already "succumbed" to rationalism, the basic outlines of this genealogy are undoubtedly correct, and despite the hostility of imperial Europe toward communism, the *Manifesto* circulated quite widely. By the late nineteenth century, the communist movement had persuaded a large section of the reading public that, just as capitalist imperialism was successfully colonizing the non-European world, the universality proclaimed by European moral judgment had been completely colonized by capitalism, as Marx's 1844 notebooks reveal: "The morality of political economy is *gain*, labour and thrift, sobriety—and yet political economy promises to satisfy my needs. The political economy of morality is the wealth of a good conscience, or virtue, etc. But how can I be virtuous if I do not exist?" (Marx, *Economic and Philosophical Manuscripts* in Marx 1974: 362). Thus political economy takes precedence over morality, and indeed lays claim to morality's previous universality as the essence of human subjectivity:

> Money has not been transcended in man within the credit system, but man is himself transformed into *money*, or, in other words, money is *incarnate* in him. Human individuality, human *morality*, have become both articles of commerce and the *material* which money inhabits. The substance, the body clothing the *spirit of money* is not money, paper, but instead it is my personal existence, my flesh and blood, my social worth and status.
> (Marx, "Excepts from James Mill" in Marx 1974: 264)

Morris was friends with Engels and admired Marx's writings, so it is no surprise that his romances reflect the influence of the Marxist account of moral evolution explained by the history of political economy.

A generation after Marx and Engels, and contemporaneous with the emergence of science fiction out of scientific romance and fantasy out of Christian romance, Friedrich Nietzsche takes Marx's critique a step further by asking not merely how and why have moral values changed throughout history, but "under what conditions did man devise the value judgments good and evil? *and what value do they themselves possess?*" (Nietzsche 1968: 453). These questions give rise to Nietzsche's famous differentiation of master morality from slave morality, first articulated in the chapter "What Is Noble" in *Beyond Good and Evil* (Nietzsche 1968: 394–8) but most fully explored in the first essay of *The Genealogy of Morals* (1887), "'Good and Evil,' 'Good and Bad'" (Nietzsche 1968: 460–92). Both sets of values are expressions of specific life forms, in this case distinct human types. In the "first type of morality the opposition of 'good' and 'bad' means approximately the same as 'noble' and 'contemptible,'" and it is expressed from a perspective of self-confidence that is "*value-creating*. Everything it knows as a part of itself it honors; such a morality is self-glorification" (Nietzsche 1968: 394–5), and everything outside it is denigrated as a consequence. The second type, slave morality, is reactive rather than active and self-asserting, and it is

> the origin of the famous opposition of "good" and "evil": into evil one's feelings project power and dangerousness, a certain terribleness, subtlety, and strength ... According to slave morality, those who are "evil" thus inspire fear; according to master morality it is precisely those who are "good" that inspire, and wish to inspire, fear, while the "bad" are felt to be contemptible.
> (Nietzsche 1968: 397)

The slave conception of "good" finally emerges as a back-formation consequent to "evil," "because the good human being has to be *undangerous* in the slaves' way of thinking: he is good-natured, easy to deceive, a little stupid perhaps ... " (Nietzsche 1968: 397). The ultimate triumph of this latter form through its universalization in Christianity, which Nietzsche provocatively labels the "slave revolt in morality" (Nietzsche 1968: 470–9), is the lesson of his beast fable of the lamb which, to preserve its own existence, seeks to persuade the bird of prey not to eat it by redefining the bird of prey as an undifferentiated, universal moral subject that could refuse to eat lambs just as lambs do not eat one another, thus establishing a single moral standard, that of the lamb, for vastly different entities. "[T]he belief that *the strong man is free* to be weak and the bird of prey to be a lamb" gives the lamb "the right to make the bird of prey *accountable* for being a bird of prey" (Nietzsche 1968: 481). Deleuze glosses this fable cogently: "As soon as forces are projected into a fictitious subject this subject proves to be blameworthy or deserving—blameworthy if active force performs the activity which is its own, deserving if reactive force does not perform the activity which it ... does not have" (Deleuze 1983: 124).

This logic of false universality constitutes the root not only of theological universalism but also the anthropocentric positivist conception of disinterested scientific objectivity, and thereby draws the decognitive and anethical strands of our analysis together. Building upon his pluralist ethical perspectivism, in the third essay of *Genealogy of Morals* Nietzsche deconstructs the impersonal notion of objectivity as a residuum of divine transcendence, an attribute attainable only by an imaginary deity, and proposes an alternative for human knowledge:

> to see differently in this way for once, to *want* to see differently, is no small discipline and preparation of the intellect for its future "objectivity"—the latter understood not as "contemplation without interest" (which is a nonsensical absurdity), but as the ability *to control* one's Pro and Con and to dispose of them, so that one knows how to employ a *variety* of perspectives and affective interpretations in the service of knowledge.
>
> (Nietzsche 1968: 555)

He concludes his decognitive demonstration by asserting that "There is *only* a perspective seeing, *only* a perspective 'knowing;' and the *more* affects we allow to speak about one thing, the *more* eyes, different eyes, we can use to observe one thing, the more complete will our 'concept' of this thing, our 'objectivity,' be" (Nietzsche 1968: 555). There are as many ways to see and to be affected by events and experiences as there are kinds of entity to be affected, as Spinoza already knew, so cognition must be as plural as ethics.

With the results of our philosophical investigation in hand, let us know turn back to the question of weird fiction's differentiation from fantasy. Consciously inspired by Marx and Engels, Morris's rejection of universal morality in favor of socially and historically determined ethics as the basis for fantastic narration parallels the relativization of scientific knowledge that, as we saw above, inaugurates the critique of positivism at the start of the twentieth century. Nietzsche's contemporaneous investigation of the value of such values and the logical sleight of hand that transforms immanent and local good v. bad into transcendent and universal Good v. Evil deconstructs these fundamental binarisms into a dialectically irreducible difference of forces corresponding to different forms and conditions of life: the aggressive, affirmative bird of prey v. the resentful, doubly negative lamb. Weird fiction, then, goes further than the historical relativism of fantastic romance to take up Nietzsche's challenge by extrapolating ever greater divergences of life conditions between the human narrator/reader and the unhuman entities it encounters, and consequently ever greater divergences of value, ethics, and sensation that produce incomprehension and fear but also Lovecraft's sense of "adventurous expectancy" as well as Hodgson's hope. Adoption of a Nietzschean pluralism of cognitive operations and ethical values, in fact, helps to explain the sharp division we have already noted between idealist weird writers such as Machen and Blackwood on the one hand and materialist weird writers such as Lovecraft and Hodgson on the other. In essays such as "Idealism and Materialism—A Reflection" (1919), "In Defense of Dagon" (1921), "A Confession of Unfaith" (1922), and most obviously "Nietzscheism and Realism" (1921), Lovecraft openly acknowledged the Nietzschean references that appear in his own work (most clearly in "The Call of Cthulhu" [1928], "The Silver Key" [1929], and "Through the Gates of the Silver Key" [1934]). None of Hodgson's extant writings indicates a direct interest in Nietzsche, but like Lovecraft, he may well have been introduced to the German thinker's ideas by one of the first thorough studies of Nietzsche to appear in English, H.L. Mencken's 1908 book *The Philosophy of Friedrich Nietzsche*. In his preface to the third edition of 1913, Mencken notes that "a considerable public had awaited [his] effort, for the first edition was quickly exhausted and there was an immediate demand for a special edition in England" (Mencken 1913: xli), so it would have been available to Hodgson as well.

The distinction between moral and ethical fantasy will also help us differentiate weird fiction from Gothic horror. Gothic horror, and traditional supernatural horror generally, operates within a theocentric cosmos of fixed but forgotten moral values that re-assert themselves through the return of the repressed past to demand payment of the debt owed it by the present. Even when something resembling scientific cognition is implicated in this process, as it is in Stoker's *Dracula* and Stevenson's *Strange Case of Dr. Jekyll and Mr. Hyde*, it doesn't reveal anything beyond the range of human experience or knowledge; at most it restores to credibility a folk knowledge or rationalizes a superstition or myth. The folk culture of Transylvania knows how to dispose of vampires even if the English rationalists do not, and the ambiguous perversions committed by Edward Hyde can hardly surprise a Christian moralist for whom every human soul is marked by a transcendental sin. As such the Gothic debt to the past, no matter how appalling or inhumane, remains within the range of human conduct and so can be redeemed in conventional terms; the recurrence of redemptive language here is not arbitrary but essential. Conversely, weird fiction emerges in the effort to escape this repetition compulsion, to draw attention toward the radically unknown and unknowable in order not to ratify the morality we inherit from history but to challenge our ability to anticipate and adapt to a different possible future, or even a present that is other than we think (in the case of Lovecraft's monstrosities which have always already been here, although their presence has been disavowed or unthought). Just as decognition dethrones positivist epistemology, anethical critique dethrones absolutist morality, leaving the human subject to confront a multidimensional material cosmos that far exceeds the capacity of human reason to master.

Weird Materialisms

Weird fiction critically intervenes into the transition from nineteenth-century fantastika—scientific romance, fantastic romance, Gothic horror—to twentieth-century fantastika in several ways that distinguish it from science fiction and high fantasy: first, by focusing the reader's attention upon the limits of scientific rationality's ability to predict and control the world and the anxiety that the transgression of those limits produces in the subject; second, by extrapolating the unintended but imaginable consequences of such transgression for human existence in its present form; and third, by exposing the radical inability of traditional moral categories to render soluble or even graspable the conflict among forms of life at the root of non-theological fantastic storytelling. These three aspects are common to virtually all weird fiction, and they mark it as a narrative form that operates not through the cognitive estrangement characteristic of science fiction or the moral triumph of high fantasy, but decognitive and anethical estrangement, which means a methodological estrangement of cognition from itself and a psychological estrangement of the narrating and reading subjects from cognition as such, as well as an abandonment of moral judgment concerning the narrative's consequences. A few weird writers, including Hodgson and Lovecraft, go even further, subjecting the normative language of scientific cognition, everyday common sense, and conventional morality to scrutiny in order to suggest both its limitations and what may lurk outside it.

The historical emergence of weird fiction also parallels the history of anti-positivism and anti-universalism, although this is most evident in the cases of the genre's best-known figures, the ones who respectively anticipated and consolidated the field almost a century apart. Even before Comte begins his megalomaniac project of bringing modern science to a totalitarian conclusion, the weird's main precursor, Edgar Allan Poe, articulates the suspicion of and hostility to universalizing science that would later underpin the idealist mysticism of Machen and Blackwood. Poe does this in many works, perhaps most concisely in "Sonnet—To Science" (1829): "Science! true daughter of Old Time thou art!/Who alterest all things with thy peering eyes./Why preyest thou thus upon the poet's heart,/Vulture, whose wings are dull realities?" (ll.1–4, Poe 1984a: 38). Here the primary danger represented by science is the progressive disenchantment of the world: "Hast thou not torn the Naiad from her flood,/The Elfin from the green grass, and from me/The summer dream beneath the tamarind tree?" (ll. 12–14, Poe 1984A: 38). Poe would pursue this theme intermittently for the rest of his life, and that pursuit would reach a climax in his prose poem *Eureka* (1848), which defends aesthetic intuition in the understanding of the cosmos against the rigid logical methods of deduction and induction, with the ultimate aim of harmonizing art and science (Poe 1984a: 1268–71). This perspective would later become central not only to Machen's and Blackwood's weird tales, but also to Lord Dunsany's fantasies of re-enchantment such as *The King of Elfland's Daughter* (1924) and Hodgson's weird eschatology expressed in *The House on the Borderland* and *The Night Land*. In poems such as "Annabel Lee" and tales such as "Some Words with a Mummy" or "A Cask of Amontillado," Poe also reveals at least an indifference and at most an outright hostility toward traditional morality that made his works controversial in his own lifetime and a recurring inspiration for later cultural iconoclasts, among whom are the French Symbolists as well as the weird writers.

The innovator of the weird who was most explicitly dedicated to the critique of positivism and moral universality is of course Lovecraft, who followed popular accounts of the developments of relativity, quantum physics, and their philosophical consequences with as much rapt attention as he had read Nietzsche and who was one of the first writers of fantastika to wrestle with those ideas in his fiction as well as his letters. Stories such as "The Shunned House" (1924), "The Call of Cthulhu" (1928), and *At the Mountains of Madness* (1936) include details unmistakably derived from relativity and quantum theory, including non-Euclidean geometry and quantum complementarity, as well as metaphorical allusions to the enormous paradigm shift that accompanied Einstein's and Bohr's achievements. However, Lovecraft's most expansive fictional treatment of the new physics can be found in "The Dreams in the Witch House" (1933), which draws upon general relativity to depict what we would call today travel through hyperspace via wormholes, and may also contain allusions to multi-dimensional quantum event-space. Although he initially rejected the implications of relativity as irrational, Lovecraft later came to see the theory's equation of matter with energy as a confirmation of his own materialism:

> The truth is, that the discovery of matter's identity with energy—and its consequent lack of vital intrinsic difference from empty space—is *an absolute coup de grace to the primitive and irresponsible myth of "spirit." For matter, it appears, really is exactly what "spirit" was always supposed to be.* Thus it is proved *that wandering energy always has a detectable form*—that if it doesn't take the form of waves or electron-streams, *it becomes matter itself*...
>
> (Lovecraft 1968: 266–7)

Quantum theory gave him more trouble, but he ultimately accepted its implications as further evidence for his view of the cosmos too. When he sums up the change in human perspective on the cosmos since 1900, he emphasizes, "First of all, a radical increase in that element of unknowability *which we always admitted*. We are bidden to accept, as the one paradoxical *certainty* of experience, the fact that we can never have any other ultimate certainty" (Lovecraft 1971: 224). Later in the same letter he intentionally switches to Heisenberg's language: "what does the natural evidence of 1930 suggest, anyhow? Well, *uncertainty* in the first place. A definite limitation of our knowledge of what lies behind the visible aspects of the cosmos as seen by human beings from this planet" (Lovecraft 1971: 227; see also Lovecraft 2014: 180–1). The appeal of this idea to Lovecraft is straightforward: it confirms and extends his own sense of the frustrating limitations of the human mind in understanding a radically nonhuman universe, and the inability of religious faith or theological rationalization to overcome them. His 1924 "Confession of Unfaith" expresses the latter view serenely, and concludes by attributing the "perfecting" of his "cynicism" to the influence of Nietzsche and Mencken (Lovecraft 2006: 148).

Hodgson's atheist, materialist approach to the composition of weird fiction, to which we will now turn our attention, constitutes the missing decognitive and anethical link between Poe in the nineteenth century and Lovecraft in the twentieth. His short story "The Derelict" (originally published in 1912), concerning a group of sailors who come across a drifting wooden sailing ship that has biochemically mutated into a single monstrous lifeform, begins with a succinct statement of general materialist principles spoken by the narrator, who is a doctor forced by poverty to work aboard their ship:

> *Material* ... is inevitably the medium of expression of the Life-Force—the fulcrum, as it were; lacking which, it is unable to exert itself, or, indeed, to express itself in any form or fashion that would be intelligible or evident to us ... Life is a thing, state, fact, or element, call-it-what-you-like, which requires the *Material* through which to manifest itself, and that given the *Material*, plus the Conditions, the result is Life. In other words, that Life is an evolved product, manifested through Matter and bred of Conditions ...
>
> (CF 3: 235)

This insistence on the primacy of matter in the evolution of life is the more expansive and accessible corollary of Hodgson's aggressive but gnomic declaration in the story "Out of the Storm" (originally published in 1909) that "*The sea is now all the God there is! ... Listen! it is laughing again. God is it, not He*" (CF 3: 181), in other words protean matter, not anthropomorphic spirit. On this basis he pioneers a mode of narrative in which horrifying threats arise not from supernatural entities inherited from religion, folklore, or mythology but from material entities emerging at the extreme limits of scientific plausibility, the biologically alien with incomprehensible life conditions rather than the spiritually demonic hungry for human souls.

Although Hodgson's fictions are not explicitly linked in the way that the Cthulhu Mythos links many of Lovecraft's tales, they share a consistent and coherent conceptual structure. Provocative statements of principle such as "God is *it*, not He" lead ultimately to the articulation of a full-scale materialist metaphysics of the weird in the posthumously published tale "The Hog," the last of Hodgson's stories concerning the occult detective Carnacki. At the conclusion of that story, in an attempt to ground the preceding narrative of a monstrous eruption—the Hog of the story's title—into the human world and the combination of science and magic necessary to confront it (figured in his famous electric pentacle[5]), Carnacki reminds his audience that

> at one time the earth was just a sphere of extremely hot gases [which] condensed in the form of materials and other "solid" matters; but there are some that are

---

[5] Eugene Thacker discusses Carnacki's electric pentacle at length in Thacker 2011: 69–72, and Emily Alder (2020: 148–9) traces the device's derivation from Victorian scientific investigations.

not yet solidified—air, for instance ... There are [also] larger and more attenuated "gas" belts lying, zone on zone, far up and around us. These compose the inner circles. They are surrounded in turn by a circle or belt of what I have called ... "emanations". This circle which I have named the Outer Circle cannot lie less than a hundred thousand miles off the earth, and has a thickness [of] anything between five and ten million miles. ... Now the Outer Circle is the psychic circle, yet it is also physical ... [I]n the sense that electricity is physical, the Outer or Psychic Circle is physical in its constituents.

(CF 2: 313–4)

Carnacki goes on to recall, in an echo of classical materialism, that "a physical man is composed entirely from the constituents of earth and air. ... In other words without earth and air he could not *BE!* Or to put it another way, earth and air breed within themselves the materials of the body and the brain, and therefore, presumably, the machine of intelligence" (CF 2: 314). In parallel fashion, then, "the million-mile long clouds of monstrosity which float in the Psychic or Outer Circle are bred of the elements of that circle ... just as an octopus or shark is bred out of the sea, or a tiger or any other physical force is bred out of the elements of its earth-and-air surroundings" (CF 2: 314). The encounter with those intangible yet material "monstrosities" constitutes one major category of the weird, which is, as in Lovecraft, conceived not in moral or theological terms but in terms of the physical struggle for survival among forms of life:

The monstrosities of the Outer Circle are malignant towards all that we consider most desirable, just in the same way that a shark or a tiger may be considered malignant, in a physical way, to all that we consider desirable. They are predatory— as all positive force is predatory .... They plunder and destroy to satisfy lusts and hungers exactly as other forms of existence plunder and destroy to satisfy their lusts and hungers.

(CF 2: 314–5)

In other words, the monstrosities are "beyond good and evil" in the Nietzschean sense implied by the allusion to predatory positive force—like other animals they serve no dark lord, oppose no forces of light or goodness, and offer no bargains for human souls; instead, they treat humans as nothing more than raw material for the perpetuation of their own physical existence.

This atheological, materialist theory of the weird seems congruent with the framework laid out in Hodgson's major work *The Night Land* to explain how, in the far future, the earth will be transformed into an alien landscape in which humans huddle together inside great fortresses in order to survive the unleashed power of the outer monstrosities:

The evil must surely have begun in the Days of the Darkening (which I might liken to a story which was believed doubtfully, much as we of this day believe the story of the Creation). A dim record there was of olden sciences (that are yet far off in our future) which, disturbing the unmeasurable Outward Powers, had allowed to pass the Barrier of Life some of those Monsters and Ab-human creatures, which are so wondrously cushioned from us at this normal present. And thus there had materialized, and in other cases developed, grotesque and horrible Creatures, which now beset the humans of this world. And where there was no power to take on material form, there had been allowed to certain dreadful Forces to have power to affect the life of the human spirit.

(NL: 44)

This passage also introduces us to a term Hodgson coined and uses repeatedly in the Carnacki stories and *The Night Land*: "ab-human." Neither book explicitly defines the term, beyond associating it with "abnormal" (CF 2: 138), but Kelly Hurley concludes that it refers to "species hybrids, abominations of a natural evolutionary process or the products of human degeneration" (Hurley 2001: 130). I prefer China Miéville's expansion of the term's definition to refer to "teratological expressions of [the] unrepresentable and unknowable, the evasive of meaning" (Miéville 2012: 381), and we will return to this term several times in the course of this study. Now if we accept Hodgson's definition of the "Psychic Circle" as material, along with his materialist definition of human intelligence and its status as prey to the entities of that circle, then it seems fair to assume that the "ab-human" "evil" described here is physical and psychological predation, and that he intends the "human spirit" in this passage to be interpreted materialistically as well, as an emergent property of biological evolution. Indeed, *The Night Land* alone among Hodgson's major works regularly deploys the apparently moral language of good and evil, although its use is inconsistent in ways that ironically undercut it; his other novels make virtually no use of it.

Just as the weird threat to humanity is not a moral one but rather a material one, so is the defense against that threat a material one: Carnacki's electric pentacle, which is refined through experiment over the course of the stories, and *The Night Land*'s Great Redoubt itself, a metal pyramid eight miles high and defended by an electric circle powered by what Hodgson calls the "Earth-Current," a non-renewable geophysical power source which also "fructified the soil, and gave life and blood to the plants and to the trees, and to every bush and natural thing" in the hundreds of massive "Underground Fields" beneath the Redoubt. These fields straddle a "Crack" in the earth's crust through which the Earth-Current flows (NL: 50, 57). The Earth-Current, which powers handheld weapons such as the Diskos and has magnetic properties that affect compasses, seems to serve as a material figure for the inchoate "Life-Force" described by the doctor in "The Derelict," and at the conclusion of the novel it even restores life to the narrator's beloved, whose "spirit" had been attacked by the inimical forces outside the pyramid as he strove to bring her to safety following the fall of the Lesser Redoubt where she had lived (NL: 544, 575–6, 581–2). Yet the joy of her resurrection is balanced by the somber knowledge that someday the Earth-Current preserving the Great Redoubt will run out just as the current of the Lesser Redoubt ran out, and there will be no one to rescue the remnants of humanity as the narrator rescued his beloved. Physical resurrection does not entail spiritual redemption or eternal life. As in the cosmological vision at the heart of *The House on the Borderland*, here thermodynamics is the foundation of materialist cosmology as well as ontology, and entropy is the ultimate fate of the material universe and all its contents, including the human spirit.

From ontology we now turn to the phenomenology and epistemology of the weird in Hodgson's conception. In the passage from "The Hog" discussed earlier, Carnacki goes on to propose a corporeal mechanism for the human sensory experience of the weird, the "mental eye," which he describes as follows:

> When we see "ghostly" things it is often the "mental" eye performing simultaneously the duty of revealing to the brain what the physical eye sees as well as what it sees itself. The two sights blending their functions in such a fashion gives us the impression that we are actually seeing through our physical eyes the whole of the "sight" that is being revealed to the brain. In this way we get an impression of seeing with our physical eyes both the material and the immaterial parts of an "abnormal" scene; for each part being received and revealed to the brain by machinery suitable to the particular purpose appears to have equal value of reality, that is, it appears to be equally material. In the same way, were anything to threaten our psychic body we should have the impression, generally speaking, that it was our physical body that had been threatened, because our psychic sensations and impressions would be super-imposed upon our physical, in the same way that our psychic and our physical sight are super-imposed.
>
> (CF 2: 311)

This formulation seems to me to bear a remarkable resemblance to Spinoza's famous theorization of mind-body parallelism, according to which the forms of knowledge and experience accessible to the mind are strictly correlative to the actions and passions of which the body is capable, although there is no evidence that Hodgson was familiar with Spinoza's writings. Even Hodgson's language in this passage, which refers to "mental eyes" or "psychic eyes," echoes Spinoza's description of philosophical demonstration as the "eyes of the mind."[6] In any case, the immanence of Hodgson's conception here conforms to his overall materialism.

Although Carnacki the Ghost Finder, who articulates both this weird phenomenology/epistemology and the weird ontology that underpins it, encounters the weird through his work as a detective, he is a character more typical of Lovecraft's materialism of contemplation than of Hodgson's materialism of labor. As Miéville notes, "Unlike Lovecraft's effete scholars and genteel madmen, Hodgson's protagonists are kind of ... well, buff. A disproportionate number of them are sailors" (Mieville 2002a: vii). To get a clearer sense of Hodgson's unique conception of the laboring subjects of weird materialism, we can turn to several sources in different forms and

---

[6] See Spinoza, *Ethics* Part Five, proposition twenty-three (Spinoza 1985: 607–8). Regarding mind-body parallelism more generally, see *Ethics* Part Two, proposition seven and its scholium: "The order and connection of ideas is the same as the order and connection of things," and therefore "a mode of extension and the idea of that mode are one and the same thing, but expressed in two ways" (Spinoza 1985: 415). Also *Ethics* Part Three, proposition eleven: "The idea of any thing that increases or diminishes, aids or restrains, our Body's power of acting, increases or diminishes, aids or restrains, our Mind's power of thinking" (Spinoza 1985: 500).

genres. His short fiction, both fantastic and realistic, is largely populated by physical laborers, especially "shellbacks" (experienced sailors who have crossed the equator), and often concerned with conflicts over the conditions of their labor and the effects of those conditions on their somatic and psychological integrity. Particularly noteworthy in this regard are several realistic stories that narrate the revenge of mistreated workers upon their cruel or tyrannical overseers, usually achieved through hand-to-hand combat (though in one unusual and highly interesting case, revenge is exacted through crossdressing)[7]; in light of Hodgson's own negative experiences at sea, most of these stories must be viewed as quasi-autobiographical or alternately as wish fulfillments.

With the exception of the Carnacki stories, the vast majority of Hodgson's fantastic short fiction focuses on sailors who encounter weird monstrosities and disruptions of varying sorts as they work their way across poorly charted seas. Sometimes, as in "The Derelict" cited earlier or his first published novel *The Boats of the "Glen Carrig,"* the monstrosities are biological mutations that undermine the protagonists' sense of the stability of fundamental conceptual polarities like the living and the dead, organic and inorganic, human and nonhuman, or figure and ground—when a sailing ship's deck comes to life and tries to consume them, as it does in "The Derelict," it's literally as if the place where they stand, which is simultaneously the site of their labor and the basis for their survival at sea, has risen up to destroy them. In Hodgson's most famous story "The Voice in the Night" (1907, in CF 3), a shipwrecked couple is forced to survive by eating the strange fungus that covers their island refuge, only to find their own bodies becoming fungal. In other cases, such as "The *Shamraken* Homeward-Bounder" (1908, in CF 3) and "Riven Night" (posthumous, in CF 3), the weird erupts not as an isolated object or entity but as a shift in the atmosphere or environment, the crossing of an ontological and phenomenological threshold, and the sailors respond as to a dream or vision of transcendence. In the former tale a group of aged sailors mistakes a cyclonic storm for the gates of heaven, while in the latter, the sky ahead of the ship is split by an alien light that calls members of the crew to reunions with their dead, but in a profoundly ambivalent and disturbing way that echoes the narrator's brief encounter with his long-dead beloved in the hallucinatory middle section of Hodgson's novel *The House on the Borderland* (HB: 235–50)

Indeed, Hodgson's novels interrogate the effect of the weird on the worker's psyche more expansively than his short fiction does. For example, the narrator of *The House on the Borderland*, generally called the Recluse by scholars, is frightened by the appearance of the swine-things around his home, but instead of going mad he sets to work fortifying his house and takes up arms to defend it, even venturing into the things' subterranean lair to learn about them. In the course of the cosmological visions of universal heat death that overwhelm him between attacks by the swine-things, his consciousness is expanded and his emotional history plumbed in ways that can only be described as psychedelic, but his will to resist is unaffected by these psychological transformations. Although the weird, in the form of a glowing, infected wound,

---

[7] For the former, see "How the Honourable Billy Darrell Raised the Wind" (1913, in CF 5), "The Regeneration of Captain Bully Keller" (1914, in CF 3), and "We Two and Billy Dunkan" (1914, in CF 3); for the latter, "The Getting Even of Tommy Dodd" (1912, in CF 5), discussed at length in Chapter Three below.

ultimately overwhelms him, he goes down fighting. The transtemporal narrator of *The Night Land,* to whom scholars often refer as X (a "name" derived from the title of Hodgson's condensation of the novel, *The Dream of X* [1912, CF 5: 333–73][8]), is born an eighteenth-century English gentleman, but for the main narrative he is reincarnated as a far-future watchman or "Monstruwacan" on the Great Redoubt's ramparts, the security of which he must leave in order to rescue his reincarnated beloved from the ab-human monstrosities that swarm the landscape that was once the earth.[9] He too is transformed into a stubbornly resistant and ultimately heroic subject by the specialized mental and bodily labor he undertakes in order to survive his weird journey, every moment of which is exhaustively narrated in both external/physical and internal/psychological detail.

Perhaps the most interesting novel with regard to the experience of the weird through labor is Hodgson's third, *The Ghost Pirates,* originally published in 1909. Narrated in first person by the common sailor Jessop, it tells the story of the final voyage of the doomed cargo packet *Mortzestus,* a three-masted sailing ship which is slowly invaded and ultimately taken over by the title figures, which exterminate and replace the human crew. The ghosts invade the ship by occupying first its extremities, such as the rails, the upper crossbeams, and the rigging on the masts, and they are first encountered by the common sailors in the course of their duty watches on deck and aloft. The ghosts untie knots, unfurl sails, unship gear, and otherwise interfere with the crew's labor. The weirdness of those encounters stands out in sharp relief against the backdrop of Hodgson's casual precision in describing the quotidian experience of maritime labor, to which the reader's attention is first drawn by the three-page poem, "The Hell O! O! Chaunty," that serves as an epigraph to the novel. This is a rhythmic work song sung to coordinate the movements of sailors hauling up the ship's anchor or sails: "Hark to the tramp of the bearded shellbacks!/ … /O hark to the haunting chorus of the capstan and the bars!" (GP: 11–12). Such "profound nautical erudition" suffuses the entire book; indeed, Lovecraft singles out Hodgson's "command of maritime knowledge, and [his] clever selection of hints and incidents suggestive of latent horrors in Nature," as the source of this novel's "enviable peaks of power" (Lovecraft 2000: 59).

The narrator Jessop is among the first to encounter the ghost pirates while on watch, and he soon formulates a theory, which is essentially a weird materialist phenomenology, to explain their weirdness:

---

[8] In his complete rewrite of *The Night Land* (Stoddard 2005), James Stoddard gives X the name "Andros," which is Greek for "male." I compare Stoddard's rewrite to Hodgson's original in Chapter One below.

[9] Hodgson's repeated reliance on reincarnation and the persistence of mental life after death in his fiction might appear to undermine his materialism, but as Emily Alder demonstrates, the late Victorian forms of spiritualism on which he draws in his depictions were in fact attempts to give such notions an objective, concrete basis: " … if psychical ideas were, for the [Society for Psychical Research], at the cutting edge of modern scientific debates, so too was evolutionary science, and the two must be looked at in conjunction. Darwinism and the evolutionary history of humans cast doubts for many over the existence of God, heaven, or the immortal soul, but spiritualism, to an extent, allowed these same beliefs to be incorporated into a scientific and materialist world view. The progressive aspects of the evolutionary process encouraged psychical researchers to hope for the enhancement of humanity's future through the development of the human mind" (Alder 2007: 125).

> Suppose the earth were inhabited by two kinds of life. We're one, and *they're* the other ... [I]n a normal state we may not be capable of appreciating the *realness* of the other[.] But they may be just as *real* and material to *them* as *we* are to *us* ... The earth may be just as *real* to them, as to us. I mean that it may have qualities as material to them, as it has to us; but neither of us could appreciate the other's realness, or the quality of realness in the earth, which was real to the other.
>
> (GP: 101–2)

This explanation again confirms the consistency of Hodgon's ontological and phenomenological materialism of the weird. Jessop later notices that the ship has been enveloped by a mist that obscures the crew's vision of the human world, indicating that the ship is moving across the invisible threshold of the overlapping ghost world; however, it can still be seen by other ships:

> The strangeness was with us. It was something that was about (or invested) our ship that prevented me—or indeed, anyone else aboard—from seeing that other [ship]. It was evident that she had been able to see us, as was proved by her signaling ... It appeared to me, at that time, to be the weirdest thing that could happen to us.
>
> (GP: 112)

This boundary crossing that transforms their perception also explains the human crew's newfound ability to perceive the ghosts at work among them, which in turn precipitates a rising sense of panic and attempts to fight back but no outbreaks of madness à la Lovecraft, and it also presages the *Mortzestus*'s absorption into the weird world of the pirates. When the ghost pirates finally take over the ship, after having carried off many sailors from their duty stations, they also take over the labor of the human sailors they've replaced: of his period hiding from the ghosts before escaping overboard, Jessop recalls that "Scarcely were the sails set, when I heard the swish and flick of gaskets being cast adrift on the lower yards, and realised that ghostly things were at work there" (GP: 264). Just as the sailors they replace did, these ghosts work for a living, and they expertly sail the captured ship under the waves.

Like a weird version of Herman Melville's Ishmael,[10] Jessop alone survives to tell the tale, and he does so with no expectation that it will be believed; after concluding his report to the captain of the ship that rescued him, he remarks, "there's no one

---

[10] Although it is tempting to view Hodgson as a weird heir to Melville's metaphysical brand of maritime narrative (and to the American's proto-weird interest in tentacles, manifested in the "Squid" chapter of *Moby-Dick*), no evidence exists that Hodgson was familiar with Melville's work. Indeed, Hodgson's lifespan (1877–1918) corresponds exactly to the period of Melville's eclipse between 1876 (when his works went out of print) and the scholarly revival of the early 1920s. Thus the convergence must be explained some other way, perhaps in terms of their similar experiences at sea, but even that prospect appears to be limited. For example, Hodgson never worked on a whaling ship, and in his realistic story "The Mystery of Missing Ships" (1915), the narrator, a ship's captain trying to repair his damaged steam boiler before pirates attack, insists that of all the rapacious people at sea, "whalers is worst. They got a sort of free pass to loaf around the oceans doing nought, with more men an' boats than's good for 'em. It's like *asking* them to help themselves, sending hard cases to sea fitted up like that—all ready to make trouble" (CF 3: 327).

except our own selves will ever know how it happened—really. The shellbacks don't count. They're only 'beastly, drunken brutes of *common sailors*'—Poor devils! No one would think of taking anything they said, as anything more than a damned cuffer" (GP: 268). This bitter recognition of the common sailors' low social status and bad reputation, which constitutes the concluding lines of the novel, suggests that Hodgson's literary interest in representations of labor was not mere realistic detail meant to increase the verisimilitude of his weird fictions. His essays demonstrate this clearly— three of the twelve surviving texts focus on the critique of sailors' and miners' working conditions and their economic ramifications during the period of classical liberalism and imperialism.[11] The two most detailed essays offer materialist analyses of the sailor's life both before and after apprenticeship. "The Trade in Sea Apprentices" (published in *Nautical Magazine*, 1906; now in WS) demonstrates mathematically that the then-common practice of family-subsidized indenture of apprentice sailors benefits the ship owners alone, since the so-called "apprentices" are virtually never given an opportunity to learn the trade but instead are kept busy with menial tasks, while the even more polemical essay "Is the Mercantile Navy Worth Joining?—Certainly Not" (published in the *Grand Magazine*, 1905) concludes as follows:

> Of the actual wretchedness of the [officer's] life, I have said nothing. It is a life of hardness, broken sleep, loneliness, separation, and discomfort. It is indeed a thankless life, without even the common rewards of industry. It leads neither to fame nor wealth, nor, save in exceptional cases, to a sufficiency upon which to retire; and finally the officers of the mercantile marine have not that poor consolation of their Naval brethren, a certain social position. The shore-dwellers scarcely recognize any difference between the mercantile marine officer and the poor wretch they have most atrociously designated the 'common sailor.'
>
> (WS: 158)

Again, the exploitation and degradation of the "common sailor" are the points of contention, in a text with no weird overtones whatsoever. As noted above, Hodgson's own subjective experience of the sailor's life changed radically in the course of his apprenticeship as a common sailor and his career as a mate, and while his realistic fiction reflects that change directly and sometimes rather artlessly, his weird tales encode a more complex subjective transformation. Like the sailors of the *Mortzestus*, Hodgson's protagonists resist the weird physically and psychologically. Like the characters in his realistic fiction who fight their bosses in order to improve their lots, those protagonists sometimes win victories over their opponents, but the labor of those victories—and the defeats as well—transforms them into different subjects. Thus in Hodgson's work we can identify an extended parallel between the materiality of the weird and the materiality of labor, between the struggle against the weird's unhuman or ab-human

---

[11] Four other essays focus on the techniques and benefits of bodybuilding, and thus could be said to constitute an extended reflection on the "labor on the self," "care of the self," or "technologies of the self" that Michel Foucault has traced through the Western theological, philosophical, and political tradition; for a brief overview of this project, see Foucault 1988.

threat to both cognition and life itself and the struggle against exploitation—a parallel that seems to me worth further investigation.

At this point, having examined the main aspects of Hodgson's materialist approach to the weird, we must ask whether Hodgson's materialist versions of ontology, phenomenology, psychology, and epistemology, along with his focus on labor as the arena in which the weird is encountered and resisted, led him to adopt some form of the radical politics often (though not always, as Lovecraft's case proves) associated with philosophical materialism since the eighteenth century. Hodgson's published essays and stories on the tribulations of skilled labor stop well short of revolutionary agitation or organization and instead advocate refusal, resistance, and reform within the framework of liberal capitalism. However, among his posthumously published papers is a poem, which editor Jane Frank dates to around 1912, titled "Pillars of the Empire." It is a short ballad, with a chorus repeated verbatim between verses describing the suffering of laborers on ships, in factories and mines—essentially the same groups whose circumstances he analyzes in his essays.[12] Here is the text of the chorus: "*Pillars of the Empire, with their bases fixed in Hell,/Built with the bones of Workers—masonry grim and fell:/Bases that ever crumble to the dust of unnumbered dead;/Bases exuding misshapen souls of Workers working for bread!*" (WS: 217). As poetry, particularly of its era (and for comparison, Ezra Pound's Imagist volume *Ripostes,* Amy Lowell's *Dome of Many-Coloured Glass,* and Claude McKay's *Songs of Jamaica* also appeared in 1912), it is not only stodgy in form but also clumsy in rhythm and rhyme, as is much of Hodgson's verse; nevertheless, it expresses a much fiercer and more direct critique of alienated labor under imperialism than we find anywhere else in Hodgson's writings.[13] Here the problem is not presented as a case of incompetent or hostile management that could simply be resisted, corrected, or replaced; instead, the problem is empire itself, a systematic global structure of oppression founded on exploited labor, which constitutes the "Pillars of the Empire." It is a system that produces "misshapen souls" of all genders, races, and ethnicities not as an unintended consequence but as an overt means to the end of profit. In relation to Hodgson's better-known work in weird fiction, this image implies that capitalist imperialism itself "weirds" subjectivity, transforming and distorting it through the labor process just as the weird does. If this reading is valid, it suggests that Hodgson's weird materialism unexpectedly intersects and overlaps with the anti-imperialist historical materialism of his contemporaries Lenin and Rosa Luxemburg, though again no evidence exists that he was familiar with their writings (see Lenin 1967 and Luxemburg 2003: section III). Even if such insights did not lead Hodgson to embrace radical politics before the First World War broke out and overwrote those insights with the more conventional patriotism we find in his other late poems and stories, this poem suggests that his work might have developed in a more radical direction had he survived the war, and weird fiction as a tradition might have followed suit.

---

[12] In addition to the essays on the conditions of labor for sailors and officers discussed above, Hodgson also published "The Perils of the Mine," a brief compendium of mine disasters narrated from the miners' viewpoint, in the *Westminster Gazette* in 1910 (in WS).

[13] Contrast this with the idealist Machen's implicitly pro-imperialist vision of "The Bowmen" assisting British troops during the First World War (Machen 2011: 223–6).

Hodgson's weird materialism, which I have outlined in some detail here, offers readers and critics of weird fiction a conceptual framework that is as ideologically disenchanted and logically consistent as Lovecraft's cosmic indifferentism but less contemplative, as well as better informed and more progressive in terms of labor and class. We will see in Chapter Two below that Hodgson also offers us a more balanced representation of racial and ethnic difference than Lovecraft does. Taken together, these factors constitute both a justification for examining his work in relation to the critical materialism of science fiction and the foundation for a counter-history of weird fiction, one less compromised by Lovecraft's racism and elitism. Before we rush to celebrate Hodgson, however, the elements of paternalism in his attitudes toward women, which will be discussed in Chapter Three below, must be acknowledged; in my view this paternalism complicates and compromises his materialism but does not entirely undermine it. Nevertheless, like the works of William Morris, Edith Nesbit, Michael Moorcock, Ursula K. Le Guin, Samuel R. Delany, and others, Hodgson's fiction offers readers materials for the construction of a politically subversive alternative to the philosophical and political conservatism that dominates mainstream fantasy and weird fiction alike, and for that reason alone it deserves more critical attention.

Part One

Hope in Space and Time

William Hope Hodgson imagined and narrated remarkable things, and today he is finally beginning to be lauded for this, but his readers should not forget that he imagined them from the viewpoint of a white cisgender[1] Englishman of the stoutly imperialist Victorian and Edwardian eras, and moreover from the viewpoint of a largely self-educated skilled laborer of that era. While these circumstances make his literary evocations of the weird all the more impressive, they also mark his works with evidence of the conceptual and social constraints that defined those historical periods. Before we analyze his most original and impressive literary visions, we must collect the evidence of those constraints to see how much they affect the aims and value of his work as a whole. More than any other obligation that this study must fulfill, this one will cause us to lament the lack of letters and autobiographical writings that might have permitted us to draw more definitive conclusions regarding Hodgson's views on race, gender, and related political issues of his day. Our examination in this Part is made doubly important by the continuing influence H.P. Lovecraft's concepts and practices exert over both weird writers and weird scholars even today, a fact which has tended to discourage contemporary readers from investigating the work of other Old Weird writers who offer different possibilities for the genre. Most discouraging to such investigation has been—and remains—Lovecraft's lifelong racism, which found echoes among members of his circle such as Robert E. Howard.

Acknowledgment of Lovecraft's racism is commonplace today, but a review of its outlines will allow us to contrast it with Hodgson's attitudes more concretely. The crudest expressions of Lovecraft's views occurred early, among what could charitably be labeled his juvenilia (his first significant work of fiction, "Dagon," dates to 1919): the poems "De Triumpho Naturae" (1905, when he was fifteen) and "On the Creation of Niggers" (1912, when he was twenty-two). The former is dedicated to racist ideologue William Benjamin Smith and versifies claims from Smith's 1905 book *The Color Line* that "The savage black, the ape-resembling beast," is necessarily doomed, for "Against God's will the Yankee freed the slave,/And in the act consign'd him to the grave" because the innately inferior slave needs white mastery in order to survive (Lovecraft

---

[1] As far as we know—Kelly Hurley (2001) has called this assumption into question in her discussion of transgressive gender roleplay in Hodgson's fiction, which I will discuss in Chapter Three.

2013: 33–4). The latter poem is more concise and also more reflective of Lovecraft's increasingly open rejection of Christianity, to which the earlier poem paid lip service: instead of focusing on the perils of Black emancipation, "Creation" archly attributes the origin of African peoples to the Olympian Gods, who "conceived a clever plan" to bridge the gap between beasts and humans: "A beast they wrought, in semi-human figure,/Fill'd it with vice, and call'ed the thing a NIGGER" (Lovecraft 2013: 389). If Lovecraft's attitudes toward Blacks remained clear and consistent throughout his life, the same can't be said for his attitudes toward Jews. He brags to Rheinhart Kleiner that his "ineradicable aversion to the Semitic race" dates from his high school days, when he "became rather well known as an anti-Semite" (Lovecraft 2020: 72), though in later life he would have several close Jewish friends and proteges (including writer Robert Bloch) and even marry an assimilated Jewish woman, Sonia Greene. In any case, at the top of the human hierarchy, Lovecraft predictably placed the Aryan or Teutonic race with which he himself identified, as for example in one of his earliest published essays, "The Crime of the Century" (1915; the title refers to what Lovecraft saw as the greatest tragedy of the First World War: intra-racial warfare between the equally Teutonic British and Germans that would ultimately benefit their racially inferior rivals): "Tracing the career of the Teuton through mediaeval and modern history, we can find no possible excuse for denying him his actual biological supremacy. In widely separated localities and under widely diverse conditions, his innate racial qualities have raised him to preëminence" (Lovecraft 2006: 13). His letters to many correspondents contain similar passages.[2]

Although Lovecraft rarely made overtly racist statements in his published fiction, stories such as "The Horror at Red Hook" (1927) and "The Call of Cthulhu" (1928) turn upon the self-evident moral and physical "degeneracy" of non-white and immigrant communities, while "The Shadow Over Innsmouth" (1936) generates horror out of fears of miscegenation figured as interbreeding between humans and the fishlike Deep Ones. This rhetorical disjunction has allowed many readers to overlook, misinterpret, or downplay his views. Lovecraft's biographer and textual editor S.T. Joshi deserves credit for not merely acknowledging but highlighting and analyzing these issues across his entire corpus, concluding that

> In my view, Lovecraft leaves himself most open to criticism on the issue of race not by the mere espousal of such views but by his lack of openmindedness on the issue, and more particularly his resolute unwillingness to study the most up-to-date findings on the subject from biologists, anthropologists, and other scientists of unquestioned authority who were, through the early decades of the century, systematically destroying each and every pseudo-scientific 'proof' of racialist theories.
>
> (Joshi 2010: 938–9)

Joshi's perspective is readily defensible up to this point, but he takes his account a step further to argue that, "ugly and unfortunate as Lovecraft's racial views are, they do not

---

[2] See Joshi's discussion of these writings and related ones in Joshi 2010: 110–14, 212–18, 936–43.

materially affect the validity of the rest of his philosophical thought ... I cannot see that they affect his metaphysical, ethical, aesthetic, or even his late political views in any meaningful way. These views do not stand or fall on racialist assumptions" (2010: 939). While this assertion may be comforting to devotees, if accepted widely or uncritically, it would have the unfortunate effect of foreclosing, or at least discouraging, inquiry into possible links between Lovecraft's prejudices, his broader philosophy, and his literary achievements. Luckily, other critics—including Michel Houellebecq (2005) and China Miéville, who writes, "The very race-inflected nihilism we vigorously repudiate is simultaneously a central engine for what we admire in Lovecraft's art" (Miéville 2005: xix)—refuse to be discouraged, and their work forms a background for the highly visible interrogation of Lovecraft's racism that can be found in Matt Ruff's 2016 novel *Lovecraft Country* and the 2020 HBO television series based on it.

Lovecraft's attitudes toward gender and class receive less emphatic expression in his writings than his racial ones, but they are nonetheless relevant to contemporary reception of the Old Weird. On the one hand, in his essay *Supernatural Horror in Literature*, Lovecraft expressed his admiration for many women writers including Ann Radcliffe, Mary Shelley, and Emily Brontë, and he was one of the first critics to praise Charlotte Perkins Gilman's story "The Yellow Wallpaper" (1892). More tellingly, the Lovecraft Circle—unlike, say, the Inklings—included several active women writers, one of whom, C.L. Moore, Lovecraft greatly admired and actively encouraged in her contributions to weird fiction and science fiction (see Lovecraft 2017). On the other hand, none of Lovecraft's stories feature fully developed female characters or female narrators; the most memorable women in his fiction are probably Lavinia Whateley, the inbred backwoods albino who gives birth to the monstrous Yog-Sothoth's twins in "The Dunwich Horror" (1929), the seventeenth-century witch Keziah Mason in "The Dreams in the Witch House" (1933), and Asenath Waite, the young woman of partially nonhuman ancestry whose body is usurped by her sorcerer father Ephraim so he can survive bodily death long enough to take over another male body, that of Asenath's husband Edward Derby, in "The Thing on the Doorstep" (1937). The exact degree of Lovecraft's misogyny is much more difficult to determine than that of his racism, though many critics see the disturbingly nonhuman anatomies of his monsters as indices of an underlying disgust with the sexualized, and especially the female, body. With regard to class, Lovecraft's attitude shows a much clearer progression from youthful disdain or condescension for the working class, predicated on a snobbish sense of his family's aristocratic heritage that gradually eroded as they descended into poverty, to a guarded sympathy that is nevertheless still marked by cultural elitism as his experience of the Great Depression led him to embrace a technocratic version of New Deal social democracy. This wishful identification with the dominant class is at the root of what I described in the Introduction as the contemplative nature of Lovecraft's materialism.

As we will see in the three chapters that follow, William Hope Hodgson's attitudes to these subjects, as expressed in his fiction, differ sharply from Lovecraft's in a variety of ways, and as such they offer us a different way to look at weird fiction's emergence, as well as its entanglement with broader social and cultural conflicts, in the early twentieth century. Ultimately, I hope, such a perspective will allow us to construct a different history, to tell a different story, of the weird. This is not to say that Hodgson conforms to twenty-first-century norms of unprejudiced thinking or political progressivism; he remained a man of his era, though a highly unusual one who anticipates the future in many astonishing particulars, and some of his views are unquestionably ambiguous and unsettling. Although I intend to confront and criticize those views as directly and thoroughly as possible, I do not apologize for using the inconsistencies and uncertainties revealed by his fiction to make the most sympathetic possible case for Hodgson in this part of the book, since I see no point in denouncing the ideological misjudgments of an author whom no one at present myopically idolizes or uncritically imitates. If my efforts in this book succeed, and Hodgson comes to be more widely and deeply appreciated as a writer, or if additional historical information becomes available, then perhaps a harsher account of his historical limitations will become necessary. For now, my aim is simply to situate him in his time and in the places he knew so that the true extent of his imaginative escapes from the limitations of space and time can be assessed in Parts Two and Three. In order to understand his untimeliness, we must first measure the extent of his timeliness.

1

The Larger English

For most readers, *The Night Land*'s reputation precedes it, and that reputation is deeply ambivalent, to the point of bipolarity. On the one hand, virtually everyone who makes it through the novel admits the startling originality and scope of its fantastic, far-future setting: the dead sun, the earth's familiar landscape made radically alien, the monstrous threats, and the great fortress which preserves humankind from its environment. Hodgson's most influential heirs and admirers speak for the rest of his fans: Lovecraft describes it as "one of the most potent pieces of macabre imagination ever written" (Lovecraft 2000: 59), and China Miéville calls it "one of the most extraordinary works in the English language … a masterpiece" (Miéville 2002a: ix). On the other hand, virtually everyone also complains that the book's highly artificial verbal style interferes with the reader's access to and enjoyment of its originality, to the point that it often prevents otherwise interested readers from finishing it. Again, his most famous promoters make this case forcefully: according to Lovecraft, *The Night Land* "is told in a rather clumsy fashion, … marred by painful verboseness, repetitiousness, … and an attempt at archaic language even more grotesque and absurd than that in [Hodgson's first-published novel, *The Boats of the*] 'Glen Carrig'" (Lovecraft 2000: 59), while Miéville speculates that, "If a committee had been set up to design an unreadable book, they'd probably have come up with *The Night Land*," in large part because it "is written in a staggeringly inept cod-antique style" (Miéville 2002a: ix).

Although such assessments are not entirely unwarranted, I think they are overstated, for two reasons. The first is that other, more widely influential writers of fantastika have deployed styles of comparable artificiality, and while most of them, such as E.R. Eddison and J.R.R. Tolkien, postdate Hodgson, at least one, William Morris, predates him and possibly influenced or at least authorized his linguistic experiments. (The fact that all three were well educated in ancient and modern languages, while Hodgson was not, testifies to the latter's artistic ambitions as well as his foolhardiness.) Readers who are prepared to make allowances for these writers' artifices should not complain overmuch about Hodgson's. Second, and more relevant to the following discussion, most readers come to *The Night Land* after having read Hodgson's other three novels, either because they choose to read in the order of the books' original publication or because they begin with the shorter texts, and those novels may give the erroneous impression that *The Night Land*'s experimentation with language is an anomaly in his oeuvre, the extravagance of an overly ambitious "artist" who has mistaken his true métier, which is the direct and uncluttered narration of cosmic fear. While it is true that Hodgson's shorter novels pose few if any linguistic challenges to the reader, this does not mean that he was content to work exclusively within the constraints of standard English usage and idiomatic diction. His short fiction, especially his non-fantastic short fiction, abounds with attempts to represent foreign accents and regional dialects as variations on the "larger English" he encountered in his career as a merchant sailor. Indeed, the plots of several realist stories turn upon questions of language in ways that illuminate Hodgson's means and aims in *The Night Land*.

The phrase "the larger English" appears in the opening paragraphs of "The Captain of the Onion Boat," a sentimental tale of lovers separated by religious vocation first published in *Nash's Magazine* in 1910, as part of the characterization of the Mate who serves as the story's ethical center and goad to action: " 'Old Man's got it bad as ever,' he muttered, in an accent and language that spoke of the larger English" (CF 4: 407). The "Old Man" is his captain, Big John Carlos, son of a Spanish father and an English mother, who finds himself trapped by paternal Catholicism and the hierarchical language that abets it when his betrothed, daughter of a conservative Spanish landowner, enters a convent after Carlos is erroneously reported lost at sea. Their minds "darkened with the Clouds of Belief" (CF 4: 410), neither lover can initially imagine, much less countenance, the recantation of her sacred vows, until the Mate's oft-repeated and mildly blasphemous refrain "W'y th 'ell don't 'e get 'er out!" provides the final impetus for a shift in Carlos's perspective:

> In him as in the woman, there had been going forward, without his knowledge, that steady disruption of religious belief—the rotting and decaying of all arbitrary things, before the primal need of the human heart; so that the olden barriers of "Impossibility," were now but as shadows, that would be gone in a moment, when next the Force of his Need should urge him to take his heart's desire.
>
> (CF 4: 411)

The lovers "listened unknowingly for the coming of the unknown one who should give the little push forward, and so cause them to step over the borderland into all natural and long craved for happiness" (CF 4: 412). In the course of the story, Captain Carlos says only ten words and his beloved says nothing at all, bound as they are by the "arbitrary" religious words that separate them; the Mate is the only regularly quoted speaker, and the direct practicality of his uneducated dialect contrasts just as sharply with the circumlocutionary formality of the narrator's voice as it does with the couple's muteness. Indeed, his role is more catalytic than argumentative: in terms of speech-act theory, it is the illocutionary force of the Mate's words—the performative energy they transmit—and not their content or referents that gives Carlos the "little push" he needs to break free of his religious scruples and spring into action. "After all [that]," the narrator acknowledges, "the Rescue—if it can be named by a term so heroic—proved a ridiculously easy matter" (CF 4: 416). Once an alternate language to that of Catholicism, and with it an alternate set of presuppositions, has been revealed by the Mate's speech, action becomes not merely possible but inevitable.

Hodgson's interest in the encounter, interpenetration, and blending of different languages and dialects has largely been ignored by scholarship, despite the fact that much of his fiction manifests it (and examples can even be found in his few surviving letters [U: 37]). His ambition in this regard is comparable to Mark Twain's, although he is ultimately less successful than his American contemporary in differentiating non-standard speech patterns. In a few cases, non-standard English serves merely to intensify tragic sentimentalism, as in the speech of the mourning parents in "The Valley of Lost Children" (*Cornhill Magazine*, 1906), or to sharpen the satire of a caricature, as in the outdated slang spoken by the wizened crew of "The *Shamraken* Homeward Bounder" (*Putnam's Monthly*, 1908) as they mistake a hurricane for the gates of heaven (or hell). More often, it appears in the narrative as the association of non-standard English, especially uneducated working-class dialect, with unencumbered vision, (at least comparative) ethical clarity, and practical force. This is the significance of the half-English, half-French pidgin of the pirate Captain Dan, who posthumously avenges the middle-class slights and betrayals that drove him from home in "The Home-Coming of Captain Dan" (*The Red Magazine*, 1918); the accents of the crafty Scots sailors who rescue a group of Balkan youths from impending execution in "Merciful Plunder" (posthumously published in 1925); and the shipboard idiom of the longsuffering sailors who witness the revenge of their abused comrade on the brutal officers in "The Haunting of the *Lady Shannon*" (posthumously published in 1975). While this association of dialect and class with ethics is not unprecedented in English literature—Charles Dickens famously deployed it in *Hard Times* (1854), and it also plays a role in Emily Brontë's *Wuthering Heights* (1847)—it was often undercut in those same works when the authors further depicted their dialect-speaking characters as emotionally uncontrolled or personally eccentric so as to reduce the general significance of their claims or their suffering. Lovecraft, of course, used nonstandard English almost exclusively as a marker of a character's intellectual inferiority or ethical perversion, as we see in the speech of Old Wizard Whateley in "The Dunwich Horror." As a working-class writer himself, Hodgson seems to have rejected such a condescending view of nonstandard speech.

Two of his stories take a different, more thorough-going approach to language, inscribing a dialectic of dialect and ethics into their plots. Set during the Napoleonic Wars, "The Friendship of Monsieur Jeynois" (*The Red Magazine*, 1915) is narrated long after the events that comprise it by former cabin boy John Merlyn, who describes his younger self in gentlemanly English as "a poor and ignorant lad" who "talked a strange mixture of dialects and rough words" as a consequence of his impoverished and itinerant childhood (CF 5: 124). The tale focuses on Merlyn's admiration for M. Jeynois of the title, a morally upright and cultured Frenchman who has outfitted a brig as an English privateer against his countrymen (for reasons never explained), and who speaks much better English than any of the Englishmen aboard. Merlyn reports Jeynois's rebuke of his unreliable crewmen, spoken in "good English that no man could better; for Monsieur was French, to my thinking, only in name" (CF 5: 127). Merlyn later overhears the surly English officers plotting Jeynois's murder and, despite sharing both their English ancestry and their poor language skills, decides to inform the Frenchman of it, in the process demonstrating the "rough words" that were his only medium:

> "You're in horful danger, sir," I told him, for that was how I spoke in those days, before ever I was given the good schooling that I had later. " ... Cappen Drool is to have th' brig, an' he've offered t'others yourn share o' the prize money an' a hundred guineas, and they'm not to make no claim to own the ship."
>
> (CF 5: 129)

As a result of the boy's veneration for his noble behavior and verbal eloquence, Jeynois is awake and armed when the conspirators come for him. A lengthy and unequal battle between them erupts, which Merlyn tries to balance by aiding Jeynois. Although the pair manages to drive off their attackers temporarily, killing the ringleaders, Jeynois is mortally wounded. In gratitude to the cabin boy for his aid, Jeynois writes out an impromptu will naming Merlyn his heir (although the illiterate Merlyn "was too ignorant at that time to know what it was that he wrote"), specifying that he be sent to "a good school" (CF 5: 139), after which Jeynois dies, leaving the boy to "cry over his dead hero" and fend off the remaining thugs with threats to ignite the ship's powder stores (CF 5: 140). Upon arriving in Portsmouth, he bears witness to the mutiny, sees the surviving conspirators hanged, and only then collects the legacy from his dead friend: the education that provides him with the language skills to write the story in the first place.

Even more interesting in this regard is "The Mystery of Captain Chappel" (*The Red Magazine*, 1917), which focuses on an elderly cobbler named Juk who, despite his occupation, is asked by his policeman nephew to assist in the investigation of Chappel's puzzling murder. Like Inspector Lestrade in the Sherlock Holmes stories, the police chief wants to keep Juk's involvement "on the quiet" for fear that "maybe he'll get into a bother over lettin' an amachoor come messin' around" (CF 2: 401). Juk is an unconventional private detective, ambivalent about his abilities ("'I'm not struck, nevvy, on detectiven' ... I got the gift, I know; but it's a sneakin', pryin', think-evil-of-yer-feller-men sort of job, an' no work for a decent-hearted man'" [CF 2: 401]) and given to lengthy, digressive diatribes in very broad working-class dialect. While Juk is investigating, a second man is killed the same way Chappel was, then he and his nephew witness a third murder, carried out by a croaking black creature of enormous stature, that they are unable to prevent. All the clues in the three cases lead Juk to suspect some kind of revenge plot, so he and his nephew stake out a nearby pub in search of the killer. They find him soon enough, "a big negro" who "looked rough and powerful, and had something of the appearance of a mariner who had made enough money to live ashore in comfort; for he was wearing quite a well-cut suit, double-breasted, with an inflamed tie, and a tie-pin that winked like a true diamond" (CF 2: 411). When they attempt to arrest him outside his lodgings, he easily overpowers them, knocking the nephew out cold but treating the old cobbler gently: "the negro proved himself no brute, now that he had only the one small opponent. He freed himself with a swift, easy strength, without attempting to strike, much as a grown man might free himself from the grip of a boy" (CF 2: 411). Here Hodgson inverts the traditional racist trope that labels an adult Black male a "boy" subordinate to the "manhood" of the white, foreshadowing the story's surprising denouement.

At the tale's conclusion Juk reveals that the three murdered men had previously been partners who owned and operated a ship that was rumored to be crewed by seal poachers and pirates, hence guilty of their own share of murders. The well-dressed Black man, Juk deduces, must have

> been concerned in their sealin' business, and maybe worse; an' when I thinks of it, I gets wonderin' if they'd cut the poor heathen's tongue out, so as he couldn't give 'em away; yet so as they could use him. What so be it is they done to him and others, I'm mighty sure it was as bad as could be.
>
> (CF 2: 416)

The loss of his tongue would explain the croaking sounds he made during the third murder, when he wore a stuffed seal's head on his own head to terrify his foe. Juk concludes his speculations by admitting, "If he's caught, maybe we'll learn, an' maybe we won't. But I hopes as you policemen, you'll never lay a hand on him. I'd be very well pleased. I believe he gave them three divvils no more than was comin' to them; an' he let me off gentle tonight. I don't forget that" (CF 2: 416). Despite not having "enough knowledge ... to be what you'd call scientific" (CF 2: 401), Juk out-thinks and out-maneuvers the police to identify the killer, and despite referring to his quarry three times as a "nigger," Juk not only articulates an ethical (though not legal) defense for him that he would have been unable to speak for himself (if in fact he lacked a tongue), but also acquits him of culpability for the crimes and wishes him well. This is not a matter of Juk speaking *for him* or *in his place*, but rather speaking *in support* of him. In this story, the rough-spoken—or even unspoken—but practical ethics of the lowly, both Black and white, unites them in solidarity even as it trumps the stiffly correct language and self-satisfied legalism of the police and the courts.

These patterns of association between language, perception, social status, and ethical judgment also manifest themselves in Hodgson's weird fiction, though far less often. In *The Ghost Pirates* (1909), for example, the narrator Jessop first learns of the *Mortzestus*'s reputation for minor misfortune and possible haunting from the cockney Williams, who tells him, "There's too many bloomin' shadders about this 'ere packet; they gets onter yer nerves like nothin' as ever I seen before in me nat'ral" (GP: 19). Williams's foreboding is soon amply confirmed by his and other crewmen's experience, although he does not live to see it, and Jessop, who ends up being the ship's only survivor, bitterly admits that his crewmate's testimony would count for nothing with the authorities because of his status, which is clearly marked in his speech: "They're only 'beastly, drunken brutes of *common sailors*'—Poor devils! No one would think of taking anything they said, as anything more than a damned cuffer" (GP: 268). Such linguistic difference does not constitute a significant aspect of this novel, however, aside from Hodgson's careful effort to represent several different versions of non-standard English accents and idioms among the officers and crew of the *Mortzestus*.

Stronger evidence showing the importance of linguistic multiplicity to Hodgson's conception of the weird can be found in one of his very few incomplete manuscripts to survive, "Captain Dang." As Sam Moskowitz noted when he first published it in 1996, this text seems to be the beginning of a novel that is somehow related to the short story "The Habitants of Middle Islet," itself not published until 1962. Moskowitz speculates that "Hodgson's lack of financial success with his novels caused him to drop this as an unprofitable venture" (Moskowitz 1996: 86), although it is impossible to determine whether "Captain Dang" is an unfinished expansion of the unsold short story or the story was an unsuccessful attempt to salvage the basic plot of the abandoned novel. The short story involves a group of men who sail to the "Middle Islet" off the coast of Nightingale Island, in the isolated Tristan da Cunha archipelago of the South Atlantic, in search of the lost ship that carried one man's fiancée. There they find the dismasted ship with his beloved's belongings and day calendar, inexplicably set to the very day they arrive, in a tidy cabin, but no sign of survivors. When two men decide to spend a night aboard the derelict, they encounter a terrifying species of carnivorous humanoid sea monster that can hypnotize humans into seeing familiar faces in place of their inhuman visages, a trait they use to lure the grieving fiancé to a violent death. Although the story contains several effective details, such as the calendar and the dreamlike hypnotism passage, it concludes abruptly with the surviving searchers' frantic departure, which leaves the mysteries unexplained; perhaps this haste is why it failed to sell.

The draft opening section of "Captain Dang" incorporates the most striking events of the short story, slightly modified and shifted to the South Pacific, into an eyewitness report summarized by Dang to his Second Mate Morgan (the narrator) as an explanation for why he has taken their ship off course to search for an unmapped island. While Morgan, who introduces himself as a newly certified Mate in search of a berth, is clearly a fictionalized version of the young Hodgson, who had earned his own Mate's certificate in 1897, Dang seems to represent Hodgson's masculine ideal, which is expressed through his mastery of languages as well as his physique (both Morgan and Dang, like Hodgson himself, are scientific body-builders and skilled boxers). When Morgan first meets Dang to apply for the position of Second Mate on Dang's ship, he observes that

> never a note of the sailor was there in him, from knight-heads to half-round, as one might say nautically … In short, so far removed was he from the "odour of salt" that, but for his stern face, I should have named him as a frequenter of Bond Street and other haunts, in Piccadilly and elsewhere, of the Smart and Fashionable.
>
> (CF 5: 246)

Morgan assumes that he has accurately determined Dang's station and role, but when the captain emerges from his cabin after the ship departs London, Morgan is stunned by the change in his appearance. The "Smart and Fashionable" gentleman has become a "stout-seeming, enormously broad, unshaven man, dressed in heavy, blue pilot-cloth, with a peak-hat pushed back on his head ... His walk had lost its swift precision and had given place to a careless roll that yet had a cat-like note of quickness in it" (CF 5: 248–9). Only Dang's incongruous lavender kid gloves remain to remind Morgan of his previous appearance.

Just as Dang's appearance switches from dandy to salt and back again, so does his speech switch back and forth between the idioms of the aristocrat and the skilled laborer. When he takes Morgan to the shipping office to sign his contract, he speaks as lord and master to a servant, peremptorily advising his First Mate, "I shall be down again tonight, Mister ... Tell the steward not to turn in till I come" (CF 5: 247). When Morgan next sees him, however, Dang genially tells him, "You'll be pickin' your watch, laddie, in a moment; be sure to pick Turrill, that lanky, daft lookin' devil for our side. I want him in our watch" (CF 5: 249). This code switching involves not just Dang's grammar and diction, but even the timbre of his voice: "His very voice was different. It had lost its note of culture and its crispness. It sounded deeper, more mellow, slacker" (CF 5: 248). The unusual relationship between Dang and Morgan comes to be defined by this switching of the codes that conventionally articulate distinctions of class, educational level, status, and, most importantly in this case, the institutional authority of command. Dang's voices signify on the one hand his legal right as captain to give orders that his subordinates must carry out, and on the other, his ethical responsibility as an accomplished sailor to give only appropriate orders that his subordinates can respect. This balanced mixture—"what [Morgan] considered was his assumed 'rough speech' was not homogenous but hybrid" (CF 5: 255)—reveals Dang to be an ideal officer whom Morgan comes to admire and wish to imitate. Dang's willingness to step across the boundaries between levels in the shipboard hierarchy to demonstrate his qualifications extends even to the treatment of his body: after watching Morgan knock an aggressively insubordinate Russian named Jarkoff unconscious (CF 5: 264–5), Dang feels his blood "stirred" and goes forward to offer the regular seamen the chance to box with him, although they only accept the offer when he allows three of them to team up against him alone. Even so, he quickly dispatches all of them, and after sending them to the steward for bandages and rum, Dang "shout[s] the cheeriest of good nights to the men in the fo'cas'le, the same being answered with the utmost heartiness and respect" (CF 5: 266–7).

Realizing that Dang's alternation of speech and bodily codes, which Morgan describes as "the man of culture ... peeping out unwittingly through the rind of rough, pilot-clad sailorman" (CF 5: 253) and vice versa, has become the norm aboard his ship, Morgan assumes it can be discussed meta-linguistically as well, but he is mistaken. While listening to Dang tell the sea monster story, Morgan notices what he takes to be a slip in the level of the captain's speech and says, "You've altered again, Sir ... " Dang asks, "'What's that, laddie?' ... But somehow there was something at the back of his tone that warned me I'd made a mistake to venture what I had said" (CF 5: 255). For reasons never explained in the fragment, Dang is unwilling to acknowledge his unusual linguistic practice or explain its origin; similarly, no explanation is offered for the First Mate's advice "never [to] say a word again' wimmen where he [Dang] can hear you, or he'll plug you sure as fate" (CF 5: 250). The unfinished manuscript breaks off shortly after Dang finishes telling Morgan the tale he has heard of the missing ship's rediscovery and the frightening creatures occupying it; his decision to see it for himself seems to be motivated purely by curiosity and a craving for adventure, although his unexplained reverence for women may point to a planned but unwritten revelation of more directly personal interest. Such a conclusion would converge thematically with that of the short story version as well as a similar tale, "The Finding of the *Graiken*" (*The Red Magazine*, 1913), although neither of those tales includes code-switching. Had it been completed, "Captain Dang" would almost certainly have taken Hodgson's experiments with dialects, linguistic markers of social distinctions, and artificial extensions of English to a higher level of originality and sophistication that may well have vindicated, or at least clarified, his widely derided and misunderstood efforts in *The Night Land*.

As I noted at the beginning of this chapter, many reviewers and critics, including Lovecraft, have contended that Hodgson's style in *The Night Land*, which is apparently intended to suggest the formal diction of the seventeenth or eighteenth century, constitutes both an intrinsic artistic flaw and a major obstacle for readers that has prevented him from attaining the literary recognition that his fantastic themes and concepts deserve. The most remarkable consequence of this widespread judgment is the attempt by fantasy novelist James Stoddard to rewrite *The Night Land* scene by scene in a more conventionally idiomatic style. Far from more successfully realizing Hodgson's aim, as he states is his intention, Stoddard's rewrite—or rather reboot, as I will explain later—conventionalizes and normalizes much of the weirdness of Hodgson's text, effectively "unweirding" it. This well-intentioned unweirding, which, surprisingly, mirrors and extends Hodgson's own efforts to get his work published almost exactly a century earlier, demonstrates the extent to which weird fiction must be defined, appreciated, and studied not merely as a specific range of possible thematic and symbolic contents (involving, as we have already seen, a radical extension of or estrangement from human cognition and experience as well as the presentation of non-, un- or ab-human experiences, the last being Hodgson's own preferred term[1]) but also as a set of stylistic and formal strategies centered on the problem of how to refer to or represent the non-/un-/ab-human. In the terms that structural linguistics taught us, the weird materializes as much in the signifier as in the signified of such fiction, just as class did in realist fiction, and both signifier and signified impose a new kind of interpretive labor upon the reader.

Hodgson's four novels were originally published between 1907 and 1912, but despite positive reviews, they were not financially successful, and after his death they soon went out of print and probably would have been forgotten if not for the place of honor given them in the revised version of Lovecraft's influential essay *Supernatural Horror in Literature*. Of Hodgson's work in general Lovecraft writes, "Few can equal him in adumbrating the nearness of nameless forces and monstrous besieging entities through casual hints and insignificant details, or in conveying feelings of the spectral and the abnormal in connexion with regions or buildings." He describes Hodgson's last-published

---

[1] On Hodgson's conception of the ab-human, see Hurley 2001: 130–40, and Miéville 2012: 379–82.

novel *The Night Land* as "one of the most potent pieces of macabre imagination ever written," and provides a capsule summary that would be difficult to better:

> The picture of a night-black, dead planet, with the remains of the human race concentrated in a stupendously vast metal pyramid and besieged by monstrous, hybrid, and altogether unknown forces of darkness, is something that no reader can ever forget. Shapes and entities of an altogether non-human and inconceivable sort—the prowlers of the black, man-forsaken, and unexplored world outside the pyramid—are *suggested* and *partly* described with ineffable potency; while the night-bound landscape with its chasms and slopes and dying volcanism takes on an almost sentient terror beneath the author's touch. Midway in the book the central figure ventures outside the pyramid on a quest through death-haunted realms untrod by man for millions of years—and in his slow, minutely described, day-by-day progress over unthinkable leagues of immemorial blackness there is a sense of cosmic alienage, breathless mystery, and terrified expectancy unrivalled in the whole range of literature.
> (Lovecraft 2000: 59–60)

This description has prompted thousands of readers, including August Derleth, who brought Hodgson's novels back into print for the first time in 1946, to seek out Hodgson's works, and has kept them in print now for three-quarters of a century.

However, Lovecraft also offers a caveat that is the basis for our discussion here: *The Night Land*, he notes, "is told in a rather clumsy fashion, as the dreams of a man of the seventeenth century, whose mind merges with its own future incarnation; and is seriously marred by painful verboseness, repetitiousness, artificial and nauseously sticky romantic sentimentality, and an attempt at archaic language even more grotesque and absurd than that in [Hodgson's first-published novel, *The Boats of the*] '*Glen Carrig*'" (Lovecraft 2000: 59). In a letter to James F. Morton, in fact the last letter Lovecraft wrote before his death in 1937, he goes much further, asking in exasperation,

> what sort of insanity gets hold of some of these birds (W.H. Hodgson is the classic & memorable offender ...) when they try to represent the diction of an age which after all is, historically speaking, essentially modern? Haven't they ever read Goldsmith & Fielding & Johnson & Gibbon & Sterne & Smollett & dozens of other prose writers of that fairly recent yesterday? What in Yuggoth's name causes them to drag down from the remoter regions of antiquity a cobwebbed jargon more Chaucerian or Elizabethan than anything else, & serve it up as contemporary with Burke's speeches & the seditious Declaration of Independence?
> (Lovecraft 2011: 399)

Most later readers of *The Night Land* agree with this view,[2] and even Hodgson himself appears to have recognized the difficulty that his chosen style posed; in a 1905 letter

---

[2] Among the few to dissent from it are Ian Bell (Bell 1987: 37–43), Michael Moorcock (Moorcock 2004: 51–2), and James Cawthorn (Cawthorn & Moorcock 1988: 65–6).

Hodgson reports that his novels *The House on the Borderland* and *The Ghost Pirates* have been rejected by publishers twenty-one and fourteen times respectively, and concludes that "I've tried hard to be commonplace in [my writing]; but, I'm afraid, with but poor success. I cannot ride [sic] above that failing of mine which urges me to write original stuff" (U: 34).

Perhaps an example of Hodgson's "original stuff" will make the case clearer. Here is a passage that Sam Gafford cites as typical in his important essay "Writing Backwards: The Novels of William Hope Hodgson" (to which I will return in a moment). The passage is drawn from chapter four of *The Night Land*, "The Hushing of the Voice," and depicts the situation within the Great Redoubt following the departure of an unauthorized rescue party to assist the inhabitants of the distant, threatened Lesser Redoubt:

> And in thiswise passed three days and nights; yet both in the sleeptime and the time of waking did great multitudes cease not to watch; so that many went hungry for sleep, as in truth did I. And sometimes we saw those Youths with plainness; but other times they were lost to our sight in the utter shadows of the Night Land. Yet, by the telling of our instruments, and the sense of my hearing, there was no awareness among the Monsters, and the Forces of Evil, that any were abroad from the Pyramid; so that a little hope came into our hearts that yet there might be no tragedy.
>
> (NL: 87)

This passage shows some of the ways that Hodgson manipulates syntax, diction, and vocabulary to create an effect of readerly defamiliarization or estrangement, including syntactic inversion ("cease not to watch"), mixed metaphor ("hungry for sleep"), terminological archaism ("thiswise"), and neologism ("sleeptime"). Over the course of 500 pages, that estrangement becomes rather severe. Andy Sawyer somewhat hyperbolically describes Hodgson's style in this novel, which seems to find justification if not actual inspiration in William Morris's quasi-medieval romances of the 1890s, as "a series of sledgehammer blows [aimed] at language itself" before concluding that, "Grammatically, this is like little ever dignified with the title of 'the English Language'—at least, to modern ears ... " (Sawyer 2014: 177–8).

Since *The Night Land* was the last published of Hodgson's novels, critics have long assumed that it was also the last written, and thus represents the final flowering of his cosmic imagination before he resigned himself to focusing on realistic tales of seafaring. However, in his essay Gafford argues, on the basis of recently discovered letters, that in fact it was written first, perhaps as early as 1905 (Gafford 2013b: 24). If this is correct, it means that Hodgson's idiosyncratic artistic development did not culminate in *The Night Land*, but instead that he "moved away from [*Night Land*]'s quasi-science fiction scenario (which contained an astounding number of original conceptions) and toward [*Boats of the 'Glen Carrig'*]'s more basic adventure slant" (Gafford 2013b: 25). According to Gafford, "It is only in [*Boats of the 'Glen Carrig'*] that Hodgson hits a medium, combining his imagination with a flat, but readable, style" (Gafford 2013b: 23). That "flattening" is achieved primarily through the return to conventional syntax, but also through a drastic reduction in the density of metaphysical language of the sort analyzed in the other sections of this study. In short, the repeated rejection of his stylistically more difficult novels by publishers gradually drove Hodgson to adopt a more idiomatic, accessible, and contemporary style—in other words, to begin a process of "unweirding" his own writing at the stylistic level.

However, Hodgson apparently did not go back and rewrite his earlier novels in the "flat, readable" style that he had arduously and belatedly achieved in *Boats of the "Glen Carrig."* That task, which we might see as the completion of the process I've just outlined, would fall to another of Hodgson's later admirers, the contemporary American fantasist James Stoddard. Best known as the author of the *Evenmere* trilogy (consisting of *The High House*, which won the Compton Crook Award for Best First Novel in 1998 [Stoddard 1998]; *The False House* [Stoddard 2000]; and *Evenmere* [Stoddard 2015]), Stoddard wrote a Master's thesis on Ballantine's Adult Fantasy series of the nineteen-seventies, which had published *The Boats of the "Glen Carrig"* and *The Night Land* in paperback for the first time. Even before writing his *Evenmere* books, though, Stoddard had embarked on his rewrite, which is effectively a reboot, of Hodgson's *Night Land*. In his introduction to it, he insists that he was motivated by a desire to broaden the popular appeal of a novel he considers a "masterpiece":

> Unfortunately, a book that should be considered a classic is mostly unread and forgotten, for Hodgson chose to write it in a difficult, archaic style. Editor Lin Carter, while praising the book when he oversaw its paperback publication in 1972, said, "*The Night Land* is a work of sustained imaginative vision without equal in literature, but it is dreadfully overwritten, overlong, and verbose to the point of shameful self-indulgence."
>
> (Stoddard 2011: v)

Stoddard goes on to describe the stages of his project, which took nearly a decade to complete:

> I began by rewriting the book, paragraph by paragraph, but soon discovered that Hodgson's prose did not hold up to direct "translation." I grew bolder and began adding dialogue (Hodgson had none), character motivation, and even brief scenes not in the original volume, but necessary to support the logic of the story line. I was forced to name the main character, who [sic] Hodgson left nameless. I have divided the book into more chapters than in the original, breaking the action at various points to slow the relentless pace, and have renamed several chapters to avoid giving away the plot. I have striven to use Hodgson's thoughts (sometimes only bare hints) to recreate his world.
>
> (Stoddard 2011: v–vi)

Of course, Hodgson's "thoughts" are only accessible in the form of his words on the page, which are what Stoddard found wanting and set out to change. The result is a book that incorporates all the main plot points of the original in roughly two-thirds the number of pages, written in a contemporary, idiomatic style that is easily readable—a style that, I note parenthetically, seems considerably less ornate and expressive than that of Stoddard's own *Evenmere* books.

In order to compare Stoddard's version with Hodgson's original, please recall the passage quoted earlier (page 44 above) as an example of the latter's style. Here is Stoddard's version of the same passage:

> From the time the travelers left the pyramid, onlookers thronged the embrasures and Viewing Tables, anxiously awaiting word. Sometimes we saw the company plainly, other times they remained lost in the grotesque shadows of the Night Land. According to our Instruments and my Night Hearing the monsters and Forces of Evil remained unaware of them, and we began to hope that tragedy might be miraculously avoided. Three days and nights passed, and I scarcely slept at all, for as I sat in the Tower of Observation I knew there were mothers and fathers keeping vigil below me at the northern embrasures.
>
> (Stoddard 2011: 46–7)

Notice that Stoddard has eliminated the archaisms, circumlocutions, and syntactical inversions of the original, which reduces the texture of the prose nearly to neutrality and smoothness.

But that passage is only minimally weird even in Hodgson's version. Other passages, more central to the evocation of the ab-human, suffer a stylistically similar but conceptually and symbolically more dismaying fate. Here is Hodgson's description of the advent of the monsters and ab-humans that we examined in the Introduction from the viewpoint of his materialist metaphysics:

> Of the coming of these monstrosities and evil Forces, no man could say much with verity; for the evil of it began before the Histories of the Great Redoubt were shaped; aye, even before the sun had lost all power to light; though, it must not be a thing of certainty, that even at this far time the invisible, black heavens held no warmth for this world ... The evil must surely have begun in the Days of the Darkening (which I might liken to a story which was believed doubtfully, much as we of this day believe the story of the Creation). A dim record there was of olden sciences (that are yet far off in our future) which, disturbing the unmeasurable Outward Powers, had allowed to pass the Barrier of Life some of those Monsters and Ab-human creatures, which are so wondrously cushioned from us at this normal present. And thus there had materialised, and in other cases developed, grotesque and horrible Creatures, which now beset the humans of this world. And where there was no power to take on material form, there had been allowed to certain dreadful Forces to have power to affect the life of the human spirit. And this growing very dreadful, and the world full of lawlessness and degeneracy, there had banded together the sound millions, and built the Last Redoubt.
>
> (NL: 44–5)

And now Stoddard's version:

> Of the coming of the monstrosities, we knew little, for the evil began before the histories of the Great Pyramid were written, before the sun had even completely faded. We believed the trouble arose in the legendary Days of the Darkening, when ancient science disturbed powers beyond the earthly plane, allowing the monsters and Ab-humans to pass an unseen barrier previously protecting mankind. Grotesque and horrible creatures materialized to assault humanity, while those entities lacking the power to assume physical form grew into Forces capable of influencing and destroying the human spirit. As civilization descended into lawlessness, the surviving millions banded together in the twilight of the world to build the Last Redoubt.
>
> (Stoddard 2011: 25–6)

The rewrite condenses the original to half its length and smooths out its idiosyncrasies of syntax, diction, and vocabulary, such as circumlocution ("before the sun had lost … warmth for this world") and temporal paradox ("olden sciences that are yet far off in our future"). It also eliminates the parenthetical aside on the growing religious skepticism of modernity and the concluding language of physical and social degeneration. Whereas the purely linguistic modifications minimize the stylistic distance between the original text and contemporary usage, and consequently reduce the estrangement that the reader experiences, the deletions serve to reduce the symbolic complexity and erase both the historical specificity and the metaphysical weight of Hodgson's prose.

The result is a severe "unweirding" of *The Night Land* at the level of language and form. Although Stoddard strives to preserve the weird themes and imagery of the original text, which he feels make it a masterpiece, his revisions conventionalize and normalize the textual materials that most obdurately resist standard habits of reading contemporary prose narrative, which is to say the small-scale formal elements that foreground and intensify the weirdness of Hodgson's thematic imagination. In this way Stoddard completes the process of formal and stylistic "unweirding" that Hodgson himself inaugurated in response to publishers' indifference to his most original work. This systematic revision reveals itself to be a reboot, a narrative reset intended to serve as the starting point for further narration set in the same fictional world, when we note that it is dedicated to four people whom Stoddard credits with keeping Hodgson's work in print—H.C. Koenig, who lent Lovecraft his Hodgson collection in 1934 and thus made possible the comments in *Supernatural Horror in Literature* that have led so many to read *The Night Land*; August Derleth, who republished Hodgson's works after the Second World War; Lin Carter and Betty Ballantine, who published them in paperback for the first time—and one, Andy Robertson, "who created The Night Land website and publishes original anthologies based on the book" (Stoddard 2011: iii). Thus Stoddard addresses his rewrite specifically to readers of Hodgson who also aspire to write pastiches of Hodgson, perhaps as a shortcut for those who find the original text too hard going.³ This may be why Stoddard's book jacket is graced with a laudatory blurb from the Paranormal Romance Guild. If half a century of Lovecraft pastiches have taught us anything, however, it is that such shortcuts hardly ever lead to genuine literary achievement.⁴

To conclude this chapter, let me turn back to Lovecraft for a moment. Although he was one of the readers who objected most strongly to Hodgson's stylistic and formal choices in *The Night Land*, and presumably one of those who would have preferred a less estranging style, he himself has often been ridiculed and marginalized for his own stylistic choices. Edmund Wilson's well-known denunciation of Lovecraft's work as "bad taste" manifesting itself in "bad art" (Wilson 1950: 288) can stand in for a whole tradition of criticism that relegates him to sub-literary status because of his reliance on laborious descriptions, obscure adjectives (like "eldritch") and a proliferating series of abstract negations ("unnamable," "unspeakable," etc.). Despite his critique of Hodgson, Lovecraft was well aware of the need to escape the confines of idiomatic contemporary language and challenge his audience's reading techniques in order to successfully evoke the non-/un-/ab-human. In a 1934 letter to Duane Rimel, an aspiring writer who had asked him for advice about how to compose weird fiction, Lovecraft described his rationale for giving his most famous creation an almost unpronounceable name:

> The word [Cthulhu] is supposed to represent a fumbling human attempt to catch the phonetics of an *absolutely non-human* word. The name of the hellish entity was invented by beings whose vocal organs were not like man's, hence it has no relation to the human speech equipment. The syllables were determined by a physiological equipment wholly unlike ours, *hence could never be uttered perfectly by human throats*. In the story, we have human beings who habitually use the word as best they can; but all they can do is to *approximate* it. This they accomplish by using their throats in a queer way to imitate the original sound as their ancestors heard it from non-human throats. This queer use of the human throat makes a sound something like the original non-human sound, *but it is not like any human speech or sounds that we commonly hear*. It is an alien, unfamiliar sound that human beings can only make with an effort, and that they would not ever think of making if they were not imitating something non-human .... My rather careful devising of this name was a sort of protest against the silly and childish habit of most weird and science-fiction writers, of having *utterly non-human entities* use a nomenclature of *thoroughly human character;* as if alien-organed beings could possibly have languages based on *human* vocal organs.
>
> (Lovecraft 2016: 194)

---

[3] Andy Robertson, who died in 2014, published two anthologies of *Night Land* pastiches, *Night Lands Volume I: Eternal Love* (Robertson 2003) and *Night Lands Volume II: Nightmares of the Fall* (Robertson 2007). One of the contributors to these volumes, Brett Davidson, has also published a full-length pastiche novel, *Anima* (Davidson 2015). The most prominent contributor to these volumes is probably Nebula Award nominee John C. Wright, whose Hodgson pastiches have been published separately as Wright 2014.

[4] In addition to pastiches and fanfic, Hodgson's work has inspired a number of aesthetically interesting homages, which will be discussed in the Envoi at the end of this study.

The key sentence here is the middle one: "It is an alien, unfamiliar sound that human beings can only make with an effort, and that they would not ever think of making if there were not imitating something non-human." The material effort that a human writer must make to speak or write a non-human word (which can only be approximate, since an *absolutely non-human word* is by definition beyond our capacities) must be matched by the material effort human readers make to speak that word to themselves as they read. That effort, shared by author and reader, is a crucial aspect of the labor that makes weird fiction weird; linguistic unweirding deprives readers of the opportunity—or obligation—to perform that labor and thereby dispels much of the weirdness while claiming to save it from itself.

We can compare Lovecraft's formulation to Viktor Shklovsky's well-known assertion in "Art as Technique" that "The technique of art is to make objects 'unfamiliar,' to make forms difficult, to increase the difficulty and length of perception because the process of perception is an aesthetic end in itself and must be prolonged" (Shklovsky 1965: 12). Like the representation of class dialect, weirding the signifier defamiliarizes or estranges it from conventional usage, demands more attention from perception, and thereby foregrounds the *formal* literariness of the fiction, whether realist or weird. From Hodgson's mannered stylistic challenges to Lovecraft's complex rhetoric of unnamability and beyond, the "pulp modernism"[5] of weird fiction constitutes an explicitly self-reflexive and experimental genre that is, in its own unique ways, comparable to the broader formal experiments of high modernist and postmodernist fiction that developed alongside and after it.

Andy Sawyer comes at this issue from a slightly different direction in his comparative study of Hodgson and H.G. Wells, but his conclusion confirms my claim: unlike Wells, who always wrote in a direct and idiomatic style,

> Hodgson ... took the more audacious step of attempting to manipulate the language and structure of his novels in order to create a verbal analogue of the spiritual dislocation embodied within them .... [He] stands at the head of a more fractured approach to language and narrative, an approach designed to create atmosphere and underline what is said rather than to describe accurately and in scientific detail.
>
> (Sawyer 2014: 180)

Like Sawyer, I have argued elsewhere (see Murphy 2009) that William S. Burroughs, Michael Moorcock, and J.G. Ballard are the indirect literary descendants of both Hodgson and Lovecraft, writers who took their precursors' formal and stylistic experiments as much as (perhaps more than) their thematic concerns as points of departure for new weird fictions that forego the comforts of pastiche in favor of an

---

[5] I am referring to Leif Sorensen's [2010: 501] extension of a term originally coined by Paula Rabinowitz (2002). Mark Fisher appears to have independently coined this term to describe the music of British postpunk group the Fall, which was inspired by Lovecraft and M.R. James; see Fisher 2006.

ever-greater estrangement from the conventionally human. Although this is not, strictly speaking, an entirely cognitive form of estrangement, its aim to find a way of representing the radically alien through and against standard language allies it with the aims of more conventional science fiction in a project of further enlarging—and thereby weirding—the English language.

2

Spoken to My Own Brother

Questions of ethnicity, race, and racism have loomed large in recent critical discussions of weird fiction, primarily as a consequence of renewed controversy over racist ideas expressed in H.P. Lovecraft's letters, essays, and poetry. Hodgson, born thirteen years before Lovecraft in 1877, grew up in a different cultural environment in the UK, where chattel slavery had been legally abolished a generation earlier than it was in the United States. However, lingering elements of slavery in British colonies, as well as the imperialist and Orientalist racism that accompanied the management of the Empire (which Rudyard Kipling had aimed to justify as the "white man's burden" in his 1899 poem of that title), meant that British attitudes toward people of color remained inextricably bound up with questions of white nationalism, religion, and political authority throughout Hodgson's lifetime. In the absence of letters, poems, or essays that address these questions directly, we have no recourse but to examine Hodgson's fiction for indications of his views, and most of the tales that are relevant to the issue are not the weird fiction for which he is renowned. Among his most influential tales, the only one with immediately identifiable racial overtones is *The House on the Borderland*, which critics such as Iain Sinclair (1990: 185) and Jonathan Newell (2020: 147) argue establishes a symbolic equation between the Irish peasantry among whom the manuscript's finders are camping in the frame tale and the monstrous swine-things that emerge from the pit beneath the house to torment the Recluse in the main narrative.

The evidence for this claim lies in two details readers encounter near the novel's beginning. First, upon arriving at the fictive Irish village of Kraighten on a fishing trip, the presumably Scandinavian narrator Berreggnog quips, "there was no joke in sleeping in a room with a numerous family of healthy Irish in one corner, and the pig-sty in the other" (HB: 3), thereby locating the Irish in a living space shared with swine and implying a similarity between the two that foreshadows the appearance of the anthropomorphic swine-things later in the novel. Second, Berreggnog describes the spoken Gaelic of the Irish he encounters as "jabbering" (HB: 5), and the Recluse's manuscript uses the same term to describe the voices of the swine-things (HB: 55). At the time Hodgson was writing, prior to the Easter Rising of 1916, the Irish War of Independence (1919–21), and the establishment of the Irish Free State in 1922, Irish people, and especially the rural Irish, were often lampooned in British books and newspapers as an intellectually inferior "race" closer to animals than to their imperial overlords, much as Blacks were in the United States. Conversely, Berreggnog also notes that the eponymous house where the swine-things lurk "was a place shunned by the people of the village, as it had been shunned by their fathers before them … In the village it was a synonym of all this is unholy and dreadful" (HB: 298). None of Hodgson's other works make use of racist depictions of the Irish, although he does use stereotypes such as the Irish policeman in a few stories set in the United States. Thus, we must examine his less famous texts for the clearest clues regarding his views on racial and ethnic difference.

These views, which are sometimes marked by a categorizing racial essentialism but don't necessarily descend to the level of overt racism, are evident in Hodgson's very first published short story, "The Goddess of Death," which appeared in *Royal Magazine* in 1904. A simple tale of apparently supernatural danger that is ultimately revealed to be an ingenious deception, its emphasis on uninterrupted action, lack of individualized characterization, and somewhat anti-climactic structure mark it as an apprentice work. Derived from a tall tale that Hodgson had originally made up to entertain his younger siblings in Blackburn (M1: 29, E: 5) and possibly influenced by Edith Nesbit's 1887 story "Man-Size in Marble," "The Goddess of Death" is narrated in the first person by the traveler Sir Herton, who finds the English country town of T-worth "almost in a state of panic" over a rash of murders supposedly committed by an animated statue from the town park (CF 2: 317). With his friend Turner, Herton investigates the park, where they find the statue's pedestal empty and then are briefly chased by a giant figure which abruptly disappears. Somewhat ashamed at their flight, they return to the park to find the pedestal occupied by a white marble statue wearing a strange black headdress, but no footprints in the surrounding snow to indicate how it might have descended or re-ascended. Turner calls it a god and explains how its original owner, a former British Army colonel who had been stationed in India, had left both it and his estate to the town for a park after he was found strangled to death. Herton suspects the statue to be a female figure, although neither can identify it. The next morning another victim is found strangled, and Herton assembles a group of men to follow the tracks left near the body, which lead to a retreating figure that looks exactly like the statue. The men pursue the figure back to the park, where it disappears into the lake adjacent to the pedestal after Herton and Turner fire upon it with pistols. Puzzled by the mystery, Herton pores through the late colonel's library for clues, and finally locates documents that explain the statue's provenance: while leading part of the British Raj's campaign against the Thugs or Thuggees, the organized criminal gangs of India that had become infamous in the UK as stranglers, the colonel had pillaged it from one of their temples that he had destroyed. It represents "another—and, to Europeans, unknown—form of Kali, the Goddess of Death" (CF 2: 325), who would later appear among the "Beast-gods, and Horrors" surrounding the spectral house on the red plain in chapter three of *The House on the Borderland* (HB: 38–40). The colonel's papers also conveniently reveal the mechanical secrets of the pedestal, which allow the statue to disappear and reappear and at the same time lead to an underground room connected to the lake. The room shows signs of occupancy, and a body disguised to resemble the statue is fished from the lake; further research among the colonel's papers suggests that this is probably the high priest of the plundered temple, who followed the colonel back to England in order to take elaborate revenge, disguised as his deity.

Despite being such an early story, "The Goddess of Death" displays many features of Hodgson's treatment of racial difference that would become characteristic of his more polished mature works. First and foremost, it makes no claims regarding the superiority of Christian religious beliefs over Hindu ones: although the pillaged temple is described as "a sort of Holy of Holies of Thugdom, where they carried on their brutal and disgusting rites" (CF 2: 325), the colonel's theft of the statue is straightforwardly described as "sacrilege" against Kali (CF 2: 328). The high priest is described without any other physical details as an "enormous Hindoo" whose impersonation of the goddess almost succeeds because of the superstitious gullibility of the English townsfolk, including even Herton and Turner for a time. When Herton first hears of the killings and their reported cause, he thinks, "Good Heavens! What ignorance, what superstition! … As I strolled through the town I laughed, picturing to myself the absurdity of some people believing in a walking marble statue. Pooh! What fools there are!" (CF 2: 317). After pursuing and then losing the huge figure, though, he begins to doubt his own rationalist skepticism—"The shock had thoroughly upset me, and a sense of helplessness assailed me" (CF 2: 324)—until the idea of consulting the colonel's papers occurs to him, and what he learns from them restores his confidence in reason. Despite this, when faced with the submerged mask of Kali on the dead priest's face, he experiences "a horrible sensation of fear and awe" that momentarily revives his own irrational "fancy" (CF 2: 327). This evocation of rational skepticism's fragility in the face of inexplicable phenomena, and the concomitant reversibility of doubt into belief and vice versa, would become central to Hodgson's later series of Carnacki the Ghostfinder stories.

A story set in British India, which can't be dated accurately because it was first published posthumously in 1988, takes up several of the same issues that drive the plot of "The Goddess of Death": "The Heathen's Revenge," also known as "The Way of the Heathen." This short tale is narrated by Burton, a senior officer in the "Police Secret Service" who is charged, among other things, with keeping English visitors to "a little East of the Near East" safe from the natives. The tale itself focuses on the English missionary Hallett, who had "done his vigorous utmost during one long year … to create for himself and his Cause a healthy and well-deserved hatred—that is if you view his 'work' from the heathen's side of the road" (CF 2: 457). Oblivious to the antagonism he has inspired in the natives, Hallett then committed "one more act of idiocy to crown his twelve months' vigorous war with the religious self respect of the heathens": he sent for his fiancée Mary Kingston to join him and "I suppose, live happy ever after" (CF 2: 458). She disappears shortly after her arrival, and although Burton is certain that the native priest Jurwash is responsible, he keeps this information from Hallett so that the latter won't do anything rash. Unfortunately, Jurwash himself sends word that lures Hallett into a trap set for his capture, forcing Burton to gather a troop of men for a pursuit that lengthens into months. When Burton foolishly takes a small group of his men out on a reconnaissance mission, he is captured by natives who bring him to Jurwash at a secret underground temple. The priest invites him to "learn how the gods of the heathens deal with those who treat them with indignity," and "The sneer in his voice when he used our own words 'gods of the heathens' told me I must prepare myself for his vengeance" (CF 2: 461). That vengeance is then displayed: the English woman is brought before the god's statue and beaten repeatedly—with the same kind of wooden wands that Burton had previously used to extract information from natives as well as discipline his own men (CF 2: 458–460)—by other priests while a "thing lying in its chains and whining," which Burton recognizes as Hallett, struggles to free itself with a "blackened stump" for a limb (CF 2: 462). Jurwash informs Burton that this spectacle has occurred "At dawn, each day" since Hallett was brought to the temple, and serves as a kind of ritual exorcism for British colonialism. The conclusion of the tale comes in a hasty rush of violence that, along with a few scattered inconsistencies, may account for its failure to sell to the magazine market during and after Hodgson's lifetime: Hallett abruptly breaks his chain and kills Jurwash and the other priests with it, then frees Mary and flees the cavern, leaving Burton to escape by himself. He and his men are never able to locate the cavern thereafter, and both Hallett and Mary, resettled in England, repress their experiences in order to focus on their roses and potatoes, which are "far more important in [Hallett's] present life than ever the heathen's soul will be. So far as he is concerned, the latter can continue in his own particular brand of sin, calling it religious self-respect, or whatever he likes" (CF 2: 464).

"The Heathen's Revenge" is, if anything, even more explicit in its critique of British imperialist attitudes than "The Goddess of Death" is. Although Burton is an agent of imperial military rule who utilizes violence and torture without scruple or apology in order to achieve his aims, he has not been blinded by imperial ideology and readily admits that "there are details of life [in the East] that differ somewhat from what the white man considers to be the right and proper order of things," even if "These facts ... are ignored by a large proportion of our stiff-necked countrymen who never venture off our tight little island." The priest Jurwash, for example, would seem "a somewhat ragged native in the eyes of any European but the holiest priest of a tribe of priests, in the eyes of the native" (CF 2: 457), and Hallett's blindness to this difference, along with the arrogance of his Christian missionary zeal, inspires what Burton candidly describes as the natives' "healthy and well-deserved hatred." The natives see through Hallett's narcissistic philanthropy to the disavowed military force that both enables it and uses it as humanitarian cover for the material realities of imperialist rule. In other words, the natives recognize Hallett's zeal as a self-deceiving ideological smokescreen worthy only of their contempt, an opinion that Burton seems to share. This contempt contrasts with Jurwash's and Burton's grudging mutual respect as clear-eyed and pragmatic antagonists, which is expressed in the former's promise to the latter, after he is captured, that "'You shall suffer no harm if you obey,'" which Burton, "having heard a good deal about the methods of Jurwash and seen the results of his handiwork during many years in the S.P.," decides to accept and obey (CF 2: 461). As such the tale could serve as a critical allegory of imperialism's devastating and inevitable consequences for both colonized and colonizer.

Compared to other contemporaries such as Kipling or Arthur Conan Doyle, Hodgson wrote few stories set in India or involving characters of Indian descent, a fact that perhaps reflects a knowledge of the colony that was probably limited to a few (if any) landfalls at Indian ports, interactions with Indian sailors, and/or his reading of British books and journalism on the subject. Aside from the two tales already discussed, the only others that contribute to an understanding of their author's attitudes regarding British India are two published in *The Red Magazine* during the same year, 1913, although otherwise they are quite different from one another. "Kind, Kind and Gentle Is She," which takes its title from a sentimental "Scotch ballad" composed by William C. Peters to lyrics by Gabriel H. Barbour in the 1840s, concerns a handsome, burly English sapper or military engineer named Jell Murphy stationed at an unnamed army garrison in India. His captain assigns him to sing the title song on a musical program that is being organized by the captain's fiancée, Lady Mary Worthington, and in the course of their rehearsals he falls hopelessly in love with her. While she also finds herself drawn to his brawny masculinity, she restrains herself from crossing the barrier of social class that separates them. Murphy ultimately fails similarly to restrain himself and kisses her at the climax of their final rehearsal, after which he disappears into the night and returns the following morning experiencing "a severe attack of his old plain fever" that leaves him hospitalized (CF 4: 465). To this point the Indian setting has been largely irrelevant to the plot, but that changes when a false report arrives that nearby "hillmen," presumably referring to tribal groups of the northern Punjab region (presently divided between northern India and northwestern Pakistan) or perhaps Assam (in far eastern India), about neither of which Hodgson could have had first-hand knowledge, are "out on the bloomin' rampage," so the garrison's regiment is sent to intercept them, leaving the garrison poorly defended against a surprise attack by the hillmen.

The rationale posited for the attack is somewhat condescending: the hillmen carry rifles but don't fire them, leading the sergeant to infer, in broad dialect, that

> Them's new smuggled-in German or Roosian rifles, same bore as the [British Army] Service pattern—rotten made they is, too, sir. But the amminition's gone astray somewhere or t'other; an' that bloomin' well explains them monkeyin' in 'ere, like I never 'eard the likes of, not since the bad year. It ain't their way. But they couldn't stand 'aving them rifles and no bloomin' amminition; an' it's all a plant to get the station amminition, so as they can play 'ell with them new playthings they got.
>
> (CF 4: 467–8)

Although weakened by fever, Murphy defends Lady Mary and the other women with "a big sapper's ax, but no rifle" (CF 4: 467) because the British troops have rapidly exhausted their own ammunition. He then leads a sortie to get more bullets from the garrison armory, but gets cut off. This sets up his death scene, which rivals the most over-the-top battle sequences that Robert E. Howard would compose for Conan the Barbarian.

> The big axe swung amid a hail of German rifle-butts, yet the huge sapper was untouched. The porch gave him just room for his weapon, and no more, and not one of the attackers could get in at his side or back. And presently even the hillmen tired of rushing in on that one little spot of certain death, and gave back a while to confer … Twice more during the next half-hour the hillmen rushed Jell Murphy, and each time the big sapper built him a semicircle of dead round about the stone porch, though by the end of the second attack he was bleeding in a dozen places.

Then Hodgson goes a step further than Howard ever does. The other soldiers see

> the gigantic sapper, head and shoulders bigger than any man in the square, driving through the heart of the natives, the big axe swinging and circling and dripping. And as he swung the great axe, in a voice that could be heard above all the roar of the fight they could hear him chanting a curious medley of words:
> "Ha, ha! Gentle is she,
> Mary, my darling!"
> And with each chanted word the four-foot axe swung and circled and struck—a dripping baton beating a melody of death.
>
> (CF 4: 471)

Lady Mary, the object of this song, is unaware of it since she is caring for her wounded fiancé in an inner room, and the narrator informs us that "the words ... held for [Murphy's] particular soul no single trace of irony," so only the reader can appreciate the shift from cartoon heroism to bathos.

The role played by racial difference in this tale is much harder to parse than in the previous two stories. Only one of the hillmen, an old holy man who tries to drive away the "devils fightin' with" Murphy, is individualized in any way; like the high priest in "Goddess," the rest are described simply as physically imposing, to highlight the bravery of the Englishmen who fight them, without any other clearly racialized adjectives added. Unable to fire the weapons they carry, they act less like human beings and more like swarming insects or even forces of nature "flooding" the garrison. Even the sergeant's baffled hypothesis to explain their actions treats them as an irrational or childlike group normally governed by habit or tradition: "It ain't their way" to attack like this, unless we view their rifles as "new playthings" they can't resist trying out. Such a paternalistic interpretation would make "Kind, Kind and Gentle Is She" the one story of Hodgson's that might be assimilated to the genre of "white man's burden" adventures set in India, although clearly its main focus is the sentimental tragedy of Murphy's socially unacceptable and unrequited love that leads to his death, and not the responsibilities of British imperialism. Hodgson had already experimented with its unusual synthesis of chaste romance fiction and gory battlefield action, to much greater effect, in *The Night Land*.

Hodgson's only other story involving a significant character of Indian background is the Orientalist pulp melodrama "Jack Grey, Second Mate," first published as "Second Mate of the *Buster*" in May 1913. Set on a merchant ship out of San Francisco, it focuses on the relationship that develops between a passenger, the aristocratic Miss Mary Eversley, and the reserved but physically intimidating mate of the title, a relationship that is complicated by the presence of another passenger, the "gross, burly-looking" Mr. Pathan, who speaks English with an odd accent and is later described as a "half-breed" (CF 3: 399, 404). Pathan is more commonly the name used in India to refer to the Iranian ethnic group historically labeled Afghans and normally referred to today as Pashtuns; they are native to a region that now comprises parts of southern Afghanistan and northwestern Pakistan, but at the time of the story's composition their homeland was part of British India. Mr. Pathan's odd accent may imply that he is a native speaker of either Pashto or Persian, like many Pashtun residents of the Indian subcontinent then and now. Pathan has apparently followed Miss Eversley aboard in order to press a marriage proposal she has previously rejected, although this is never fully explained. At any rate, when Pathan attempts to take her hands, saying, "What are your hands, when I am to have the whole of you?," she unexpectedly punches him in the mouth, and when he moves to strike her, the mate intervenes to incapacitate him with a chokehold (CF 3: 403).

The enmity between the two men grows following the ship captain's sudden death, and Pathan begins to establish friendships with the "dagos and mixed breeds" (most of whom are apparently Europeans) the ship took on to replace sailors who took higher-paying berths in San Francisco (CF 3: 404). He urges the new seamen to mutiny against the First and Second Mates, which they do, murdering the timid First Mate and others in the process. Miss Eversley, who had previously treated Grey as a servant, begins more fully to appreciate his masculine virtues when they seek refuge together from the mutineers, and the spiritedness that her punch showed grows, along with the affection between them, as she assists him in holding off Pathan and his henchmen. She even fires a pistol at Pathan, but is prevented from bloodying her hands by a cartridge misfire (CF 3: 429). In the final confrontation, the wounded Grey and Mary (as he is now permitted to call her) play dead to lure Pathan into their refuge, and when he enters Grey leaps up to beat him to death before bludgeoning the other mutineers into submission with a steel door. The story ends with Grey lifting Miss Eversley in his arms, and "Master of his ship, he carried her aft to the cabin" (CF 3: 432) to consummate the implied marriage that should follow his rescue of her from the threat of interracial matrimony and sexual violence. This trope, which was already well established in popular fiction by the first decade of the twentieth century, marks "Jack Grey, Second Mate" as the most conventional, indeed stereotypical, of Hodgson's tales that include important non-white characters, though as in the tales previously discussed, he does not fill this text with the derogatory descriptives associated with racial hierarchies.

Indeed, the only one of Hodgson's tales that conforms closely to emerging pulp standards in the use of stereotypical language and imagery for depicting non-white characters or communities is the borderline science-fiction story "Diamond Cut Diamond with a Vengeance," first published in *The Red Magazine* in 1918. Set in England, it focuses on an American couple, Nell Gwynn and Tony Harrison, who are both chemists working on a formula for producing synthetic diamonds that they hope will provide them with the funds to marry. They enter a contract with a Jewish gem dealer named Moss, who finances their experiments in hope of profiting from the new source of gemstones. While the months-long pressure cooking of the raw material proceeds, Moss presses the couple for more detailed information about their formula and at the same time makes advances to Nell when Tony is absent. Strange sounds coming from the house adjoining their lab lead Tony to investigate, and upon entering the house he discovers an exact duplicate of their secret synthesizing apparatus. He and Nell deduce that Moss plans to substitute his own unsuccessful result for their successful one in order to avoid paying them for the synthetic diamonds, so they arrange a prior substitution of worthless material in order to turn the tables on him.

The concluding line of the story describes the couple heading home with enough money to marry, "leaving a fat, furious Jew-man beating a two-foot lump of pig iron savagely with a hammer" (CF 5: 213). Although several references to Moss as "the Jew-man" who "means to jew us" are attributed specifically to Tony, who also calls Moss "a hog of the very first water" (CF 5: 210), it is in fact the third-person limited narrative voice that first introduces the pattern of referring to Moss simply as "the Jew" in the story's second sentence, and continues that pattern all the way to the end. Thus the anti-Semitism expressed through both this language pattern and the stereotypical image of the cheating Jewish financier cannot be blamed on Tony's subjective prejudices alone, even though he explicitly confirms the purpose behind it when he exults, "It makes me feel virtuous to think that we've got the best of a brute like that!" (CF 5: 212). The total absence of any similar racialized patterns of verbal reference in Hodgson's other stories—he almost always uses comparatively neutral terms like "native" in his India tales, for example, and we have already examined his ironic usage of "heathen"—as well as the syntactical crudity of the recurring phrases "the Jew" and "the Jew-man" arouses a suspicion that this story might be either a very early one that was circulated and purchased for publication unrevised, or perhaps one that underwent some unfortunate editorial modification. No evidence exists to prove or disprove such suspicions, however. In any case, as Moskowitz notes, "Of all Hodgson's voluminous production, both published and unpublished, this is the only story found with either overt or covert anti-semitism" (M2: 26).

A more complex and less troubling example of Hodgson's representation of non-white characters and communities can be found in the Captain Gault tale "The Case of the Chinese Curio Dealer" (*London Magazine*, 1914). The dozen Gault stories published between July 1914 and October 1917 were among Hodgson's most popular and successful, along with the earlier Carnacki stories that ran from January 1910 to January 1912. Gault is a crafty, enterprising, and surprisingly cultured ship's captain who earns extra money by smuggling expensive and/or stolen items past the police and customs services on shore, a maritime version of the charming gentleman thief popularized by E.W. Hornung's Raffles and Maurice Leblanc's Arsène Lupin. Like "Diamond Cut Diamond," "The Case of the Chinese Curio Dealer" has a double-cross at its center. As the title indicates, Gault's prospective customer in this story is a Chinese shopkeeper, though Gault encounters him in San Francisco rather than the British-occupied Chinese ports of Hong Kong or Port Edward, perhaps implying that Hodgson had no direct experience of mainland Chinese ports. The curio dealer's name is Hual Miggett, and "By the look of him, he was half Chinaman, a quarter Negro, and the other quarter badly mixed. But his English was quite good, considering" (CF 1: 265). Hual Miggett's non-Chinese ancestry is only mentioned once more, as we shall see shortly, and plays no further role in the story. He approaches Gault when the latter enters his shop, and somewhat diffidently asks him to smuggle a large box to England. Gault banters with him briefly, until Miggett shows a charm on his own coat that matches one on Gault's watchchain. What happens next is worth quoting in full:

> "Brother," I said, as I might have spoken to my own brother, "let us prove this thing completely." And, in a minute, I could no longer doubt at all. This stranger, part

Chinese, part Negro and part other things, was a member of the same brotherhood to which I belong. Those who are also my brothers will be able to name it.

"Now," I said, "tell me all your tale, and if it is not against common decency to help you, you may depend on me." I smiled at him encouragingly.

(CF 1: 266)

The brotherhood in question is never identified, although the ensuing plot implies it to be a criminal organization, or perhaps a Masonic one of the sort common in nineteenth-century British fiction. In any case, unlike such fiction, their common membership in this brotherhood unites them rather than setting them into conflict. In response to Gault's invitation, the curio dealer reveals that the box contains his son, who has insulted the president of another, more ancient brotherhood from China, the "Nameless Ones," and must escape from California to avoid being murdered for the transgression. Despite their brotherhood, and the presence in the shop's backroom of "the biggest Chinaman I ever saw in my life [holding] the longest and ugliest-looking knife I've ever set eyes on" as he awaits the son's return (CF 1: 268), Gault is not fully convinced of Miggett's candor, so he takes a day to investigate the situation. Back on his ship, his binoculars show him a constant watch being kept on the curio shop, making the secret extraction of a large box impossible. His second visit to the shop, disguised as a European tourist, reveals that the dealer has not been totally honest, however.

Inside the box to be smuggled is a mummy case that conceals Miggett's son's drugged form, as expected, but also "the most magnificent carving I could ever have dreamed of, in old amber, of the nameless god, Kuch, of the Blood Lust." Although this sentence appears to contain a contradiction, Gault's ensuing explanation shows that it does not: "Kuch" is not the name of this deity, but only a phonetic approximation, since "There is no real equivalent in the letter sounds of any nation for the guttural which indicates this embodiment of the most dreadful of the Desires—the elemental appeal of the Blood Lust" (CF 1: 276). Had he been aware of it, Lovecraft would have appreciated this precedent for his naming of Cthulhu, which (as we saw at the conclusion of Chapter One) was "supposed to represent a fumbling human attempt to catch the phonetics of an *absolutely non-human* word [that] *could never be uttered perfectly by human throats*" (Lovecraft 2016: 194). Gault quickly deduces that the namelessness Kuch shares with the brotherhood seeking revenge on Miggett's son marks it as the Nameless Ones' deity as well as a valuable piece of their property, which the son stole. By smuggling both the son and the idol to England, Miggett can simultaneously save his offspring's life and earn himself a fortune selling the idol to a collector. Gault is not entirely surprised to learn that Miggett has lied to him, but he "can understand Hual Miggett, senior, being so eager to send mummy-case, and all, abroad. But if I save his son tomorrow, the god shall certainly not come with us" (CF 1: 277) in any way that generates profit for Miggett. Gault's elaborate plan, involving a racing boat and a very fast crossdressed sprinter to distract the Nameless Ones watching the shop, succeeds, but prior to that he had surreptitiously transferred the Kuch idol from the mummy case into a hollow bronze goat idol that he returns the next day to purchase, thereby gaining the potential profit for himself. Any superiority that Gault feels at the case's close flows from a personal moral judgment passed on an untrustworthy "brother" and fellow smuggler, however, and not from racial prejudice as in "Diamond Cut Diamond."

Another tale, "The Sharks of the *St. Elmo*" (unpublished in Hodgson's lifetime), confirms this at least with regard to Chinese people. It focuses on huge schools of sharks that mysteriously impede the sailing of a ship that is ultimately revealed to be surreptitiously returning political dissidents, who have been kidnapped, drugged, and sealed into barrels, to China so that the "present figurehead" government (which during Hodgson's writing career was controlled by European imperial powers and the United States) can "make an example of them." The fact that "The Chinese government had no power to touch them so long as they remained in 'Frisco, as theirs was a political offense" (CF 3: 533), may imply that the kidnapped men were Chinese nationalists. In any case, once the mystery of the sharks is solved and the men are released from the barrels, the sharks disperse and the ship returns the men to California.

As we have already seen with regard to "The Mystery of Captain Chappel," discussed in the previous chapter, Hodgson's attitude toward racial differences reveals its most progressive, or at least open-minded, aspects in his tales involving Black sailors, who are depicted as enduring hardships and abuse that surpass anything Hodgson himself experienced. Later stories (at least in terms of publication date) develop this perspective further by deepening the mysteries they include to the point of weirdness. While the cobbler Juk's reconstruction and subsequent approval of his quarry's revenge upon his former exploiters derive at least in part from his victims' own prior criminal acts as pirates, poachers, and likely murderers themselves, the Black sailor's killer in "Old Golly" (posthumously published in 1919) is not one readers would have immediately recognized as a career criminal, but simply a "hard-case" captain who treats his entire crew with contemptuous violence. The story opens with recently hired crew members questioning a hand who had been aboard at the time about Old Golly's murder. The hand, named Johnstone, tells them that the captain "Got him in the back of the neck with an iron pin. Hove it at him, you know … Old Golly just went at the knees all in a heap, and never said a word 'cept 'Golly'!" (a habit that had earned him his nickname). Golly hadn't done anything that the crew knew of, but "the Old Man'd been drinkin' some, or he'd never have let fly just goin' into harbour." Since the port they entered was San Francisco, however, the captain faces no punishment: "he'd have got his bloomin' neck jolly well stretched, I'm thinkin', if it had been a British port. I s'pose they thought one nigger more or less didn't matter all that much. Anyway, he got off" (CF 3: 465). The next day, strange, seemingly supernatural events begin to take place aloft, among the sails and rigging where the sailors do most of their work. First Johnstone hears a voice, and then he is struck in the eye; although the other sailors mock him, the older Scottie shares his concern, and they both agree the events must be connected to Golly's murder. Johnstone asks, "What would old Golly want to do it for? … We treated him fair and square in the fo'cas'le. I guess he'd want to get even with the Old Man, not us sailormen forrard." Scottie replies, candidly, "We tret him pretty fair, lad, 'cause we *had* to, and part 'cause he wasn't a bad sort. But he could lick any man in here, an' I guess that was what made us pretty civil," rather than any commitment to liberal principles (CF 3: 466–7). When we recall that Hodgson himself took up body-building in order to defend himself against the physical assaults of both officers and common sailors, this characterization of Old Golly as a powerful fighter implies a greater degree of sympathy and identification with him than Juk expressed with the voiceless Black gentleman in "The Mystery of Captain Chappel."[1]

As more sailors report encounters with a monstrous presence in the rigging, including one who falls to his death in the sea after shouting, "Don't touch me, Golly! I never did nothin' to you!" (CF 3: 467), the officers become concerned enough to try and reduce the sailors' anxieties, but the captain refuses either to believe the reports or to respect his crew's fears, yelling, "Nigger! Nigger be damned! … Funk and fancy, that's all the ghosts there is aloft in this packet, an' I don't allow *them* to bother me in my ship" (CF 3: 470). He drives the men up the masts, and when they stop in the lower rigging, he swarms up to berate and beat them,

> but before he could hit again, the men heard something say, 'Golly! Golly!' quite softly out of the shadows of the maintop. The Captain hove himself round and then—how it happened no one ever knew—he had missed his grip and was falling. He fell over the forward end of the top, and the bight of the clew-garnet caught him and broke his back. They found him hanging there, limp and silent, when they raced down from the threatening heights of the lofty main mast.
>
> (CF 3: 471)

Days later, the First Mate (now Captain) and the Boatswain discover that the ship's newly installed scoop-pump, which draws in water from under the vessel and comes up inside the hollow steel main-mast, makes a noise that sounds like "Golly! Golly!" when its scoop slips open. Once it's closed, they receive no more reports of ghostly speech aloft. Nevertheless, "not a man in the forecastle believed it … As Johnstone put it: 'I told you he'd go up. Old Golly'd never have rest till he got level. If he hadn't got him that time, he'd have got him in the end!' And all the men nodded back in solemn assent" (CF 3: 472). Even though the crew is by no means free of racism, they clearly acknowledge the justice, whether supernatural or simply poetic, of the Captain's belated punishment for murdering Golly.

The careful balance between supernatural and prosaic explanations found in "Old Golly" gives way to full-blown weird fiction in "Demons of the Sea" (posthumously published in 1923), which is narrated in the first person by a sailor called Darky who has a very dark complexion, although he is never explicitly labeled Black, nor is he subject to abuse. Indeed, Darky is a highly respected crew member, though not actually an officer, of a ship that encounters strange sights produced by an undersea earthquake. Most alarming of all, he notes, "Suddenly out of the depths, right before us, there arose a monstrous black face. It was like a frightful caricature of a human countenance" that another sailor likens to "the devil himself." As in "Old Golly," the

---

[1] This identification may be explained, at least in part, by Moskowitz's report that Hodgson's "entire family was off-beat and eccentric, a non-conformist group; and to add to the suspicion with which they were viewed was the fact that many of them were of dark complexion" (M1, 16). Unfortunately, the available biographical sources contain no further references to this, although if true, it would also clarify the interpretation of "Demons of the Sea," discussed below.

captain initially dismisses their report, sneering to Darky, "You've been looking at your own ugly reflection in the water." The other sailors too wonder if "it couldn't have been a reflection by any chance, could it?" Darky replies, "Ask [the other witness] Stevenson," implying that if this were the case, the white or light-complexioned sailor Stevenson would have seen a white reflection, which he did not (CF 3: 475). Soon after this, they spot another ship looming out of the fog rising from the overheated sea, but when they hail it, they get no response. As the other ship approaches, Darky sees that it is swarming with "the most horrible creatures I had ever seen," which look just like the face he and Stevenson saw earlier. He describes the creatures at length:

> Their bodies had something of the shape of a seal's, but of a dead, unhealthy white. The lower part of the body ended in a sort of double-curved tail on which they appeared to be able to shuffle about. In place of arms they had two long, snaky feelers, at the ends of which were two very human-like hands equipped with talons instead of nails ... Their faces which, like their tentacles, were black, were the most grotesquely human things about them, and the upper jaw closed into the lower, after the manner of the jaws of an octopus.
>
> (CF 3: 479–80)

These creatures, which Darky and the crew hold off with axes and firearms until their own ship can pick up enough breeze to escape the overrun ship, resemble nothing so much as the Weed Men of Hodgson's novel *The Boats of the "Glen Carrig"* (1907). The officers report the encounter when they reach San Francisco, but a gunboat sent to investigate finds nothing, leaving the threat the creatures pose open.

The absence of explicitly racialized terms and descriptions in this story, as in others by Hodgson, makes it challenging to interpret from the viewpoint of racial difference. If we read Darky as a Black sailor, then it is possible to see the story as one that subordinates human racial differences to the more immediate danger of threatening nonhuman entities, especially in light of the contradictory mixture of racialized imagery used to describe the "demons": the combination of unhealthy, corpse-like white bodies with "grotesquely human" black faces and arms could almost serve as a satirical commentary on the grotesqueries of blackface minstrelsy, although nothing else in Hodgson's surviving works parallels this in any obvious way. If, on the other hand, Darky is not a sailor of African descent but instead a dark-skinned European or American, his nickname would serve as an ironic commentary on racial categories and terms, since "darky" was the more aristocratic or "genteel" alternative for "nigger" at the time of the story's appearance.

Unlike Lovecraft or Robert E. Howard, who left behind clear evidence of their racial antipathies in letters and poems, Hodgson's surviving writings do not provide us with a simple key to his attitudes toward ethnic and racial differences, and the relatively sympathetic outline I have sketched here could no doubt be countered with a more damning interpretation using many of the same sources. Nevertheless, the ambiguities in Hodgson's representations of racial difference speak to the changing status of the British Empire in the world of international commerce that he encountered in his travels as a merchant sailor, and to the lessons he drew from his own experiences with people of different racial backgrounds. As Bloch reminds us, "The emotion of hope goes out of itself, makes people broad instead of confining them ... The work of this emotion requires people who throw themselves actively into what is becoming, to which they themselves belong" (Bloch 1986: 3), and Hodgson's depictions of racial mixing, conflict, and uneasy alliance clearly testify to his timely immersion in his era's process of becoming.

3

Teach Him to Know a Man

In contrast to issues of race, which readers encounter comparatively seldom in Hodgson's fiction, issues of gender difference can be found in many of his tales, even those that take place in completely masculine milieux such as the Victorian merchant navy. Indeed, the exclusively masculine spaces privileged in nautical fiction like Hodgson's generally function as arenas for the production and reproduction of conventional models of masculinity. As a body builder both before and during his writing career, Hodgson lays special emphasis on physical strength, dexterity, and endurance as manifestations of masculinity, all of which can be found most directly represented in his stories centering on boxing as a discipline that enables abused men to avenge themselves on their tormentors: "How the Honourable Billy Darrell Raised the Wind" (*The Red Magazine*, 1913), "The Regeneration of Captain Bully Keller" (*The Red Magazine*, 1914), and "We Two and Bully Dunkan" (*The Red Magazine*, 1914). Fighting prowess as a measure of a man's worth also contributes to the plots of "The Friendship of Monsieur Jeynois," "The Mystery of Captain Chappel," "Captain Dang," "Kind, Kind and Gentle Is She," and "Jack Grey, Second Mate," discussed in previous chapters. As a result of the conventionality of the gender roles they depict, these tales may be less interesting for contemporary readers than Hodgson's stories involving the challenges that femininity and unconventional forms of masculinity pose for an apparently cisgender male author working within a patriarchal social order that was just beginning to confront its own irrational assumptions regarding gender.

In his essay "Hodgson's Women," Sam Gafford argues that "Hodgson's fictional conception of women changed over his writing career. The 'romantic' view of *The Night Land* gives way to a more 'courtship' slant in the short stories and eventually to the extremely cynical depiction" of the Captain Gault stories (Gafford 2014: 128). The centrality of traditionally gendered romantic relationships to three of his four novels (only *The Ghost Pirates* lacks one), published between 1907 and 1912, has often been interpreted as a weakness by predominantly male critics of science fiction and horror such as Lovecraft, and even the few critics who take a more positive view of those relationships, such as Kelly Hurley, acknowledge the odd ways Hodgson chooses to represent them. Close study of his earliest fiction and poetry, written and in some cases published before his first novel appeared, offers elements of context for those unusual choices that help explain their function in his major works.

On the basis of documents originally assembled by Sam Moskowitz, Jane Frank states that "Hodgson wrote most of his poetry between 1899, when he returned from his last tour of duty in the Merchant Navy, and 1906, whilst living in Blackburn" (LP: vi), although almost none of it was published during his lifetime. This is the same period in which Hodgson wrote all his novels, according to letters discovered by Sam Gafford; his difficulty finding publishers for them was the immediate cause of his nearly complete shift to the writing of short fiction thereafter. Thus it seems safe to assume that any conclusions regarding Hodgson's views on gender that emerge from the poetry will be at least partially applicable to the novels, and also to the short fiction that dominated his later career. All Hodgson's novels are narrated in the first person by their male protagonists, as are many of his short stories; conversely, his few tales that focus on female characters are uniformly narrated in third person. In contrast to Lovecraft, whose fiction eschews female narrators and protagonists, Hodgson's diffident embrace of the latter but not the former may imply a reluctance to adopt female personae, perhaps as a consequence of a lack of confidence in his ability to present them believably. This makes the eight poems he wrote from a first-person female viewpoint especially important for determining what his ideas about women and their roles were. These poems fall into three thematic categories: two, "I Come Again" and "Listening," lament a lost or inconstant lover; two, "How It Happened" and "I Have Borne My Lord a Son," focus on moments of shared joy in courtship and childbirth; but the remaining four, "Ballade," "My Babe My Babe," "Thou, Who Art Jesu's Mother!," and "Little Garments," all bemoan the deaths of infants or young children. Hodgson's third published story, "The Valley of Lost Children" (*Cornhill Magazine*, 1906), constitutes a deeply sentimental fantasy upon that same subject: in it, a pair of indebted tenant farmers are unexpectedly blessed with a son in their middle age, but he dies very young of an infected wound from a thorn. An old man is the only other person to attend the child's burial, and though he is a stranger, they allow him to perform the service for the dead. Afterwards, he tells them, in dense working-class dialect, of a dream vision the Lord gave him of his own dead daughter happily playing with other children in the afterlife, for "ther leetle folk whom ther Lord teketh pass not inter ther Valley o' ther Shadder, but inter ther Valley o' Light" (CF 5: 4), which is also called the Valley of Lost Children. Years later, after being evicted from the farm where their child is buried, the mother dreams a similar vision of finding her son happily playing in the Valley, and it is a dream from which she never awakes.

Sam Moskowitz plausibly argues that this story, like the poems, was written for Hodgson's beloved, longsuffering mother and constitutes an honest attempt to sympathize with her pain and offer her solace: "Though his mother had nine living children, she never ceased to mourn the three [sons] that had died during infancy. To comfort her, Hodgson wrote a short fantasy titled 'The Valley of Lost Children'" (M1: 36). This interpretation also explains the uncharacteristic emphasis, in both tale and poems, on the certainty of God's justice and mercy, which Hodgson himself consistently denied but his mother, the widow of a clergyman, believed fervently. In contrast, Hodgson wrote only two poems from the viewpoint of a father mourning his dead son, and both "My Son! My Son!" and "Boy Billy Boo-Hoo" suggest more ambivalence in that relationship than in the mother-son relationship: the father knows that "for me thou hast/Leavened thy love with something less than fear" (LP: 70), perhaps because he has treated his son as "Always a-needing to be told not to do/ The thing you'd find him doing;/And to be as good as gold,/Which he'd have never been at all, young or old" (WS: 197). These details lend credence to both Moskowitz's and Everts's assertions (M1: 15; E: 3) that Hodgson did not get along well with his father, Anglican minister Samuel Hodgson, despite the fact that the son dedicated *The House on the Borderland* to his late father, "Whose Feet Tread the Lost Aeons" (HB: v). Perhaps this is also why Hodgson wrote no tale from the viewpoint of a grieving father, although he did write one focused on a grandfather mourning his drowned grandson: "Sea Horses" (originally published in *London Magazine* in 1913; CF 5: 49–68). Aside from this, the main interest these linked writings have for contemporary readers is their exploration of maternal grief through fantastic tropes: in addition to the dream vision in "The Valley of Lost Children," "My Babe My Babe" depicts the dead child as a ghostly "silent shadow" haunting the mother (LP: 16) and "Little Garments," the most overwrought of the poems, begins its distraught meditation on the dead child's clothing by addressing the drawer in which it is preserved as a coffin-like "Chest of terror where they lie!" (LP: 68).

Although it contains no fantastic elements, the story "Judge Barclay's Wife" (*London Magazine*, 1912) extends these earlier investigations of maternal psychology. Its California Gold Rush setting and theme of rough-and-ready frontier justice make it particularly anomalous in Hodgson's oeuvre. Its protagonist is Mrs. Anna Barclay, a "hard-faced, big-boned, childless woman of sixty" who is "vigorous and a ruler of men, her husband in particular" (CF 5: 23). Judge Barclay's only deviation from his wife's rule lies in his tendency to temper the harsher demands of the frontier legal system with mercy, a conventionally feminine trait she deplores as both a moral weakness and a failure of professional responsibility, leading her to take steps to "stiffen his backbone" whenever possible. If the phallic language is not sufficiently clear, the narrative explicitly attributes her inflexibility and lack of sympathy to the "frozen womanhood" of "her denied motherhood." For his part, the judge has tried, unsuccessfully, to show her what goes on "behind the sentence," the "agony and shame and degradation of the poor human in the Machinery of Correction" (CF 5: 24), so that she will better understand the justice of his rulings. However, her unplanned participation in the abortive execution of a young miner, whose guilt is uncertain, succeeds where her husband's arguments fail. The sight of the miner's mother's extravagant grief, which is intensified by the knowledge that she herself inadvertently led the posse to her son's hideout, "thaws" Mrs. Barclay's womanhood—she wonders, "Was there often this weight of terror and complete HORROR bred into being by the deliberate doings of Man, for any purpose whatever—call it Justice or by any other name?" (CF 5: 30)—and inspires her, rather implausibly, to grab the sheriff's gun and hold the posse at bay so that the miner can escape. Once he has gone, she offers herself in his place, as if to confirm the completeness of her change of heart: "if you must hang somebody, hang me; not a bit of a young boy like that!" (CF 5: 33). Although Gafford correctly notes that Mrs. Barclay is shown to be "wrong because she does not agree with the men" (Gafford 2014: 126), the men in question are displaying virtues that are traditionally gendered female, and her change of heart brings her into agreement not only with the men, but also with her own disavowed and repressed but ultimately more generous feminine self. In its derivation of a general principle of mercy available to both men and women from the (vicarious, in this case) maternal feeling of responsibility for a child's life, this tale can be read as an indirect sequel to "The Valley of Lost Children," and thus as evidence of Hodgson's ethical growth as a writer.

Many of Hodgson's short stories, both weird and realist, include female love interests for the male characters, and by far the majority of those roles and relationships are presented in entirely conventional terms which do not interest us here. The Captain Gault stories, however, openly address and take sides in the gender conflicts of Hodgson's day, such as the struggle over women's suffrage, and as such they can serve as the closest substitutes we have for essays or letters expressing the author's own views, provided we read them carefully. While the inventive and witty Gault, a classic loveable rogue, is an attractive character in many ways, his views on women are not among his most endearing traits for readers today, even if some of them, spoken as performances intended to further criminal smuggling schemes, may be intended to be deceptive or even ironic to some degree.

Gafford observes that the Captain Gault tale "My Lady's Jewels" was one of the last published, in *London Magazine* in 1916, yet it "leads off the collection *Captain Gault*, which shows the esteem in which Hodgson held the story" (Gafford 2014: 126). In it, Gault agrees to assist the rich young widow Mrs. Ernley smuggle a million-dollar diamond necklace into New York past the customs officers. However, just before they reach this agreement, Mrs. Ernley denounces the import duty she is supposed—but refuses—to pay, saying, "It's a mighty wicked tax ... If we women had the vote, we'd alter things. I s'pose you don't think a woman's fit to vote, Captain. But let me tell you, she's a heap fitter than half the men." At the time of publication the United States was still four years and the UK twelve years away from granting the vote to women over twenty-one, so this would have drawn attention as a controversial remark. To this pro-suffragette provocation Gault replies that he is not against women voting, "under conditions that are fair to the men." Such conditions, he goes on to say, require acknowledging that "The suffrage is largely the modern equivalent of physical force. Women have less of it by nature, than men, and consequently there is a certain artificiality in the situation of a woman voting on equal terms with a man ... " Mrs. Ernley protests that "Might's not right! ... A clever woman has more brains than a labourer. Yet you give *him* the vote!" Gault responds that "The vote is might as well as right" because "Nowadays, when a man wants a thing, he votes for it, instead of fighting for it. In the old days, he fought for it, and would today, if his vote were outvoted by a lot of people who were *physically* midgets" (CF 1: 364). Their political debate breaks off at this point, before the absurdity of Gault's position becomes apparent—should physically weakened old men or physically disabled men lose their right to vote?—so that they can reach a practical agreement on how Gault will conceal the necklace and how much he will be paid for the risk he's taking: 2.5 percent of the necklace's cost.

The disagreement re-emerges in different language a few pages later, after Mrs. Ernley belatedly realizes how much 2.5 percent of a million dollars is and decides to back out of the deal without informing Gault; she gives him a cut-glass replica necklace to conceal and keeps the diamond one in her own possession, believing she can smuggle it without his aid and thereby avoid paying him. He notices the substitution and upbraids her for all it implies:

> You have shown not only meanness, but, a thousand times worse, you have lied to me, lie after lie; and with every lie you hurt me badly; for you blackened not only yourself in my eyes; but, at the same time, you blackened all of your sex; for a man judges women through the goodness or badness of the women he gets to know personally.
>
> (CF 1: 371)

Somewhat paradoxically, Gault the professional criminal uses a biblical allusion to sharpen the point of his ethical attack on her: "God made Adam, and the Two of Them made Eve—I guess that's why the result's been a spot uncertain … [Adam] was too much of an amateur, and left out the governor," logic, that would have allowed women to set their own moral compasses as accurately as men presumably do (CF 1: 370). Shamed and mortified, Mrs. Ernley retreats to her cabin for the rest of the voyage, at the end of which her hidden necklace is duly located by the customs officer. Gault takes pity on her, however, and successfully improvises a way to get the real necklace past them. When he visits her at home later, she admits to having learned a lesson: "I suppose being rather well-off *does* make one inclined to grow soft, morally." He agrees, though in rather curious terms. The central issue is not the morality of obeying the law, as one might expect from her statement, but rather the ethics of physical survival: "Life is either Training or Degeneration … But smuggling diamonds isn't necessarily degeneration. It consists largely of *using* Circumstances. But it's a man's job. A woman's too much given to expecting heads I win, tails you lose. And that's just *dodging* Circumstances. And dodging Circumstances is just plain Degeneration" (CF 1: 378). In other words, despite being illegal, smuggling isn't necessarily ethically wrong, if one does it well and with a respect for the different roles and capacities of the parties involved; Mrs. Ernley's transgression lay not in smuggling the necklace per se, but in failing to respect those roles and capacities, just as her support of women's suffrage failed to respect men's different roles and capacities in self-government, at least as Gault defines them. Gault adopts a tone of disinterested ethical didacticism here that his obvious financial interest in the situation's outcome would belie, if it were not for his concluding admonition to Mrs. Ernley to donate his fee to the Sailors' Home, where "They need the cash pretty bad, I know" (CF 1: 380). Thus the tale concludes in a bewildering aporia of materialist ethics and gender difference.

A second Gault story that is also directly relevant to this discussion of gender is "The Painted Lady," first published in *London Magazine* in November 1915 but almost certainly written a year earlier, in response to the intensive newspaper coverage of the Mona Lisa's return to the Louvre over two years after it had been stolen by Italian glazier Vincenzo Peruggia, who had tried unsuccessfully to return it to Italy. In Hodgson's version of the case, an American art dealer named Black has masterminded the theft of Da Vinci's masterpiece in order to make half a million dollars profit from a private collector and, in an ironic nod to Peruggia, "to have this bit of goods in the little old U.S.A" because "It's too fine for any other nation on earth" (CF 1: 334). Following a detailed exposition of how Black fooled the authenticators of the "recovered" painting with a forgery, an impressed Gault agrees to help him smuggle the original past US customs. Gault's unexpectedly philosophical musings on the painting's female subject first introduce gender roles and relations into the plot:

> It's as if the elemental female smiled out in her face—not what we mean nowadays by the word *woman*, but all that is the essential of the *female*. The smile is conscienceless; not consciously so, but naturally. It's as if the unrestrained female— the "faun" in the woman—the subtle license in her—the subtle, yet unbridled, goat-spirit of her was spreading out over her face, like a slow stain. It's the truth about that side of a woman that the best part of a man insists on turning his blind eye to. The painting ought to be called: "The Uncomfortable Truth!"
>
> (CF 1: 336)

Although at the time Hodgson wrote this story the Mona Lisa was not yet the most famous and popular painting on earth, it had already been described by critics as a depiction of the mysterious "elemental female" or "eternal feminine" lauded by Goethe as the essence of wisdom and creativity. Gault's account differs from Goethe's by emphasizing uncontrolled female desire—the "faun"—instead of creativity, and the stereotype of the "femme fatale," widespread in Victorian culture, is undoubtedly implied in Gault's description too.

Gault's (and Hodgson's) most likely source for this interpretation is the celebrated passage from the "Leonardo Da Vinci" chapter of Walter Pater's influential essay collection *The Renaissance* (first edition 1873) which describes the face of the painting's subject as follows:

> All the thoughts and experience of the world have etched and moulded there, in that which they have of power to refine and make expressive the outward form, the animalism of Greece, the lust of Rome, the mysticism of the middle age with its spiritual ambition and imaginative loves, the return of the Pagan world, the sins of the Borgias. She is older than the rocks among which she sits; like the vampire, she has been dead many times, and learned the secrets of the grave; and has been a diver in deep seas, and keeps their fallen day about her; and trafficked for strange webs with Eastern merchants; and, as Leda, was the mother of Helen of Troy, and, as Saint Anne, the mother of Mary; and all this has been to her but as the sound of lyres and flutes, and lives only in the delicacy with which it has moulded the changing lineaments, and tinged the eyelids and the hands.
>
> (Pater 1980: 98–9)

If Gault's language is less sensual and evocative than Pater's, it is in the same measure more direct, as befits its genre and expected readership: by reading the painting unambiguously as an image of unrestrained, amoral desire, Gault establishes a narrative link between the two meanings of the story's title: a "painted lady" is literally a painting of a woman, but figuratively the term is a euphemism for a prostitute.

Gault makes this first speech to Black alone, before the ship departs, but once they are at sea, he observes that Black has begun to spend time with a young woman named Lanny whom Gault suspects of being part of a group of art thieves, and his later remarks are directed primarily at her. He starts an argument with her regarding the artistic merit of the Mona Lisa, which he derides as "not a *complete* work of art" because "It is the product of a twisted art and a very great handicraft." Specifically, he insists that the female figure depicted "is a twisted fragment of a woman—the produce of a twisted nature. I understand, I guess, because I'm a bit twisted myself; it's only in odd moments that I can fight down the twist in me, which makes me see every woman worse even than she is" (CF 1: 340–1). Gault's diction here makes it difficult to determine whether he attributes the figure's "twisted nature" to Da Vinci's failure as an artist or to his success in depicting the woman's innate licentiousness, and both Black and Lanny assume that he is merely generalizing from a personal experience with a "bad woman." In a low voice Black can't hear, Lanny also offers to show Gault what a "really nice woman" is like. However, Gault is actually laying a trap for Lanny, into which she falls: Black's cabin was ransacked the previous day, while he was out on deck with Lanny, by people looking for the painting, and since they found nothing, Gault expects them to ransack his own quarters next, as soon as Lanny can lure him away. He shows her his apparent weakness—his own "twist"—to draw her out, she takes the bait, and he then reveals the plot to Black. Lanny takes the unmasking of her fraud calmly, leading Gault to admit, "Let me tell you, man, I admire that woman. She's got the real female brand of pluck, and full strength at that" (CF 1: 343). As in the tale of the Chinese curio dealer, a thief whom Gault robbed even as he helped the man's son escape certain death, the cat-and-mouse game Gault plays with other criminals in this tale renders his comments on gender unreliably ambiguous: does he view women as conscienceless goat spirits or as strong, plucky opponents to be admired even as he tries to defeat them?

Curiously, Hodgson published an alternate version of this story, "Captain Gunbolt Charity and the Painted Lady," in his collection *The Luck of the Strong* just six months after the earlier appeared in *London Magazine*. The earlier version was subsequently reprinted in the collection *Captain Gault* in 1918. While the plot, dialogue, and characterization are otherwise identical between the two versions, the later variant expands, clarifies, but also complicates the argument between the Captain (here renamed in conformity with the tale's new title) and Lanny over what the painting shows. It starts the day before Black's cabin is ransacked, and is interrupted by the Captain when it starts to get "a bit too serious. I felt if the young lady came out with any more of that cheap Suffragette I'm-better-'n-any-man-that-steps-the-earth kind of thing, I should begin to feel like the giant, when the boy slapped him with his own hair-brushes" (CF 5: 406). Although he says nothing aloud, he goes on to express further anti-feminist sentiments in much cruder terms than he used with the suffragette Mrs. Ernley in "My Lady's Jewels," concluding with the ironic self-assessment, "Lord! Doesn't that sound narky!" (CF 5: 406). These defensive insertions somewhat undermine his subsequent confession, already quoted above from the earlier version, that he "respect[s] her courage [and] real female brand of pluck" (CF 5: 414).

However, the section of the tale that is expanded the most is the next day's argument, after the ransacking, over the degree of artistry that is on display in the painting. Whereas the first version left the blame for the female figure's "twisted nature" uncertain, this version lays it squarely on Da Vinci himself: "The da Vinci johnny was too busy looking out for his abysmal depths of human nature, to remember the heights! ... He was like a painter, with his eye glued into a sewer, painting and sweating himself into eternal fame—that is in the eyes of other Perverts like himself ... " (CF 5: 409). This assertion (which transposes into popular fiction some of the negative reactions Pater's essay itself generated, from George Eliot among others), and the resistance it provokes in Lanny and Black, leads the Captain to expound a general theory of art, including literature, that takes up two dense pages of text and serves no obvious purpose in advancing the plot, which turns on the Captain's trap for Lanny just as in the earlier version. The Captain insists that a great artist must be "a man of great feeling, and intellectuality combined—that is to say, a Compleat Personality" (CF 5: 409). Furthermore, "If the artist's personality is a great personality and a balanced one, it will express itself in and through his subject in a great and balanced way" as great art, which can only be "the great, wise, compleat human personality, vital and therefore creative, expressing itself through some medium ... " If, on the other hand, "the artist has a twisted personality, the twist will express itself in and through his work, and the work will be as much out of perspective in its deviation from compleat sanity and truth, as it would be technically, were the artist an indifferent craftsman" (CF 5: 410). He gives the example of a book, which is "great or not, in so far as it says much or little, and says it truly or askewly, completely or incompletely. And that simple little test is the test for all art—painting, sculpture, prose, poetry, music—all of it; for if a 'work of art' says nothing, it is nothing" (CF 5: 411). From this principle he deduces that the inadequacy of the Mona Lisa lies in the fact that

> it says only part of what it should say; and the part that it does say is no more a compleat measure of a woman, than a pint-measure approximates to a furlong ... It no more approximates to a normal or compleat human woman, than a male, portrayed in a moment of murderous fight, approximates to a normal or compleat human man.
>
> (CF 5 411)

The implication here seems to be that an image of a woman that focuses solely on her lust is just as much a caricature as an image of a man focused solely on his bloodlust would be. This critique concludes in a final peroration that seems more appropriate to *The Night Land* than to this unpretentious tale of smuggling:

> As opposed to this inadequacy, the Greatest Art is complete, in the sense that it shows a Man or a Woman or a Moment in such a way that you see, with the great and particular insight of the artist who created the work, the thing you are shown, plus all the rest, which it makes or aids you to comprehend also. It portrays the Man, the Woman, or the Moment, in such a way that you realise, as you look, all the potentialities of the Man, the Woman, the Moment—the greatness and

absurd weakness of the Man; the infinite tenderness and incredible meanness of the Woman; and the aeons of Eternity that lie in wait behind the Moment.

(CF 5: 411)

After this lofty philosophical vision, the closing of the Captain's trap feels not only like an abrupt collapse of the tone but also a radical deflation of the aesthetic claims just made. Were they, too, nothing more than lines uttered to pull off a confidence trick? However they are interpreted, they unbalance and impair this version of the tale in comparison with the earlier one.

The length and abstraction of this digression suggest that the later appearance of the story may in fact represent the original draft, which Hodgson cut for the earlier appearance, on the advice of his editor or on his own, in order to produce a tighter sequence of action, and then he restored it when he got an opportunity to publish the story under a different title. If this interpretation is plausible, it further implies that the aesthetic theory articulated here was not intended simply as an elaborate con with no larger purpose, nor as the quick paraphrase of Pater that might explain the shorter Gault version, but actually represents something close to Hodgson's own philosophy of art and literature. Certainly it encapsulates both the goals attempted and the means employed in his most ambitious weird novels—what are the immense time scales of *The House on the Borderland* and *The Night Land* if not "aeons of Eternity lying in wait behind the Moment" of romantic connection? Who are the brave Recluse and his beloved in *The House on the Borderland* or the unnamed narrator X and Naani in *The Night Land* if not something akin to archetypes of man and woman?—and significantly complicates Gafford's view of the Captain Gault stories as "extremely cynical."

Possibly the most surprising of Hodgson's stories with female protagonists is the posthumously published "A Timely Escape" (1922), which Gafford does not discuss in his survey of Hodgson's female characters but which may contain a self-reflexive meditation on Hodgson's own sense of his situation as an unsuccessful fantasy writer. The tale's protagonist is Madge Jackson, who is engaged to marry Dicky Temple, an aspiring young writer who "had written some exceedingly good stuff of a somewhat fantastic nature" and seemed "to be truly bubbling over with ideas" (CF 4: 476). Unfortunately for both of them, however, Dicky admires the older writer George Vivian to the point of idolatry, driving Madge to view Vivian "as something of a rival; though, indeed, this sounds a queer thing to say when the saying concerns a man and woman" (CF 4: 475). Madge derides the "general threadbareness and commonplaceness" of Vivian's work, but Dicky "mistook the finicking smartness and re-dressed 'mouton' of his friend for something that indicated powers far beyond his own," and Vivian cultivates this hero-worship in his young admirer (CF 4: 476). The disagreement over Vivian's talent results in a quarrel between the lovers, and Dicky begins to spend even more time with the older writer. Much of the story focuses on Madge's increasing worry over Dicky's refusal to reply to her messages and the alarming physical changes she observes when seeing him out walking: "she noticed afresh with shocked feelings how dead white and spiritless was his face, and the utter slackness of his whole attitude" (CF 4: 478).

Finally, driven past the bounds of both decorum and legality (not unlike Mrs. Barclay or Mrs. Ernley, but for different reasons), Madge and her sister Gertrude climb up a pillar onto the roof of Vivian's veranda in order to peer into his upstairs window, where they think Dicky is staying. What they see abruptly changes the tale from one of "queer" courtship rivalry to something closer to a mad scientist story: Vivian has strapped Dicky into a black vulcanite chair with head rest, which presses his closed eyes against metal balls suspended from the ceiling, and armrests that hold his hands against electrodes. Thus restrained and electrified, Dicky recites in a voice "dead and lifeless, every word spoken without inflexion, with a constant slow drop, drop, as if they fell leaden upon the air from something without life" while Vivian transcribes his words, which Madge and Gertrude recognize as part of a fantasy story Dicky has been writing, into a notebook (CF 4: 483–4). By means of the machine, Vivian is literally "picking his brains" for stories that the older writer can claim as his own. Madge rushes in to rescue Dicky from the strange machine while Gertrude retrieves the notebook, along with several others, from Vivian, who puts up no resistance beyond saying, "Of his own free will entirely" (CF 4: 485). After he has recovered, Dicky confirms this, adding, "Why was I like that with you—blest if I know, Madge. I suppose it was with all that trance business. Perhaps there was some 'suggestion' about it … old Vivian wouldn't want you interfering—eh? Wanted to keep you away and have me to himself till he'd sucked me dry" (CF 4: 486).

The reversal of conventional gender attributes and roles here—Madge's subjective agency in rescuing the passively worshipful Dicky from an unscrupulous, vampiric male rival to both of them—is only the most immediately striking of this story's unexpected features. In addition, there is the closing reference to hypnotic "suggestion," which may indicate the influence of Poe's "Facts in the Case of M. Valdemar" (1845), a tale similarly focused on a voice speaking from the border between life and death. Most revealing, however, is the abrupt and near-parodic metafictional transformation of a sentimental but otherwise realist romantic story about a budding fantasy writer into a fantasy story about a machine that plagiarizes fantasy stories from the writer's mind. The theme of fantastic plagiarism introduces an autobiographical aspect into the tale that may allow us to interpret it as a meditation on Hodgson's own frustrations over his career. In a letter to Coulson Kernahan dated November 17, 1905, Hodgson writes,

> In one of the late numbers of SKETCHY BITS (ye gods!), a friend of mine called my attention to a story, entitled "The Raft," signed only by the initials C.L. The thing bears internal evidence that the writer has read at least one of my "weed" stories, and here, in such piffle as this, am I to be robbed of the *original* element, which is my birthright. If the story had been merely about the Sargasso Sea, I should have thought nothing; but they have embodied in it at least two of my ideas. That the story is *not* evolved from the brain of C.L., I have proof, for the writer betrays ignorance of his subject in every other paragraph. The story is, of course, different from mine, that is, superficially; but the deeper thing—the conception is mine. Damn him! The Sargasso, *of my stories*, is mine own happy hunting ground. I have invented it, and have a right to hunt in it.
>
> (U: 38–9)

Hodgson is particularly incensed here because, when he wrote this letter, none of his Sargasso Sea stories had yet appeared in print, although one or more were already being considered by magazines, and hence could have been available for imitation by writers with better editorial connections than his. The first such story to be published would be "From the Tideless Sea," in April 1906. This feeling of being plagiarized or "robbed" explains why he continues,

> If only I could at least have the chance, in a better mag, which this rotter has in his poorer, but no! I must be a dumb pen, whilst he, or she (wonder who it is) takes all the freshness and newness and sense of originality out of my yarns. Then, when mine come out, they will say that the stories owe their conceptions to an "unknown writer who wrote up the subject in SKETCHY BITS."
>
> (U: 39)

In the same letter he complains of having received his 427th refusal to publish his stories from an editor; even if this is an exaggeration, one can sympathize with the mounting frustration that drove him to cease writing "for nearly two whole days, and sit before my machine, coining new and perilous curses" like the one for literary pirates, who will be "buried to their neck [sic] in pits filled with the MSS from which they have pirated their ideas, and each MS has *teeth*—sharp ones!" (U: 38).

From such fantastic curses to a fantasy of rescue like "A Timely Escape" is a comparatively small step, and we can speculate that it helped Hodgson restore his resolve by allowing him to objectify and work through the subjective feeling of powerlessness to which his inability to publish his stories sometimes gave rise. If this hypothesis is accepted, it may also allow us to extrapolate an explanation for Madge's role as protagonist. This story was not published in Hodgson's lifetime; it appeared four years after his death thanks to his widow Bessie Farnsworth Hodgson's dedicated efforts to secure him a posthumous readership. In his thorough and sympathetic account of Bessie's work on behalf of her late husband's reputation, Moskowitz hypothesizes that "before he met and married Bessie, Hodgson might have felt he was little more than an automaton whose function was to provide words and that his marriage to her made him whole again" (M2: 55). Moskowitz's suggestion, which sounds almost like something quoted from one of Hodgson's own stories, was made prior to the discovery and publication of Hodgson's letters, including the one quoted above, which permit us to refine the suggestion further. Clearly Hodgson felt not only disheartened and unappreciated as a result of his initial inability to get his work published, but also cheated and robbed of his most original ideas by other writers. Bessie, who had worked as an advice columnist for the British women's magazine *Home Notes* before their marriage in 1913 (M1: 105), could provide him not only with companionship and emotional support but also with practical advice on his writing as well as insight into the inner workings of the editorial offices to which he sent his stories. Just as the sensible Madge "wakes" the dreamer Dicky from his hero-worshipping trance, pragmatic Bessie could open idealistic Hope's eyes to the quotidian realities of publishing as a business.

One final story deserves attention to conclude this discussion of Hodgson's attitudes toward gender as expressed in his fiction: the 1912 tale "The Getting Even of Tommy

Dodd," originally published in *The Red Magazine*, which makes far more extensive use of crossdressing and gender role-play than "The Case of the Chinese Curio Dealer" discussed in Chapter Two. The crossdressing described in "Curio Dealer" is merely a quick and temporary female disguise that allows Captain Gault's accomplice, the runner Billy Johnson, to sneak into Miggett's shop past the Nameless Ones' sentinels, swap clothes with Miggett's son, and then lead the sentinels away so that the son, now dressed in women's clothes, can calmly escape on Gault's arm (CF 1: 274, 278–81). In "Tommy Dodd," however, the title character's performance as his own invented cousin "Jenny Dayrin" constitutes the entire story, and its satirical play on Victorian gender roles and stereotypes bears comparison with the celebrated "Sarah Williams" episode in chapters ten and eleven of Mark Twain's *Adventures of Huckleberry Finn* (1884), which features Huck attempting to pass as a girl in order to gather information about his faked death and Jim's escape. Huck's subterfuge fails because he tries to pass himself off as a girl to an observant woman, who devises several simple tests—threading a needle, throwing an object at a rat, and catching an object dropped into the lap—that reveal he's actually a boy, whereas Tommy Dodd undertakes his crossdressing to fool the abusive male officers of the ship on which he's been apprenticed, and he succeeds beyond all expectations.

Let me take a moment to establish some historical context for Hodgson's comic tale of crossdressing. Female characters had been played by boys or young men in English theaters until around 1660, when Charles II took the throne following the death of Oliver Cromwell and the end of the Commonwealth period. By the late nineteenth century, when Hodgson was growing up, stage crossdressing was mostly limited to highly conventionalized holiday pantomimes that would be more accurately categorized as drag performances (i.e., crossdressing intended to be recognized as such, as opposed to crossdressing intended to allow the performer to be accepted as the other gender). Crossdressing in English-language literature was even more limited: aside from Don Juan's forced feminization when he is confined to the Sultan's harem in Cantos V and VI of Lord Byron's *Don Juan* (1819–24) and Rochester's brief disguise as a female fortune teller in Charlotte Brontë's *Jane Eyre* (1847), the only significant examples are the tale of the rector's son Peter Jenkyns in chapters five and six of Elizabeth Gaskell's *Cranford* (1853) and farm hand Gregory Rose's impulsive adoption of a female nurse's guise in order to care for his dying beloved Lyndall in Part Two, chapter twelve of Olive Schreiner's *The Story of an African Farm* (1883).

Of all these, Gaskell's episode (along with Twain's, already noted) is clearly the most relevant for Hodgson, for several reasons. First, practical joker Peter's spontaneous decision to dress up in his domineering sister Deborah's old gown and bonnet and then take a pillow wrapped up in swaddling to look like a baby out for a public promenade is clearly motivated by a satirical impulse "to make something to talk about in the town" (Gaskell 2005: 210), namely an appearance of scandal to mortify his more conventional sibling. Unfortunately, Peter's father returns home in the middle of his performance, and, enraged, "tore the clothes off [Peter's] back—bonnet, shawl, gown and all—and threw the pillow among the people over the railings; and ... before all the people he lifted up his cane, and flogged Peter!" (Gaskell 2005: 210). Mortified by this final humiliation at the hands of a father who had always expressed disappointment in him, Peter runs off to sea, which breaks his doting mother's heart and leads to her early death of grief (Gaskell 2005: 213–4). If we set aside the crossdressing episode for a moment, this tale corresponds remarkably well to what is known about Hodgson's own childhood: his father was a rural minister with whom he often disagreed and quarreled, and he too ran away to sea, against his parents' wishes, in early adolescence. In light of *Cranford*'s popularity, which peaked and inspired several stage adaptations at the turn of the century, it seems reasonable to posit that Hodgson, who grew up and lived much of his life far away from the metropolis in small villages similar to Cranford, may well have read it and recognized something of himself in it, perhaps his own fundamental inability to fit into conventional rural and bourgeois roles. This, in turn, might help account for the tone of good-humored indulgence and even identification with the protagonist that suffuses "The Getting Even of Tommy Dodd."

The story begins with Tommy expressing his implacable intention to get revenge on the officers for "that gross injustice which is dealt out so liberally to the boys in some ships" (CF 5: 35), a frequent object of Hodgson's ire. Most of Tommy's run-ins are with the bosun and the third mate, whose physical abuses are condoned by the ship's captain, and after his most recent drubbing, he threatens all of them: "I told [the captain] that, after I'd wiped the deck with them, I'd make him kiss my feet to teach him to know a man when he saw one" (CF 5: 36). Tommy tells his fellow apprentices that "I make a spiffing girl when I've the right togs on. I've acted often at home," and sure enough, as soon as he dons the dress and accessories his friends chip in to buy for him, "a queer silence possessed the glory hole; for Tommy, when finally dressed, from pretty shoes—which his slender feet and years allowed to be surprisingly small—to his mop of naturally curly, golden hair, made so dainty a girl that his fellow 'prentices felt all at once different towards him" (CF 5: 37). At this point the third mate barges in, forcing Tommy to improvise an explanation for the situation by claiming to be Jenny Dayrin, Tommy's Australian cousin. Both the mate and later the captain are fooled by Tommy's performance, the former offering to show "Jenny" the ship and the latter inviting her to join him for tea. Unlike Huck Finn, Tommy is apparently an acute observer of women's behavior: during tea, for example, "He took moderate bites and sips, and remembered in time that rigid but nameless article [a corset] which held his small and muscular waist so stiffly. Because he remembered, he stopped in time!" (CF 5: 42). This accuracy allows him to maintain the deception over many weeks.

For the duration of the ship's stay in Melbourne, Jenny keeps the captain and third mate on their toes by inquiring after the apprentices' lodging and meals and by inviting Tommy and his mates ashore, but the revenge plot only begins in earnest when the ship departs. Tommy is soon reported lost overboard, and two days later Jenny emerges from the hold to proclaim, "'I always meant to be a stowaway' … It was obvious that Tommy was enjoying himself, and that he had not been brought up with 'elder sisters' for nothing!" (CF 5: 43). In the course of the voyage, Jenny catches the third mate kicking the apprentices, and her outrage at this—along with the mate's insubordinate remark, which makes the captain feel "insulted before the girl"—drives the captain to knock the man unconscious. When she is informed of her cousin's supposed drowning, she opines that he was "driven to it by the brutality of the third mate" and refuses to dine with him, so the captain sends him off to eat alone. Jenny commends the captain for these acts, overlooking his lie that he himself would never strike a boy, for "He had done her heart's desire that day, and she could forgive much … Thus did Tommy go forward along the path of virtue, leaving vengeance unto those best able to dispense it" (CF 5: 44–5). Jenny's next achievement is to persuade the captain not simply to make the bosun himself scrub out the ship's pigsty, as he had tried to make Tommy do, but to lock him into the sty until the job is done (CF 5: 47). Her final triumph fulfills Tommy's original vow:

> Miss Jenny held the skipper religiously to his "paternal and benevolent" attitude toward his "young gentlemen," whilst that same captain, though the father of a large family, grew daily more enamoured of his fair passenger. One morning, when the decks were being wet down, and Miss Jenny was paddling about gaily with bare feet in the cool water, the captain's affections got the better of his discretion, for having gallantly offered to hold Miss Jenny's shoes for her, whilst she sat and dried her feet, he so far forgot himself as to stoop quickly and kiss her "pretty toes," as he called them.
>
> (CF 5: 47–8)

Sham-outraged at the uninvited and legally unsanctioned expression of physical desire, Jenny storms back to her cabin, where Tommy tells himself, "I said I'd make him [kiss my feet] … And I guess I'm squared all round now," so he lets the captain in on the performance, out of gratitude for his punishment of the third mate and bosun, and promises not to tell anyone else about the deception to avoid marring the captain's reputation. The tale concludes as "the skipper, dumb with emotion of a strong and varied kind, shook hands, speechlessly, with this pretty girl, who assured him that she was Tommy Dodd, his youngest 'prentice" (CF 5: 48).

Tommy can get his enemies to take revenge on one another for him because he understands not only how to perform as a woman, but also how the men will perform for him if they believe he is a woman. His performance of femininity effectively seduces or coerces them into performing their masculinity, despite their occasional reluctance, in order to avoid appearing weak, crude, immoral, or any other trait they deduce "she" will find undesirable. This is the ironic sense in which the vow Tommy makes to "teach [the captain] to know a man when he saw one" is kept: not by Tommy himself performing conventional masculinity through violence and forcing the captain to kiss his feet, as one might initially expect, but rather by his demonstration that none of the officers is able to recognize a male body when it displays the conventional visual and audible cues and performs the ritualized gestures of femininity. They quite literally don't know a man when they see one, because they recognize both men and women solely by means of conventional signs that are not merely stabilized by imitation but in fact constituted by imitation, as Judith Butler has taught us. Although Hodgson probably wouldn't have endorsed the conclusion Butler draws from this, that gender has no material essence and hence is entirely performative, the fact that he not only recognized the centrality of performance to both male and female gender roles but also constructed an entertaining and subversive narrative around that recognition makes him seem much more like our contemporary than many of the other attitudes expressed in his fiction.

Furthermore, perceptive readers will have recognized that these very same indices of gender performance were deployed by Hodgson earlier in his writing career, in fact in his earliest novel, *The Night Land*, where they serve mixed purposes. In the premodern opening chapter, the narrator X at one point finds the neighbor with whom he is falling in love, the Lady Mirdath, consorting with "a very clever-drest man, that had the look of the Court about him" (NL: 21); this makes X jealous, so he avoids her for many weeks, until finally he overhears her singing a sad love song and calls her to him so they can reconcile. Immediately thereafter, in response to his question about the "man of the Court," she takes him into her home and introduces him to Mistress Alison, who "was a dear and bosom friend, and she it was that had been drest in the Court suit to play a prank for a wager with a certain young man who would be lover to her." Because X had been "so speedy to offence that truly [he] never saw her face plain, because [he] was so utter jealous," he frankly acknowledges that "the Lady Mirdath had been more justly in anger [with him] than [he] supposed" (NL: 27). Like the captain and officers in "The Getting Even of Tommy Dodd," X doesn't know a man, or rather a woman, when he sees one, if she is displaying the conventional signs of masculinity. To heighten the joke, before revealing his rival's real identity Mirdath encourages X to perform his own masculinity by taking "down two great pistols from an arm-rack, that [he] fight a duel to the death" with Mistress Alison (NL: 26). A more adaptable man than the ship captain in "Tommy Dodd," he takes this revelation of his misperception with good humor, and considers the episode nothing more than another example of Mirdath's characteristic impudence and mischief, which later helps him to confirm that Naani is Mirdath's reincarnation, since she is similarly mischievous.

Moreover, perhaps the most often repeated and memorable of X's later demonstrations of his love for Naani is his wish to kiss her feet, which first happens in a scene remarkably similar to the conclusion of "Tommy Dodd": "while that we talked, I bathed the little feet of Naani; and surely, as I dried them upon my pocket-cloth, I was taken that I should kiss them; and surely I kist them, and they did be very shapely and dainty" (NL: 363). This fetishistic action, which functions as a kind of surrogate for intercourse, is repeated several times in the course of their journey back to the Great Redoubt (NL: 397, 438, 492), and gives their romance a much more tactile eroticism than the comparatively chaste interactions between the Recluse and his beloved in *The House on the Borderland* (HB: 162–7, 239–44), between Samuel Philips and his bride Mary Knowles trapped aboard the *Homebird* in the Sargasso Sea in the two "Tideless Sea" stories (CF 1: 135–74), and between narrator John Winterstraw and Mistress Mary Madison in the concluding chapters of *The Boats of the "Glen Carrig"* (BGC: 220–52). Unlike the captain's kissing of Tommy/Jenny's feet, which is met with a performance of outrage, X's actions in these scenes are encouraged and welcomed by the recipient as the signs of loving self-abasement he intends them to be. Thus the very same action, kissing feet, has antithetical meaning and consequences depending upon the nature of the relationship between the parties involved. Although this perspective does not entirely erase these scenes' oddity for contemporary readers, it does suggest a wider, more sensitive, and more sophisticated context through which to interpret them.

Kelly Hurley clearly emphasizes the profound ambivalence of Hodgson's representations of gender when she notes that "it is easy to read the scenes in which Naani is disciplined for 'naughtiness' as thoroughly misogynist ... But it is also possible to read them as something like camp parody—the parody of a man who was not particularly invested in the distinction between masculinity and femininity, and understood them as performative rather than essential identities" (Hurley 2001: 144). Hurley further points to Hodgson's comic role-play in his 1905 letters to Coulson Kernahan, in which he jauntily assumes a female persona to express his gratitude to one of the few editors to accept his stories for publication: "May the gods cease not to smile upon his kindly old head. I wish I *were* a girl, I'd go up and insist on marrying him" (U: 35; see also U: 28). If we follow this line of argument to its conclusion, we would have to acknowledge that *The Night Land*'s "stereotypes of masculinity and femininity are taken to such outrageous extremes as to explode them" (Hurley 2001: 145). This marks the sharpest possible contrast with Lovecraft, whose narrative representations of gender rely upon the ossified stereotypes of the dispassionate scientist, the over-sensitive aesthete, and the uncouth workingman for masculinity, and the witch, the victim, and the predator for femininity. Our closer inspection of gender's vicissitudes through a wider array of Hodgson's tales bears out Hurley's claim, although it doesn't give us any more grounds than Hurley had for deciding whether or not "he was heterosexual throughout his life, despite his marriage at age 36" to Bessie Farnsworth (Hurley 2001: 144). Even if it did, it's not clear what consequences this would have for our reading of his works, beyond adding another aspect to his already well-known and significant deviation from the social and cultural norms of his era, which we can already view as untimely anticipations of a time to come.

Part Two

Hope Out of Place

In order to articulate the full significance of Hodgson's approach to space and place, I first need to sketch a critical taxonomy and conceptual framework for the interpretation of comparable features in the adjacent genres of science fiction, fantasy, and weird fiction. Hodgson's texts are among the earliest to be constructed around the impossibility of achieving the type of narrative closure that is normally characteristic of science fiction or fantasy, and my claim is that this refusal of closure—I suggest we call it "foreclosure"—is explicitly figured in the tales' spatial settings. As cartographers know, the mapping of space is not a neutral process; physical spaces can be mapped in many different ways, depending on what the map is intended to accomplish. As art historians know, every physical space is transformed into a figurative one when it is represented aesthetically, for example in a painting or photograph; the same is true when it is represented in narrative, whether literary or cinematic. Think for example of the symbolic significance of Mary Shelley's decision to set the extended colloquy between Victor Frankenstein and his creature among the precipices and icefields of the Swiss Alps, or Ursula K. Le Guin's decision to set *Always Coming Home* in the Napa Valley following a global environmental catastrophe. In what follows I will use the term "landscape" to refer to such transformed spaces. Now both the intentionality and the figuration to which physical spaces are subjected when they are transformed into landscapes are constrained by the physical and historical limits of these real spaces; authors can only partially modify those spaces if they want the spaces to retain their recognizability and realist functionality. In fictions set in invented spaces, imaginary landscapes in other words, such constraints are loosened, though not necessarily abolished. However, in non-mimetic fiction like science fiction, fantasy, and weird fiction, unearthly landscapes are necessarily intentional landscapes in that the spatial settings are not pre-existing backdrops that resist modification but instead malleable performative contexts that actively co-produce important elements of the narrative.[1]

---

[1] My usage differs from that of film theorist Martin Lefebvre, who uses this same term, "intentional landscape," to describe cinematic situations in which "the spectator imputes to the film (or to its director) the intention to present a landscape," for example, the physical reconstruction of the settings of Van Gogh paintings in Vincente Minelli's *Lust for Life* (1956) and Akira Kurosawa's *Dreams* (1990) (Lefebvre 2016: 30–1). For a broader examination of the relationship of landscape to language and narration, see Roskill 1997.

In science fiction the landscape's intention is generally cognitive or epistemological: the aim of the characters converges with that of the reader to construct reliable knowledge of the imagined geography and its contents, so exploring and mapping constitute the privileged means of cognition in Darko Suvin's or Carl Freedman's sense. Somewhat polemically, we can call this practice cognitive mapping (implying thereby that it anticipates and possibly influences Fredric Jameson's appropriation of that term from Kevin Lynch [Jameson 1988; Jameson 1991: 50–4, 412–8]), and it can be seen at work in founding texts of science fiction like Jules Verne's *Journey to the Center of the Earth* (1864) and *20,000 Leagues Under the Seas* (1870). The latter, especially, is a narrative structured around the tour of the fanciful "underseascape" that Captain Nemo gives Professor Aronnax (and through him the reader), revealing in the process the marine geography's potential for appropriation, production, and exploitation. Some editions of the novel even include maps of the *Nautilus*'s travels to emphasize this. Or consider H.G. Wells's first major contribution to science fiction, *The Time Machine* (1895): although it would be more accurate to describe its figural order as topographic rather than geographic, the puzzle of humanity's fate that lies at its core is only resolved through spatial cognition. On a ridge above the Eloi's communal residences the Time Traveler finds a mock-throne from which he can "survey … the broad view of our old world under the sunset of that long day" (Wells 1934: 23). Although he sees the cupola-covered "wells" that will eventually lead him to the puzzle's solution, he doesn't understand their significance until after he has descended into the Morlocks' underworld and discovered what they eat. The geographical focus on cognition by means of encounters with previously unknown landscapes continues through the modern works of Ray Bradbury (*The Martian Chronicles* [1950]) and Arthur C. Clarke (both *2001* [1968] and *Rendezvous with Rama* [1973]), William Gibson's and Bruce Sterling's cyberpunk,[2] and leads directly to the evolving maps of Kim Stanley Robinson's celebrated Mars trilogy (1993–6).

While most important works of science fiction conclude with the successful production of a cognitive map, to the point that this may be identified as the genre's defining characteristic, a few works do not; instead, they draw attention to the epistemological limits of human knowledge construction by foreclosing any completed cognitive map. Algis Budrys's *Rogue Moon* (1960), Stanislaw Lem's *Solaris* (1961), and the Strugatsky brothers' *Roadside Picnic* (1972) present paradigmatic case studies of such foreclosure, which we might call, contra Lynch and Jameson, decognitive mapping. In Budrys's novel, the discovery of a deadly maze on the moon that remains utterly inexplicable, an "enormous puzzle" (Budrys 1960: 166), at the book's conclusion despite the protagonists' successful navigation of it, poses a paradoxical existential question: does the experience of personal duplication and death, undergone repeatedly by the protagonists so that they can ultimately navigate the maze, teach or otherwise transform them cognitively? In other words, if the sacrifice of death does not open up the way to knowledge, what if anything can do so, and what, then,

---

[2] As the *Encyclopedia of Science Fiction* notes, "many of Sterling's novels may be seen as tours conducted around fields of data by protagonists whose main function is to witness them for us" (sf-encyclopedia.com/entry/sterling_bruce). Gibson's depictions of cyberspace often operate in a similarly cartographic fashion.

does death accomplish? The maze has been mapped physically and experientially, but emphatically not cognitively. In Lem's novel, the infinitely mutable seascape of the planet-organism Solaris and the revenants it sends to haunt the human characters imply purposiveness and cognition, but never provide those implications with any stable form or content. By the end, the protagonist Kris Kelvin is no more capable of answering even the most basic questions about the oceanic mega-organism than is the degenerating science of Solaristics he is sent to evaluate. The unmappable surface of Solaris provides a figure for the instability and unreliability of human cognition, a decognitive map of scientific failure, that anticipates Lem's merciless investigation of the "myth of our cognitive universality" in *His Master's Voice* (Lem 1968: 26–7). Although the Strugatskys' novel opens with the voice of physicist Valentine Pillman describing the astronomical coordinates whence came the alien visitation that produced the incomprehensible "Zones" on which the book focuses, that information marks the limit of scientific cognition within the narrative; the plot actually follows the efforts of the stalker Red Schuhart to profit from the inexplicable artifacts he pilfers, at great personal risk, from the Zone—thus exploitation is presented as independent of cognitive mastery, at which no one ever arrives. As the brothers' original notes for the story insist, the narrative dramatizes "a decline in the stature of science" (Strugatsky 2012: 196) in the face of its cognitive incapacity to map the Zone, in other words an inescapable foreclosure of its cognitive aim.

As Stefan Ekman notes, in fantasy as in science fiction, "Exploring has become tantamount to mapping, turning the empty margins and blank areas of terra incognita into familiar terrain" (Ekman 2013: 14). However, in fantasy the landscape's intention is generally moral/ethical rather than cognitive or epistemological: the aim of the reader converges with that of the characters to (re)establish justice throughout the realm, so struggle constitutes the privileged means of redeeming the landscape. Note that this moral/ethical intentionality of the landscape in fantasy is usually predicated on a logically prior cognitive or quasi-cognitive mastery, although this may only gradually become clear to the reader through their surrogates within the text. The lands of fantasy are almost always already known to someone, hence the ubiquity of maps in fantasy fictions, and the terms of their moral/ethical redemption are usually already known too. As was the case in science fiction, we can see this process operating in many of the foundational texts of the genre such as William Morris's *Well at the World's End* (1896) and J.R.R. Tolkien's *Lord of the Rings* saga (1954). As I suggested in the Introduction, Morris's romance offers an *ethical* landscape of redemption, one predicated on the immanence and materiality of social practice rather than on the transcendence and ideality of divine revelation (following Spinoza's, Nietzsche's, and Deleuze's definitions of ethics). The book's protagonist Ralph leaves his peaceful homeland of Upmeads in search of chivalric adventure, and the farther he gets from home, the more corrupt and dangerous the societies he encounters become, culminating in the despotic state of Utterbol, from which he must escape in order to complete his quest for the Well of the title. Beyond Utterbol lies the Wall of the World that separates human historical reality from its underlying but generally forgotten sources, both social (the primitive communism of the Innocent Folk) and natural (the ecological spectrum that links the deadly Thirsty Desert to the life-giving, seaward-flowing Well itself). After drinking from the Well, which grants Ralph and his beloved Ursula no magical powers other than abundant life, their physical and ethical example inspires local forces along the road of corruption to rise up and overthrow their tyrants. The romance concludes with Ralph and friends expelling a despotic occupying army from Upmeads, thereby bringing the ethical redemption of the landscape full circle.

In contrast to Morris, Tolkien's work provides an example, and a much more widely imitated one at that, of a *moral* landscape of redemption, which is the contrary of an ethical landscape, to wit, one predicated on the transcendence and ideality of divine revelation rather than on the immanence and materiality of social practice. The creation myths "Ainulindalë" and "Valaquenta," included in the *Silmarillion* (Tolkien 1977), attest to the divine origin of the moral values pursued by Tolkien's heroes, from the First Age (culminating in the War of Wrath against Morgoth) to the Third Age (culminating in the War of the Ring against Sauron). This absolute morality is clearly inscribed in the landscape of Middle Earth itself: unmapped (by Tolkien, anyway) Valinor in the west remains the geographical locus of moral right throughout the entire saga (explicitly so in the First and Second Ages, implicitly so in the Third), while the locus of evil shifts from far north Beleriand (Thangorodrim) in the First Age to the far east of Mordor in the Third. Tolkien even provides his own critical term for narrative moral redemption in "On Fairy Stories" (1966): "eucatastrophe," which is explicitly modeled on Christ's Passion. The travels of the Fellowship of the Ring recapitulate much of Morris's intentional geography—movement from west to east, from the Shire to Rohan and Gondor and ultimately to Mordor, reveals an intensification in corruption and evil, and the hobbits' return after Sauron's defeat culminates in the "Scouring of the Shire," which echoes Ralph's expulsion of the occupying army from Upmeads. In both cases, the geographical circularity of the narrative reinforces the redemptive aim of the plot.[3]

While most major works of fantasy conclude with successful moral/ethical redemption of the landscape and its occupants, a few important ones do not; instead, they draw attention to the irreconcilable antagonism between moral transcendence on the one hand and ethical immanence on the other, and this results in the radical deferral and often the foreclosure of redemption. Among the better-known examples of this moral/ethical foreclosure are Charles G. Finney's *Circus of Dr. Lao* (1935) and Michael Moorcock's Eternal Champion cycle (1961–). In Finney's work the circus brings magical beings from diverse global cultural traditions to the outskirts of a small, fictional Arizona town in order to challenge the isolation and complacency, both intellectual and moral/ethical, of its inhabitants. Geographical isolation becomes a figure for spiritual poverty. A young schoolteacher is seduced by the Greek god Pan, to whom she had been introducing her students in lit class; an intelligent, amoral, talking sea serpent undermines the anthropocentrism of a local as it struggles to free itself from its display tank; the ancient sage Apollonius of Tyana performs assorted miracles, which are ironically trivialized; and the circus comes to a climax in a bewilderingly anachronistic reenactment of human sacrifice to the fictional god Yottle in the fictional land of Woldercan, a sacrifice which fails to restore the fertility of the waste land in

---

[3] For a more thorough explication of this contrast between Morris and Tolkien, see Murphy 2019.

the face of the double audience's skepticism and even indifference. The townspeople are confused as well as unmoved by this mock-transcendence, and so remain willfully unredeemed. As Dr. Lao says, "The world is my idea; as such I present it to you. I have my own set of weights and measures and my own table for computing values. You are privileged to have yours" (Finney 1935: 126).

Moorcock's work is at once more direct in its presentation of the antagonism between immanence and transcendence and more complex in the variations of that antagonism which it stages within different subseries of the meta-series that is the Eternal Champion Cycle. For clarity's sake I will discuss only two of the best-known subseries, Elric and Hawkmoon. The Elric cycle culminates in the composite novel *Stormbringer*, which was originally published before most of the other Elric tales. At its conclusion, the albino anti-hero Elric, who was conceived as a point-by-point antithesis to Robert E. Howard's heroes like Conan and to the fantasy clichés associated with Tolkien, must betray the lords of Chaos to whom his people have sworn allegiance by calling the banished lords of Law back for an apocalyptic battle that will expel both sets of forces from the world. This conflict results in a near-*tabula rasa*, a highly differentiated global geography melted down to its raw materials and recast for a fresh start: "The stuff of the Earth alone remained, but unformed. Its components were still in existence, but their new shape was undecided" (Moorcock 2008: 427). Its moral/ethical blankness is marred only by the survival of the Black Sword Stormbringer itself, which, having swallowed Elric's soul, stands as "the last manifestation of Chaos which would remain with this new world as it grew" (Moorcock 2008: 433). The landscape is thereby seeded with resistance to any future redemptive project.

The Hawkmoon books begin with a more clearly satiric evocation of intentional landscape: in a direct inversion of Morris's and Tolkien's implied geography, the despotic empire of Granbretan, whose armies are sweeping across an imaginary Europe, has gained control of the Germanian hero Duke Dorian Hawkmoon by affixing a Black Jewel, amulet of Chaos, to his forehead. Hawkmoon intends to serve the Runestaff, image of the Cosmic Balance between Law and Chaos, and he struggles for several volumes to escape Granbretan's influence. He ultimately succeeds not only in overthrowing Granbretan, but in the final novel of the Eternal Champion cycle as a whole, *The Quest for Tanelorn*, he joins Moorcock's ur-hero Erekosë (from *The Eternal Champion*, the formal though not historical starting point of the cycle) in destroying both the Black Jewel/Black Sword and the Runestaff/Cosmic Balance. This leaves the unmappable multiverse bereft of all transcendence, and hence all possibility of moral redemption; a subordinate character rebukes Hawkmoon by saying, "You have rid the world of gods, but now you rid it of order, too," to which he responds: "Only of Authority" (Moorcock 2013: 386). Somewhat paradoxically, we could say that here, the human landscape has been redeemed from the logic of moral redemption itself, and any ethical redemption will have to depend, beyond the conclusion of the cycle, on immanent and unforeseen human choices. This is clearly Moorcock's aim.

Since weird fiction combines elements of science fiction and fantasy into an untotalizable whole, we might expect its landscapes to combine, or rather clash, the epistemological/cognitive and the moral/ethical, which they often do. Among Old Weird writers, Arthur Machen's work in "The Great God Pan" and *The Three*

Impostors and Clark Ashton Smith's Averoigne, Zothique, and other series epitomize this combination: for Machen, acknowledgment of the limits to human knowledge following their transgression restores the mystical enchantment of the natural world, though only as the result of blood sacrifice, whereas Smith's Decadent skepticism celebrates the ultimate meaninglessness of the world through the collapse of all ethical absolutes. In the New Weird, China Miéville's Bas Lag novels are good examples of this same melding: the complex set of cognitively rationalized and exploitable magics, especially the "Crisis Energy" that drives the plot of *Perdido Street Station* (2000), the "possibility mining" that impels the Armada's quest for the ontologically ruptured seascape in *The Scar* (2002), and the "golemetry" that protects the exiled train of radicals in *Iron Council* (2004), balance equipoisally between science fiction and fantasy, and although no character or collective thereof succeeds in actually redeeming the world of Bas Lag, the specter of that future ethical (and indeed political) redemption hovers over the conclusions of all three novels, most powerfully in the "time golem" into which Judah Low transforms the train at the climax of *Iron Council*. However, the foreclosure of both cognition and redemption—decognitive mapping combined with anethical geography—is a far more common outcome in weird narrative than in either of its constituent genres, to the point that it should be considered the conventional conclusion of such narratives and perhaps their defining characteristic. This double foreclosure can be identified in both the classic Old Weird of Algernon Blackwood and H.P. Lovecraft and the New Weird of Jeff VanderMeer.

Blackwood's "The Willows" (1907, Blackwood 2002) tells the story of an encounter with the radically alien amidst the transitory sand islands of the Danube in floodtide. Although this is nominally a real landscape, its geographical instability transforms it into a predominantly imaginary one, less constrained by real history than its namesake. The alien presence becomes perceptible—though never intelligible—first through the disturbingly intentional movements of the willow bushes, and later through the appearance of funnel-shaped pits in the sand, the production of which is never explained; those funnels reappear on the face and torso of the dead man whose unintentional self-sacrifice saves the protagonists' lives at the story's climax. The unreadable alien code inscribed on the landscape and the human body remains radically anethical as well as resistant to cognitive mastery or mapping. Lovecraft was a great admirer of Blackwood's work, especially "The Willows," and he created his own version of a decognitive, unredeemed landscape in both "The Call of Cthulhu" (1928) and *At the Mountains of Madness* (1936). In the latter work, scientists discover an ancient alien city on a high plateau in Antarctica, and in the city they find mural sculptures that disclose the history of its occupants, the Old Ones. The discovery of maps showing the Old Ones' former empire, which stretched around the globe, and of evidence that the Old Ones genetically engineered all terrestrial life radically undermines the epistemological assumptions of human cognitive and geographical mastery, to the point that China Miéville describes the novella as "depict[ing] a scientific methodology presiding over the collapse of its own predicates" (Miéville 2005: xiii). It also precludes any kind of moral or ethical redemption, for us or for the Old Ones: lest the Old Ones' quasi-utopian history simply supplant humanity's as the evolutionary master narrative of cognition, the explorers learn that their civilization too was undermined and overthrown, first by their struggles with creatures so alien that they couldn't be depicted in the murals, and second by the revolt of their own shape-changing, protoplasmic slaves, the Shoggoths, which remain a threat to humanity as the tale concludes. Lovecraft stages the collapse of human epistemological and ethical categories as the repetition of the collapse of the Old Ones' far greater mastery, which is figured in the mountains that give the tale its title.

The works I've just outlined constitute some of the founding documents of weird fiction as a genre, but the pattern of decognition and non-redemption continues to dominate the field, as Jeff VanderMeer's 2014 trilogy *Area X: The Southern Reach* demonstrates. Inspired by Lem and the Strugatskys as well as Hodgson and Lovecraft, VanderMeer creates a landscape that both defies cognitive mapping and evades moral and ethical judgment. Area X is a region of the North American coastline, apparently in Florida, that has been absorbed into another world with a different set of physical laws that do not appear to be stable; alternately, Area X may be less a material geography than a geographical manifestation of a radically alien lifeform. Time passes irregularly there, and humans mutate into reptilian, avian, and mammalian forms as well as utterly non-terrestrial ones. At the trilogy's close, the boundary of Area X is on the move, swallowing more of North America, and other portals across that boundary begin to appear at widely scattered sites. As in the works of VanderMeer's precursors, the unthinkable and anethical alien landscape infects, transforms, and threatens to supplant the one we know, this time not in the distant past or far future, but in the present.

If Sam Gafford's conclusions regarding the composition history of Hodgson's novels are correct, then his novel *The Night Land,* written around 1903 and published in 1912, is the earliest of all narratives that use landscape as the primary means to carry out a decognitive/anethical project. In order to grasp as fully as possible the processes of cognitive foreclosure and non-redemption operating in that novel, though, we must follow the development of Hodgson's use of settings across the full range of his fiction. In the terms defined in the Preface, we could say that his profound untimeliness depends in large part upon an equally profound dis-placement or ex-stasis, so that moving out of place makes moving out of time possible. While it is clear that all the genres we have just discussed include major works that explicitly perform critiques of their genre's dominant logic, the recurrent overlapping or even identification of decognition and anethicality in weird fiction seems to me to imply that genre's more far-reaching skepticism regarding not only its own conditions of production, but more generally regarding human aspirations to know, to evaluate, and to control the cosmos. While science fiction will occasionally call its own cognitive focus into question and fantasy will in rare cases abandon the redemptive moral mission that motivates most of its plots, weird fiction makes such generic self-critique and undoing into its own enabling condition, and in this Hodgson's work sets a high standard for later writers.

4

The Sea Is All the God There Is

In terms of the spaces they investigate, Hodgson's weird fictions fall into three categories of increasing departure from realist conventions: traditional shipboard tales of the sea (including *The Ghost Pirates* [1909]), tales set in fantastic modifications of the seascape (including his Sargasso Sea stories such as *The Boats of the "Glen Carrig"* [1907]), and tales involving journeys across completely invented fantastic spaces (including his novels *The House on the Borderland* [1908] and *The Night Land* [1912]). According to Sam Gafford's interpretation of Hodgson's 1905 letters to Coulson Kernahan, however, the more fantastic visions were written first and the most realistic ones later, and Emily Alder has argued convincingly that "the Night Land, in essence, is conceptually a seascape" not simply because it is a hostile environment that restricts human life to an enclosed space, but also because its overall obscurity can only be observed from a high lookout similar to the crow's nest atop a mast. Since it can't be adequately mapped, it can only be navigated by combining compass readings with primitive "pilotage" using landmarks (Alder 2013: 90, 95, 98). Thus these categories comprise an overlapping continuum or spectrum rather than discrete sets. For the sake of clarity and simplicity in defining the breadth and depth of Hodgson's innovations, this discussion will begin with the most realistic and conclude with the most fantastic, even though this will sometimes require reversals of historical/biographical chronology.

The sea challenges conventional notions of setting in literature in a variety of ways. Although it is a space that humans and their stories can occupy, they can only do so long enough for storytelling with the aid of technology in the form of boats, rafts, ships, diving gear, or some form of submarine habitat. Such technological aids are necessary because sea travel reminds us that our survival needs for a breathable atmosphere, constant gravity, and a stable ground are not universally available even on our homeworld. Thus the history of sea stories is more constrained, both practically and generically, than that of tales that happen on open, walkable surfaces such as dry land, concrete, or some other comparatively stable natural or artificial substance. The challenge of such constraints accounts in part for the immense popularity and influence of Verne's *20,000 Leagues Under the Seas* (1870), which opened up new vistas for maritime narration through the invention of the elaborate submarine vessel *Nautilus*. In this regard, sea stories prefigure not only tales set on the radically changed far-future earth, but also tales set in the vacuum and microgravity of space, though Hodgson's work did not develop in the latter direction. In the aesthetic terms of landscape framing, the sea presents a wide range of sensuous aspects, from the placid to the tempestuous, but these aspects are constitutively unstable and constantly changing. This has led to its use as a figure for volatility and unpredictability. The sharp contrast between the sea's often barren surface and the tremendous range of unfamiliar things, both living and nonliving, beneath it has encouraged artists to use it as a figure of secrecy, the unconscious, and also deep time. In English-language literature, realistic depictions of life and work at sea go back at least as far as the Old English poem "The Seafarer," found in the tenth-century *Exeter Book*, and have remained consistently popular with readers, though only intermittently interesting to scholars. Hodgson's contemporary, the poet and former sailor John Masefield (1878–1967), was appointed the British Poet Laureate in 1930 at least partly in recognition of his poems and stories about life at sea, the most famous of which, "Sea-Fever" (1902), contains the well-known line, "And all I ask is a tall ship and a star to steer her by." In relation to this long tradition, Hodgson's non-fantastic tales of shipboard life contain few compelling innovations—perhaps only their regular resort to boxing scenes of revenge (which are textbook examples of wish fulfillment and can verge on the fetishistic, as in "How the Honourable Billy Darrell Raised the Wind" [1913])—to make them stand out until he began his Captain Gault series, which focuses on a charming maritime smuggler.

Hodgson's attitude toward the sea and the life of sailors was conflicted and ambivalent, as numerous scholars from Sam Moskowitz to Jane Frank and China Miéville have noted. In August 1891, before his fourteenth birthday, he began four years' apprenticeship as a seaman, and in 1897 he earned his mate's certificate, entitling him to serve as a junior officer aboard merchant marine vessels, but he abandoned that profession for good in 1899 (M 15–7, 20; E:3–5). He explained his reasons for doing so succinctly at the beginning of his 1905 essay "Is the Mercantile Navy Worth Joining? Certainly Not": "I am not at sea because I object to bad treatment, poor food, poor wages, and worse prospects. I am not at sea because very early I discovered that it is a comfortless, wearful, and thankless life—a life compact of hardness and sordidness such as shore people can hardly conceive" (WS: 155). Despite this well-founded dislike, a majority of his stories are set at sea or among sailors, and few of those are concerned with documenting poor wages or conditions. Not surprisingly, his nautical fiction often includes scenes of brutal treatment, to which his protagonists respond just as their creator did: by developing their fighting skills and soundly thrashing their tormentors. Fewer of his sea stories give any indication of what may have initially attracted him to the profession of sailor, apart from the deceptive glamor of romantic adventure that was common in popular fiction during his youth. Reports of friction with his devout and demanding father suggest that escaping from a confining home life may have motivated him as well (E:3–4).

Perhaps the story that reveals the most about Hodgson's ambivalence toward the sailor's life is "The Wild Man of the Sea," first published posthumously in 1926. Like many of his sea stories, it emphasizes the obligation that sensitive or otherwise atypical seamen have to defend themselves against the hostility and superstition of the more common types of sailor. It follows the last voyage of able seaman Jesson, whom the captain admires as the "Best sailorman that ever stepped" but the crew considers to be a "Jonah" whose presence curses the ship to dead calms, gales, and other dangers (CF 3: 483, 486). Jesson is "soaked in all the lore of the sea life and all its practical arts," such as splicing and knots, that were gradually fading away as sailing ships gave way to steam-powered vessels, and he begins to teach these arts to the much-abused ship's boy Jeb. Jesson also plays wild, half audible airs to himself on the fiddle, further highlighting his artistic bent. Almost as an aside during a lesson, Jesson encourages Jeb to "Hark to the wind ... sit on the hatch an' let the wind talk to ye," which Jeb does—"And presently, for the first time in his life, he heard *consciously* the living note of the wind, booming in its eternal melody of the Sailing-ship-Wind" (CF 3: 485). Later Jesson advises Jeb "to realise that your life is to be lived in the most wonderful and mysterious place in the world. It will be full of compensations in such lots of ways for the sordidness of the sea-life, as it is to the sailorman ... Live your own life, and let the sea be your companion" (CF 3: 487). Clearly Jesson, who is also a powerful fighter, serves as a kind of role model for Jeb, but their relationship—and by implication, the ecstatic vision of the sea that the one tries to inculcate in the other—comes to a tragic conclusion when the other sailors resolve to murder the "Jonah" and throw his body overboard. Jeb overhears the plot, warns Jesson, and attempts to help him fight off his attackers, but without success. Both are slain, but not before inflicting serious damage on their opponents, who nevertheless go on to tell their superstitious version of the story "to believing and sympathetic ears; and foolish and ignorant heads nodded a sober and uncondemnatory assent" (CF 3: 497). Such a victory of folly, ignorance, and cruelty over wonder, mystery, and beauty would certainly justify both Hodgson's farewell to a life at sea and his lifelong exploration of its concealed possibilities for fiction, although he would soon find the world of publishing in which he aspired to dwell to be afflicted with its own forms of suffering.[1]

In addition to popular realism, Hodgson's other line of experiment in sea fiction was, of course, the fantastic one, and here his innovations are more evident and influential, even in those comparatively conventional tales that take place aboard ship and among sailors. A story such as "The Haunted *Pampero*" (1918), which focuses on an apparent shipwreck survivor who is picked up by another vessel and soon becomes a suspect in the mutilation of pigs and attempts to attack the captain's wife, balances its narrative undecidably between the supernatural—the sailors imagine the survivor to be an ocean ghoul in the form of a were-shark—and the prosaic—the captain persuades himself that the survivor may simply have lost his mind during his ordeal before rescue, and the shark bites attributed to him may simply be wounds made by his shark-tooth-shaped marlinspike—according to the pattern that Hodgson had already established in his Carnacki the Ghost Finder stories. The brief, intense tale "Out of the Storm" (1909) sets up a different kind of narrative (im)balance in its verbatim transcript of a radio message from a man trapped aboard a passenger ship sinking in a titanic storm. He personifies the storm itself as a literal monster, "one of the sea's hell-orgies—one of the *Thing's* monstrous gloatings over the living," with tattered clouds that hang above him

---

[1] The ironic ethical reversal at the heart of "The Wild Man of the Sea" bears comparison with the parallel ethical reversal that drives Melville's *Billy Budd, Sailor*, in which a cruel officer is "struck dead by an angel of God [i.e. the innocent Billy Budd]! Yet the angel must hang!" (chapter 20). As discussed in note 10 of the Introduction, however, no evidence exists that Hodgson was familiar with Melville, whose works went out of print the year before Hodgson was born, and *Billy Budd* itself was not published until 1924, six years after Hodgson's death.

"like the tentacles of some enormous Horror" and breakers like teeth that "snapped at him" across the flooded deck (CF 3: 180, 182). Initially the speaker vents his fear and rage in violent diatribes against God, whom he dismisses as "no God" because He is "weak and puny beside this foul *Thing* which Thou didst create in Thy lusty youth. *It is now* God—and I am one of its children … *The sea is now all the God there is!*" (CF 3: 180-1). The monstrous storm is only one face of the inscrutable and uncategorizable counter-deity that is the sea. To demonstrate the truth of this blasphemous and amoral claim that the hostile materiality of the sea overpowers the benign spirituality of the divine, he goes on to describe a mother clinging to the ship's rail who bites her child's hand in order to make it release its grip on her arm, and a young couple who batter one another in their competition for a handhold. After the speaker strikes his head against a bulkhead and is rendered momentarily disoriented, however, he expresses regret for his blasphemy and begs God's forgiveness, attributing his own lack of pain while dying to God's "merciful" nature (CF 3: 182). The hasty and tepid conventionality of his final prayers fails to erase or even temper the intensity of his initial atheistic denunciations, however, and many readers consider this tale an important, though extraordinarily condensed, expression of Hodgson's own atheism.

Taken together, a further pair of shipboard tales explores and develops this nihilistic, anti-Christian theme more fully. In "The *Shamraken* Homeward Bounder" (1908), one of Hodgson's few outright satires, a crew of absurdly aged sailors—their "ship's boy" Nuzzie is fifty-five years old, although the rest, who are much older, believe he still "needs a tur'ble lot er sleep" for his "growin'" (CF 3: 168)—who are looking forward to retiring ashore after completing their last voyage encounter a rare cyclonic storm that they mistake first for the "Gates uv Glory" and later for the "Throne uv God" (CF 3: 175-6). The captain and crew all have biblical names—Abraham, Zephaniah, Job, Joshua, Nehemiah—and unlike younger, more boisterous sailors, they work with "wise submission" and no clear thought of the future, since "the men of the *Shamraken* lived in the past" and only skipper Abe Tombes "kept some sort of record of time and place" (CF 3: 167-8). Each man (except Job, who repeatedly boasts, "I never 'ad no wife") has apparently avoided planning for retirement because he still mourns a lost loved one: Zeph his wife Maria, Nehemiah his granddaughter, and First Mate Josh his son. When they first encounter the mist preceding the storm, Abe describes it as "mighty purty" and Josh as "unearthly … Like as of yew was in church" (CF 3: 172), and as they proceed farther into it, the storm cell appears to them as a theophanic "Piller uv cloud by day, 'n er piller uv fire by night," similar to those that guided the Israelites through the desert in Exodus. Gradually all the sailors begin to feel as if they have "come purty near ter 'eaven" and are approaching a reunion with their beloved dead (CF 3: 174-5). Refusing to listen to the surprisingly skeptical Job's suggestion that "heaven was less near than his mates supposed," they mistake the whistling wind for angelic singing, until "the wild-beast bellow of the coming Cyclone" forces them to reconsider: "'Reck'n thet's God speakin', whispered Zeph, 'Guess we're on'y mis'rable sinners" bound for hell (CF 3: 176-7). The combination of old age, submissiveness, unquestioned traditional piety, and the wish for reunion with their mourned dead makes the crew particularly susceptible to religious delusions that result from projecting their spiritual desires onto the dangerously anethical material world they must still navigate. Although they never resort to skeptical doubt, let alone blasphemy, their fate is of a piece with that of the narrator in "Out of the Storm," since the sea they sail is similarly profane, inhuman, monstrous, and indifferent to morality.

The tale "The Riven Night" (posthumously published in 1973) presents a parallel situation in more sober, indeed respectful terms, but utterly devoid of Christian iconography or language. Narrated by a young ship's apprentice tellingly named Hodgson, it focuses on a ship, commanded by a captain who has just lost his new wife, that encounters a strange light far out at sea and late at night. At first "Hodgson" dismisses it as a corposant or "corpse-candle," a small efflorescence of St. Elmo's fire superstitiously associated with imminent death, but as it grows larger, he and the ship's officers become worried and attempt to wake the captain, who ignores them. The light expands into an enormous "gulf" or "rift" through which the ship is slowly drawn into a different world in which "Time seemed to have no part" (CF 3: 512–5). Although the crew can still feel the ship all about them, they see in its place a shadowy space of ghostly peaks and glowing waves, into which "legions upon legions of ... spirit forms" float (CF 3: 515); one such form descends to deck level and reveals itself to be a lovely young girl with the handle of a sailor's knife protruding from her bosom, causing one crew member to cry out for forgiveness. When the girl turns away from him, he leaps to his death into the strange, glowing sea. Moments later, "Hodgson" sees the face of his own recently deceased mother appear, but she does not respond to his call.[2] Then the grieving captain appears on deck and, like the guilty sailor, leaps overboard, after which a "shadowy form with a face like that of the Captain's" floats upward in pursuit of a figure only he can see. If the guilty sailor's death can be counted an instance of moral justice, the same cannot be said for the grieving captain's suicide. "Hodgson" looks over the side into the unnatural ocean, where he sees "weird things that peered up at me and vanished," and after "the monotony of time passed over my head in silent aeons," something vast and distinctly un-Godlike rises from the waves: "something terrible—eyes that blazed out of mystery, and beneath, lips—white, vast and slobbering had opened, disclosing the blackness of an everlasting night" (CF 3: 516–7). When the wave ahead of the thing crashes over him, he loses consciousness, and awakens slowly to calm, daylight, and his shipmates waking around him. None are surprised to find the captain and the guilty sailor missing, but the officers simply report them as washed overboard in the ship's logbook. Unlike "*Shamraken*," this version of an encounter with the dead and the afterlife openly eschews Christian eschatology and instead retains the moral ambivalence and metaphysical mystery of Hodgson's weird novels.

Undoubtedly the most important example of Hodgson's shipboard weird fiction, of course, is the novel *The Ghost Pirates* (1909), which as its title implies combines the well-established genre of violent pirate narrative with an unusually rationalized ghost story. The narrator Jessop, newly signed onto the *Mortzestus's* homeward voyage from San Francisco, begins his account by mentioning the ship's reputation for bad luck and the opinion of the Cockney sailor Williams that "There's too many bloomin' shadders about this 'ere packet; they gets onter yer nerves like nothin' as ever I seen before in me

---

[2] The author Hodgson's mother outlived him by fifteen years (E: 24, Moskowitz 1996: 12), so the significance of this detail is unclear.

nat'ral" (GP: 19). Jessop sees his first "shadder" soon after: a manlike shape stepping inboard over the ship's rail, as if coming out of the sea. Further nebulous sightings and odd problems with the rigging follow, culminating in the disappearance of a sailor from high on the mainmast and Williams's fall to his death at the end of a ghostly encounter aloft. Although Jessop, like his creator the holder of a mate's certificate despite serving as an able seaman this trip (GP: 208), is more skeptical about ghosts than the other sailors, his speculative turn of mind leads him to a disturbing inference regarding these events:

> I believe that this ship is open ... exposed, unprotected, or whatever you like to call it. I should say it's reasonable to think that all the things of the material world are barred, as it were, from the immaterial; but that in some cases the barrier may be broken down. That's what may have happened to this ship. And if it has, she may be naked to the attacks of beings belonging to some other state of existence.
>
> (GP: 100)

This would account not only for the spate of encounters, but also for the ship's reputation for bad luck. Hodgson would provide a similar explanation of the shadow-besieged ship in the posthumously published Carnacki story "The Haunted *Jarvee*" (1920).[3] Of the beings attacking the *Mortzestus*, Jessop later clarifies that they should be considered not so much immaterial as alternatively material, in fact as occupants of a different kind of physical space that overlaps our own but remains imperceptible to humans: "The earth may be just as *real* to them, as to us. I mean that it may have qualities as material to them, as it has to us; but neither of us could appreciate the other's realness, or the quality of realness in the earth, which was real to the other" (GP: 102).

Jessop's inferences are confirmed when the ship becomes engulfed in haze or mist that prevents its crew from seeing objects nearby in the sea. Upon witnessing a passing ship vanish into a sort of shimmering heat haze, Jessop muses, "It was nothing about the other packet that was strange. The strangeness was in us. It was something that was about (or invested) our ship that prevented me—or indeed, anyone else aboard—from seeing that other" (GP: 112). More precisely, he feels "that I had looked at her from out of some other dimension" (GP: 113), which implies that the *Mortzestus* is slowly moving out of its own space and reality and into its attackers' space and reality. The accelerating pace of inexplicable deaths and disappearances bears this out, so when Jessop notices "The shadow of a ship rising out of the unexplored immensity beneath our keel," which is soon joined by three more "exact, though shadowy, representations of vessels" (GP: 216, 227), he realizes that an otherworldly trap is closing around them. One of the ghost ships' emergence onto the surface, where it is silhouetted against the

---

[3] In that tale, Carnacki speculates that the ship "possessed the 'attractive vibration' that is the power to draw to her any psychic waves in the vicinity, much in the way of a medium ... She may have developed it during the years, owing to a suitability of conditions, or it may have been in her ('of her' is a better term) from the very day her keel was laid ... A building or a ship ... may develop 'vibrations,' even as certain materials in combination under the proper conditions will certainly develop an electric current" (CF 2, 269).

setting sun (GP: 232–3), is followed soon after by the clearest sighting of a ghost pirate that the reader ever gets: Jessop

> turned sharply, and saw something peering over the taffrail. It had eyes that reflected the binnacle light, weirdly, with a frightful, tigerish gleam; but beyond that, I could see nothing with any distinctness ... The thing, whatever it was, had come more forward over the rail; but now, before the light, it recoiled with a queer, horrible litheness. It slid back, and down, and so out of sight. I have only a confused notion of a wet, glistening something, and two vile eyes.
>
> (GP: 237–8)

This encounter was likely a final reconnaissance visit, for shortly thereafter the ship is invaded by

> a queer, undulating greyness, that moved downwards inboard, and spread over the decks ... And, suddenly, all the moving greyness resolved into hundreds of strange men. In the half-light, they looked unreal and impossible, as though there had come upon us the inhabitants of some fantastic dream-world ... They swarmed in upon us in a great wave of murderous, living shadows.
>
> (GP: 261–2)

Jessop conceals himself on top of the deckhouse as all his shipmates are massacred and the ghost pirates take their places at the wheel and in the rigging, but he is forced to leap into the sea when the *Mortzestus* suddenly tips forward and, its sails filling with the wind of a different reality, dives under the waves.[4]

The oceanic space through which the *Mortzestus* sails on its final voyage is thus similar, conceptually and topographically if not geographically, to the rural space in which the Recluse's odd house sits on the borderland, as we will see shortly. Although one is land and the other sea, both consist of a relatively prosaic surface across which people regularly travel and on which people live, unaware that it is only flimsily separated from an underlying region inhabited by ab-human entities and governed by unrecognizable physical laws. Each novel begins with a local irruption of the underlying region onto the surface, proceeds through a difficult and necessarily inconclusive investigation into the underlying region's characteristics, and concludes with the absorption of the surface space where the narrative takes place into the ab-human underworld, leaving behind only a flotsam of ambiguous signs without clear referents that resist understanding. Both are excellent examples of the weird process of anethical, decognitive mapping, but they do not exhaust their author's investigations in this regard.

---

[4] In the highly condensed short story version of this plot, "The Silent Ship" (posthumously published in 1973), which is told from the viewpoint of an officer on a nearby ship who witnesses the climactic takeover, Jessop dies without telling any part of the longer story (CF 3, 140–2).

5

A Cemetery of Lost Ships and Wrack and Forgotten Things

One solution to the challenges of adapting the sea's surface to serve as a more flexible fictional setting is, paradoxically, to stabilize its fluidity, locally or temporarily, for which purpose a variety of means are available. Perhaps the most striking is the rather fanciful expedient of bringing the seafloor to the surface temporarily for human perambulation and investigation, often via the intermediary of an undersea earthquake. In weird fiction, H.P. Lovecraft is probably the best-known writer who comes to mind as a proponent of this expedient, which is used in his stories "Dagon" (1919) and "The Call of Cthulhu" (1928) as a means for staging encounters between human characters and nonhuman deep-sea entities. Hodgson developed this approach several years earlier, in his stories "The Stone Ship" (1914) and "Demons of the Sea" (posthumously published in 1923), the latter of which we discussed in Chapter Two in relation to its depiction of racial difference. The basic plot of "The Stone Ship" prefigures the climactic chapter three, "The Madness from the Sea," of "The Call of Cthulhu": a merchant ship encounters a strange rocky island, unmarked on any charts, in the middle of the ocean, and the crew's exploration of its disturbing mysteries ends in violent death. But whereas Lovecraft's tale, the namesake and cornerstone of his invented pantheon, grows increasingly weird as the action proceeds to its near-apocalyptic conclusion, Hodgson's story progressively demystifies the weirdest aspects of its titular subject, ultimately attributing all the apparent strangeness to comprehensible natural processes. The tale begins late at night, when the sailors aboard the *Alfred Jessop* (which shares a name with the narrator of *The Ghost Pirates*) are startled to hear "the infernal noise of a brook running out there on the sea, a thousand miles from any brook of earth; and away on the port bow, a vague shapeless shining" meets their gazes (CF 3: 281), while their nostrils are assailed by a charnel stench. Unable to see clearly because of the darkness and mist, the captain assembles an armed group to accompany him on a reconnaissance mission in a small boat.

As they approach the source of light and sound, they encounter huge eels and hear echoes of their own voices before discovering an oddly stout-looking ship. No one answers their hails, and once aboard the captain realizes why: "she's absolutely a stone ship—solid stone, afloat here out of Eternity, in the middle of the wide Atlantic … Why! She must weigh a thousand tons more than she's buoyancy to carry. It's just impossible ... " (CF 3: 291). In one of the cabins they find several massive human figures that are also made of stone, one of which appears to grow a mass of red hair as they watch; the mass of hair then chases them onto the deck and carries the captain overboard as the ship suddenly begins to rock while it sinks, forcing the sailors to leap into their longboat (CF 3: 296–8). The mass of hair is later identified as a carnivorous sea caterpillar that was carried up along with the sea bottom as it rose, "owing to some action of the Internal Pressures. The rocks had risen so gently that they had never made a sound; and the stone ship had risen with them out of the deep sea. She had evidently lain on one of the submerged reefs, and so had seemed to [the sailors] to be just afloat in the sea" (CF 3: 301). The narrator Duprey ultimately infers that the stone ship

> had originally been a normal enough wooden vessel of a time far removed from our own. At the sea-bottom, she had evidently undergone some natural mineralising process, and this explained her stony appearance. The stone men had been evidently humans who had been drowned in her cabin, and their swollen tissues had been subjected to the same natural process, which, however, had also deposited heavy encrustations upon them, so that their size, when compared with the normal, was prodigious.
>
> (CF 3: 303)

Thus a story which began as a weird tale ends as a neatly solved marine mystery: the brook sounds were created by seawater running out of the hulk, the shining was produced by bioluminescent organisms brought to the surface, and the stench came from rotting organic material being exposed to the air. Hodgson even inserts a "crime" into the plot, perhaps in order to ironically yet definitively resituate the tale in the detective genre: as point man of the away party, Duprey enters the cabins first, and in one of them he finds a cache of gemstones in a half-open drawer, which he pockets before his companions notice (CF 3: 295, 299, 304). He concludes the tale expressing curiosity about "how the stones and things came where I found them; but [the ship] carried guns, as I've told, I think; and there's rum doings happen at sea; yes, by George!" (CF 3: 304). Thus, according to the principles of maritime salvage, he's as entitled to the booty as anyone else.

Although "The Stone Ship" is not one of Hodgson's best-known stories, it is significant not only as a maritime example of the rationalized weird most often associated with his Carnacki the Ghost Finder stories, but also as the precise thematic counterpart of a more famous tale I discussed in the introduction, "The Derelict" (1912). "The Stone Ship" centers on the striking but fully explicable transformation of organic material—a ship's planks and masts as well as its human crew—into non-organic stone, in other words accelerated fossilization, while "The Derelict" focuses on the decidedly weird transformation of dead and inorganic matter—again, the components of a sailing ship—into a living entity. The story itself has a quasi-didactic form: it is narrated by an old ship's doctor as evidence to support his assertion that "Life is no more a mystery or a miracle than Fire or Electricity," and indeed, "So potent is the share of the *Material* in the production of that thing which we name Life, and so eager the Life-Force to express itself, that I am convinced it would, if given the right Conditions, make itself manifest even through so hopeless-seeming a medium as a simple block of sawn wood" (CF 3: 236, 235). He then tells of his own encounter, years earlier, with a bizarre derelict ship during a voyage through the Indian Ocean. He accompanies the captain and sailors of his vessel in exploring the derelict, which shows many peculiarities: it is surrounded by a viscous "scum" hundreds of yards wide that has somehow captured a ship's pigsty, its bow and stern are covered with "great clumpings of strange-looking sea-fungi," and steam or haze rises off it (CF 3: 239). Its decks, broken masts, and furnishings are covered in dirty white mold, and once the party boards, they realize that the entire ship emits a "vague, animal smell" (CF 3: 242–3). It is infested with enormous sea-lice that normally parasitize fish, and when the mold's surface is breached, it pumps out purple fluid in time with a regular thudding from below decks (CF 3: 245, 247).

By this point the reader has already drawn the conclusion that the frenetic pace doesn't allow Hodgson's characters to state outright until later: the dead matter of the ship has somehow been transformed into a living organism, complete with a beating heart, and it intends to feed upon them. One sailor gets separated from the others, and

> All about him, the mould was in active movement. His feet had sunk out of sight. The stuff appeared to be *lapping* at his legs; and abruptly his bare flesh showed. The hideous stuff had rent his trouser-legs away, as if they were paper. He gave out a simply sickening scream, and, with a vast effort, wrenched one leg free. It was partly destroyed. The next instant he pitched face downward, and the stuff heaped itself upon him, as if it were actually alive, with a dreadful savage life.
>
> (CF 3: 249)

The doctor and the crew, seeking to escape as the rest of the derelict rouses itself to motion and pursues them, leap into a lifeboat that lies against the hull, where they find the remnants of the entity's previous meal: "the bones of at least three people, all mixed together, in an extraordinary fashion, and quite clean and dry" (CF 3 253). The mold reaches for them with a fleshy protrusion that they must fight off so that they can row away, and even then, the surrounding scum holds them back for several tense minutes before releasing them to return to their own ship (CF 3: 254–6). A storm providentially intervenes at this point, and when it has passed the derelict has disappeared, to the doctor's half-regret:

> If we could know exactly what that old vessel had originally been loaded with, and the juxtaposition of the various articles of her cargo, plus the heat and time she had endured, plus one or two other only guessable quantities, we should have solved the chemistry of the Life-Force, gentlemen. Not necessarily the *origin*, mind you; but, at least we should have taken a big step on the way.
>
> (CF 3: 257)

Unlike "The Stone Ship," which ultimately provides prosaic—though highly unusual—scientific explanations for all its weird elements, the narrative of "The Derelict" accumulates and intensifies the weird features it presents, leaving the reader with an ontogenetic mystery that can only be characterized, though not explained, in the abstract, quasi-mystical terms of "Life-Force." Emily Alder suggests naming the entity with the nineteenth-century term "cryptogam," which referred to "disparate types like fungi, lichen, and slime moulds that presented similarly and were taken as sort-of plants without seeds or flowers" (Alder 2020: 175). She observes that cryptogams'

> malleability means they can easily be imagined to look like a human, or a tree, or a ship, emphasising monsters' transgressive plasticity and their resistance to classification ... Upsetting established categories of animals and plants, they cause fractures in which weird definitions of life could flourish, 'doubtful beings' could become certain, and notions of natural and unnatural, alive and not alive, or animate and inanimate, may be redefined.
>
> (Alder 2020: 177)

Cryptogams, then, perform a decognitive destructuring on the previously stable categories of nineteenth-century biology.

The weird force in Hodgson's most famous and often-reprinted short story, "The Voice in the Night" (1907), is also cryptogamic. Although the main action of this tale takes place on an island and thus it is not strictly a sea story, the narrative frame that gives the reader access to the plot is a maritime one, as well as a perversely didactic one akin to that of "The Derelict": two sailors standing a late-night watch aboard a becalmed ship in the central Pacific are hailed by a "curiously throaty and inhuman" voice from a rowboat out in the dark (CF 3: 155). The speaker, whom we later find out is named John, refuses to show himself but asks for provisions for himself and his female companion, whom he has left on an unnamed island nearby. When food is given to him, he rows away, but returns a few hours later to obey "God's wish that we should tell to you all that we have suffered" since their ship sank months earlier (CF 3: 159). Thus the island setting is doubly distanced, as it were, by the story told within the story, and its ambiguous spatiality gives John's perfervid Christian faith an ironic pedagogical value at odds with his aim. Characters who effusively praise God are rare in Hodgson's fiction, and the few we meet are generally revealed to be either deluded or doomed, sometimes both. John is no exception.

The couple's story is simple enough: abandoned by the crew when their vessel is dismasted in a storm, they construct a raft that the current carries safely to an uncharted island where a large sailing ship sits deserted in a lagoon, its sides, deck, and cabins blotched with a "grey, lichenous fungus" (CF 3: 160–1). Although they find no people aboard or ashore, they do find a little food and potable water, so they clean the fungus out of a cabin and settle there. Unfortunately, the fungus is extraordinarily tenacious, and even carbolic acid can't prevent it from returning to every surface from which it was removed, so they look for a place to sleep on the island, only to discover that "here the vile fungus ... was growing riot. In places it rose into horrible, fantastic mounds, which seemed almost to quiver, as with a quiet life, when the wind blew across them. Here and there, it took on the forms of vast fingers, and in others, it just spread out flat and smooth and treacherous" (CF 3: 162). Even though they eventually find one spot that is fungus-free where they can camp, within a few weeks both find it growing on their own bodies too. As their food supplies dwindle, John returns to their camp one day to find his fiancée eating a piece of the fungus; she tells him that "the desire for it had come suddenly," overcoming her revulsion (CF 3: 164). Disturbed by this, he takes a long walk among the huge fungal growths inland, where he is stunned to see one "swaying uneasily, as though it possessed life of its own. Abruptly, as I stared, the thought came to me that the thing had a grotesque resemblance to the figure of a distorted human creature … " When the swaying fungal shape touches him near his mouth, he tastes sweetness and is "immediately filled with an inhuman desire. I turned and seized a mass of the fungus. Then more, and—more. I was insatiable." When he can finally drag himself away, he returns to his fiancée and confesses his transgression, but withholds from her knowledge of the fungal figure because "I doubted not but that I had seen the end of one of those men who had come to the island in the ship in the lagoon; and in that monstrous ending, I had seen our own" (CF 3: 165). Soon they too will be fully transformed into fungal figures. John concludes his tale by saying, "we who had been human, became—Well, it matters less each day," and then, with a final prayer that "God, out of His great heart, bless you for your goodness," rows off before the rising sun permits the sailors to see him clearly (CF 3: 166).

Alder helpfully interprets the transformations in this story as paralleling those of "The Derelict" and, as we will see, *The Boats of the "Glen Carrig"*: "Their actions are mirrored; both fungus and human grasp and consume the body of the other. Where the tree-monsters of *Boats* [and the fungal ship in 'The Derelict'] consume humans, here the humans are equally implicated in consuming the monster. In this union, they become something new—neither human nor simply fungus" (Alder 2020: 181), just as the fungal ship constitutes an unprecedentedly new lifeform. However, her later assertion that the castaways consider themselves "'outcast souls,' beyond the reach of God or the natural order of the world associated with divine ordinance" (Alder 2020: 183), like Jonathan Newell's parenthetical observation that, "unlike Adam, [John] refuses to yield to the forbidden fruit first consumed by his wife" (Newell 2020: 143), reflects an under-appreciation of the significance of the tale's Christian language. John invokes God a dozen times in the course of the brief tale, not counting mere expostulations of the form "My God!," which is highly unusual for the nonbeliever Hodgson. The majority of those invocations are expressions of gratitude: to the listening sailors as instruments of God's mercy and charity; for his and his fiancée's safe arrival and discovery of provisions on the island; and for the strength they belatedly find to resist their desire to eat more fungus. The remaining invocations are, like the first one quoted above, more ambiguous: the events of the tale "are under a special ruling, and … it is God's wish that we should tell to you all that we have suffered" as a kind of moral lesson, while John justifies their decision not to seek escape from the island because "God would do with us what was His will" (CF 3: 163). The accumulation of these invocations encourages readers not only to interpret the eating of the fungus as an allusion to Adam and Eve's transgression, the eating of the fruit from the Tree of the Knowledge of Good and Evil (Genesis 2: 16–17 and 3: 1–13), as Newell does, but also to wonder what larger symbolic purpose that allusion might serve. The biblical parable centers on the punishment for transgressing God's explicit command, and results in Adam and Eve being expelled from the paradise of Eden when they confess their sin (Genesis 3: 16–24). Hodgson's story, however, includes no divine commands and offers neither evidence nor confession of guilt: the couple are infected with the fungus despite their strenuous efforts to remain untainted—they eat it for the first time months after they discover the first growths on their bodies, which spread in the interim—and their punishment is not to be expelled from paradise but to be confined for the rest of their lives to its apparent contrary, along with those who preceded them to the island. In virtually every detail, "The Voice in the Night" inverts the elements it shares with its purported biblical model to produce a profoundly anti-Edenic narrative.

Hodgson may well have intended the tale to inspire sympathy for the suffering couple in the sailors and the reader, but it seems equally apparent that he expected at least the reader to question and ultimately reject John's interpretation of their fate as "God's wish" and "His will." In light of Hodgson's reputation for unbelief, which is supported by many of his tales, a more likely (anti-) theological interpretation would encourage us to view the couple's unintentional infection, like their abandonment by the sailors, as an allegory for the Christian doctrine of Original Sin, which likewise assigns guilt and punishment without active transgression; since the writings of St. Paul and St. Augustine, this doctrine has traditionally been traced back to Adam and Eve's transgression and expulsion. This interpretation would further imply that the couple's ingestion of the fungus, which dominates their environment to the exclusion of almost all other nourishment, represents their reluctant but necessary acceptance of Original Sin, and the transformations they undergo thereafter mark their entry into the new, not entirely human community made up of the deserted ship's former passengers and crew. In short, the tale functions as a critical allegory—or rather a parody—of Christian conversion itself, with the ingestion of the fungus serving as the symbolic equivalent, not of the forbidden fruit from Eden, but of the ritualized repetition of the conversion experience itself, the acceptance of Christ's body into one's own in holy communion that demonstrates one's membership in the church community. The notion of Christian fellowship as a contagious fungal infection that dehumanizes its victims and isolates them from the wider human community effectively synthesizes Hodgson's reputed phobia regarding germs and infection (M1: 25) and his rejection of the faith that both his father and grandfather practiced and preached (E:1).

Just as "The Stone Ship" and "The Derelict" can be understood as thematic counterparts that depict the interchangeability of organic and inorganic, living and nonliving matter, so can "The Voice in the Night" and Hodgson's most unusual Sargasso Sea tale, "The Call in the Dawn" (which was originally published posthumously in 1920 as "The Voice in the Dawn"), be interpreted as such counterparts with respect to the possibilities of Edenic narrative. Whereas all Hodgson's other Sargasso Sea tales are plot-heavy, to the point of melodramatic absurdity in stories such as "The Finding of the *Graiken*" (1913), "The Call in the Dawn" is unusual in Hodgson's oeuvre in having virtually no plot whatsoever, which may account for his inability to sell it for publication during his lifetime. Before examining this story in detail, however, we should take a moment to explore how the set of Sargasso Sea stories contributes to Hodgson's fantastic investigation of the sea as a narrative space. Like the temporary islands thrown up by submarine earthquakes and volcanoes, the dense clusters of sargassum weed that inspired mariners to give the name "Sargasso Sea" to the mid-

Atlantic region of comparative calm and stasis lying between the Gulf Stream, North Atlantic, Canary, and North Equatorial currents provide substitute ground on which human activity can take place, thus enabling further possibilities for narrative. In *The Boats of the "Glen Carrig"* (1907), the weed is specifically described as forming both a "mainland" and "islets and banks" (BGC: 74–5) of sufficient density to capture sailing ships and hold them fast for centuries. People can survive on such trapped vessels only by enclosing themselves in wood and canvas superstructures that reach half-way up their masts, as protection from the depredations of giant "devil-fish" (octopi or squid) and crabs that abound in the weed (BGC: 74). The two "Tideless Sea" tales (CF 1: 135–74), told through messages found in bottles that have survived years at sea, document how ships come to be trapped in the Sargasso Sea and what daily life there is like, while *Boats* narrates the heroic rescue of people trapped on the weed islets for years.

As noted, "The Call in the Dawn" includes none of these things. Although it has characters—an unnamed narrator described as "a passenger ... bound down to the Barbadoes" and the ship's captain, named Johnson (CF 1: 221)—they accomplish little with their efforts aside from bearing witness to the Sargasso Sea's insoluble mystery, which appears to be the tale's primary focus. Indeed, the story begins with a peremptory address to skeptics who doubt the veracity of tales such as the one that follows:

> To those who have cast doubt upon the reality of the great Sargasso Sea, asserting that the romantic features of this remarkable sea of weed have been greatly exaggerated, I would point out that this mass of weed lurking in the central parts of the Atlantic Ocean is a fluctuating quantity, not confined strictly to an area, but moving bodily for many hundreds of miles according to storms and prevailing winds, though always within certain limits.
>
> Thus it may be that those who have gone in search of it, and not having found it where they expected, have therefore foolishly considered it to be little more than a myth built around those odd patches and small conglomerations of the weed which they may have chanced across. And all the time somewhere to the North or South, East or West, the great shifting bulk of the weed has lain quiet and lonesome and impassable—a cemetery of lost ships and wrack and forgotten things. And so my story will prove to all who read.
>
> (CF 1: 221)

This remarkable passage, which expresses Hodgson's own proprietary attitude toward the Sargasso as explained in one of his few surviving letters,[1] defines it as essentially unfixed, caught up in a process of continual displacement that foils cartographers, endangers sailors, and misleads skeptics as to both its whereabouts and its very existence. At the same time, the Sargasso acts as a repository of "wrack and forgotten things" that will also characterize the Celestial Globes in *The House on the Borderland* and the "abyss of the years" in *The Night Land*. For Hodgson, then, the Sargasso Sea

---

[1] As he writes to Coulson Kernahan on November 17, 1905, "The Sargasso, *of my stories*, is mine own happy hunting ground. I have invented it, and have a right to hunt in it" (U: 39).

is not quite a nowhere, which would literally make it a utopia or paradise, but rather always an elsewhere, a place out of place that is defined by both its capaciousness as a storehouse of memory and its concrete unlocatability.

"The Call in the Dawn" investigates the Sargasso's displacedness as well as its capaciousness in metaphysical as well as physical terms. In order to avoid a cyclonic storm, Captain Johnson heaves his vessel to, and once it has passed, he and the narrator discover that it has driven a "great, low-seeming island" of weed into their path (CF 1: 223). Contrary to Hodgson's practice in the other Sargasso stories, however, the apparition of this island is not described in foreboding terms, but rather in ecstatic ones: "Presently there was a great loom of greenness, most wondrous, in the upper sky, and from this green and aerial splendor of utter quietness there dropped curtains of lemon that enticed the sight to peer through their mystery into the lost distance, so that my thoughts were all very far from this world" (CF 1: 223). Out of this yellow light, further described as a "halo," looms the island of weed, which "doubly fill[s the narrator] with the mystery and utter hush of the dawn-time, and of the lights and of the lesson of the morning which is told silently at each dawn over the world" (CF 1: 223). This pregnant hush is abruptly broken by a small voice calling six times "out of an infinite distance: 'Son of Man!'" (CF 1: 224). Understandably startled by this, narrator and captain confer in search of an explanation, which they conclude can only be "some lone derelict held in the weed of the great island that lay Eastward of us" (CF 1: 225). With the Mate and a few sailors, they set out in a small boat to search for the speaker, taking care to arm themselves before departing. In the course of a slow circumnavigation of the "island," they note its great size and similarity to land: the weed rises "about twenty or twenty-five feet good above the ocean," and the highest inland part of it "look[s] as if it had been a low thick wood with the greater trees in the centre, and all lost in jungle of strange creeping plants." Small inlets or bays appear as "dark cavern-place[s] of dark green and gloom that went inward of the weed" (CF 1: 227). They also observe the rich biodiversity of the ecosystem: "of the life of sea animals there was no end; for all the weed, upon the outer edges seemed a-crawl with various matters; though at first we had not been able to perceive these because of the similarity in colour with the yellowness of the weed" (CF 1: 225). At one point they encounter a "devil-fish or octopus lying among the weed, very quiet, and shaded with the same gloom and colour as the weed which was its home," but instead of engaging it in battle as the protagonists of Hodgson's other Sargasso tales do, they row away just as quietly, leaving it in peace (CF 1: 227–8).

In a "deep bay" on the island's far side they find "the hull of a vessel all mastless in among the weed, near the edge, yet not very plain to be seen because it was so hidden and smothered by the weed;" this they presume to be "the place whence came that unnatural calling in the dawn" (CF 1: 228). Like the rest of the island, the hulk is overrun with marine life, largely because "the bottom of the ship was rotted nigh out of her so that the weed came upward in plenty that way with the water showing down below," leading the captain to conclude that the ship was more than 400 years old and therefore unlikely to shelter any survivors (CF 1: 229–30). Nevertheless, the call "Son of Man!" recurs the next day, in "a voice thin and lonesome, as might be thought to be the call of a spirit crying in the morning," accompanying another gorgeous dawn that manifests "a translucence of shimmering green that surely stretched to the very borders of the Eternal, in palest lights that carried the consciousness through aethereal deeps of space, until the soul went lost through the glimmering dawn, greeting unknown spirits" (CF 1: 230–1). This time the away team that is sent out brings along the ship's bell and speaking trumpet so that they can signal to the speaker, wherever he is, but again they fail to find anyone stranded in the weed. The call is repeated a third time at dawn on the third and final day of their sojourn, but it is almost drowned out by the rising wind that soon fills their sails and carries them back to their original journey from this mysterious elsewhere that no human thought or action can decipher. Just as the dawn's light grants the sailors in "The Voice in the Night" only a fleeting glimpse of John's transformed figure that deepens rather than clarifies its mystery, so the dawn's light in "The Call in the Dawn" teases the narrator—and the reader—with the imminence of a vision that never appears.

The image of dawn as a moment of mystical beauty that implies a value—and a meaning—beyond human conception is one that recurs at a number of significant points in Hodgson's work. The final stanzas of his most ambitious poem *The Voice of the Ocean*, the title of which may indicate its thematic link to the tales we are discussing, awakens the reader out of a nightlong colloquy among the Sea and the spirits of the dead with a depiction of "the dear light of dawn, that emblem of/The dawn that crown's death's night" (VO: 45) in oceanic terms: "And afar the world/Reached up her sombre hills among the glow,/Into the pure, ethereal waters of/That sea of trembling hues which spumed and beat/Softly upon the shore of night" (VO: 46). Here the shore is the metaphorical abode of darkness while the sea is the source of light. Even more resonant with "The Call in the Dawn" is a passage that appears in *The Night Land*, during the narrator X's convalescence on the island refuge to which Naani carries him following his battle with the Humped Men in the Country of Seas. In the couple's discussion of their previous lives, both together and apart, X learns that Naani recalls little of our era, which he calls "the Days of Light" and remembers primarily "by the glory of lost sunsets that had cast a holiness upon my heart, and of the hush of Dawns that had made ready my spirit in the Gone Ages to look quietly unto my death." Then he addresses the reader directly:

> And surely you to go with me in all this thing, and to have felt within your own spirit that uplifted wonder that doth shake the soul with the lost Beginning and with the unknown End, when that you have lookt through the sorrow of the Sunset, and stood silent before the Quiet Voice that doth make promise in the Dawn.
> (NL: 501)

The references to sunsets almost certainly allude to the novel's opening sentence, which concerns X's first meeting with the Lady Mirdath in their former lives: "It was the joy of the Sunset that brought us to speech" (NL: 11). The significance of this passage only increases when we recall that the Night Land knows neither sunsets nor dawns because it knows no alternation of day and night, even though X admits that in the Redoubt, "the Sleep-Time ... was, even in that strange age, by tradition called the Night," which he calls instead by his invented phrase in order "to make this history free from the confusion of 'night' and 'day,' when, in truth, it was always night without upon the world" (NL: 84).

If these passages are connected to one another substantively, and not just in their superficial figuration, then we can posit that the promise the Quiet Voice makes in the dawn is not only an expression of the hope that stands opposed to death at the end of *The Voice of the Ocean* but also somehow contained in the repeated call "Son of Man!" that punctuates and provides a title for "The Call in the Dawn." In the Christian tradition, the phrase "Son on Man" is an epithet long associated with Jesus himself but otherwise a source of still-unsettled controversy, which Hodgson may have learned from his father or grandfather.[2] Briefly, the controversy concerns the epithet's theological status: although it appears repeatedly in the Bible from the Book of Daniel onward, primarily in the Gospels, one lineage of scholars and theologians views it as an almost meaningless expression, equivalent to "someone" or "a man," that should be superseded by the more dignified, meaningful, and above all dualist appellation "Son of God" when referring to Jesus, while a contrary lineage sees it as not just meaningful but affirmatively polemical, as an antagonistic response to the sharply dualistic differentiation between God and humanity that accompanied the hierarchical institutionalization of Roman Catholicism (and, by extension, other bureaucratic ossifications of the early, communalist Christian church). The first lineage is generally called "messianic" and the second "apocalyptic." Probably the best-known member of the latter lineage is the philosopher Ernst Bloch, under whose aegis I have already placed Hodgson's paradoxical synthesis of hope and cosmic fear in the Preface. According to Bloch, "Son of Man" is "the most intimate title of the Messiah ... which shows that the Messiah is no mere ambassador from on high," but instead the return of the Primordial Man of the Kabbalah, Heavenly Adam or Adam Kadmon, who was not made from clay on the sixth day by God the Father but pre-exists the world alongside God, and who therefore represents a figure who is "almost entirely emancipated from God" and "a member of the *underground opposition movement* to Yahweh" (Bloch 1972: 146, 148, 149).[3] Heavenly Adam, the Son of Man, is himself a figure of human power and potential in no way subordinate or subservient to God, and of human hope for its own growth and flowering; in other words, he is a humanist figure in keeping with Hodgson's future-oriented atheism.

Near the conclusion of his discussion of Adam Kadmon and the Son of Man, Bloch quotes the Gnostic theologian Valentinus, as recorded by Clement of Alexandria, on the subject of apocalyptic human emancipation: "From the very beginning you are immortal; you are the children of everlasting life. You share out death among yourselves in order to exhaust it and abolish it—in order that through you and in you death may die. *You do away with the cosmos, but you yourselves remain* to rule over the

---

[2] Apropos this controversy, Delbert Burkett writes, "nineteen centuries of 'Son of Man' study have led to no consensus concerning the meaning or origin of the expression" (Burkett 1999: 5).
[3] See also Burkett 1999: chapters 3 and 7.

whole of perishable creation" (Bloch 1972: 155, italics in original).[4] The paradoxical ideas expressed here resonate strongly with Hodgson's views on life, death, and the cosmos as manifested in his writings—in the logic of reincarnation that separates and rejoins the lovers despite the apocalyptic collapse of the cosmos in both *The House on the Borderland* and *The Night Land*, and in the permutation of lives and exhaustion of death in *The Voice of the Ocean*, which we will examine at length in Chapter Eight. Although it is highly unlikely that Hodgson would have studied or otherwise known about Kabbalah or Gnosticism, the issues they address may well have found their way into his father's controversial sermons, which took place against the backdrop of late Victorian debates over the conflict between revealed religion and human science. Alternately, his documented interest in Theosophy may have led him to investigate other versions of mysticism circulating in the intellectual milieu to which he sought to contribute. In any case, the voice calling out of the Sargasso to the Son of Man is undoubtedly appealing to a humanity yet to come, a potential humanity that will attend more fully to and engage more fully with the nonhuman life that surrounds it. For such a self-transcended, and hence un(re)cognizable, human species, the errant and teeming Sargasso Sea may well constitute an Eden to be rediscovered, a treasure-house of memory to be restored, and not the frightening borderland of the monstrous that many see in it today.

This rather circuitous path brings us finally to the most substantial of Hodgson's Sargasso Sea tales, the novel *The Boats of the "Glen Carrig"* (1907), which was his first novel to be published but apparently the last one he actually wrote. It shares many features both large and small with his other novels, ranging from the general borderland settings to specific place names such as the "Country of Silence" (also used in *The Night Land*, but for a very different kind of space). Indeed, as I noted in Chapter One, *Boats* is perhaps most unique in Hodgson's oeuvre not for what it contains but for what it lacks: open metaphysical speculation. Even though this novel's characters encounter entities and situations that equal in strangeness almost anything in his other novels, they make no attempt to investigate, understand, or explain them beyond the simplest requirements of escape and survival. In comparison with *The Night Land*'s narrator X, the Recluse of *The House on the Borderland*, or Jessop in *The Ghost Pirates*, the aristocratic yet humble narrator of *Boats*, John Winterstraw, comes off as remarkably incurious about the "many-flapped thing shaped as it might be, out of raw beef" that searches for the men aboard the marooned ship (BGC: 40), the anthropophagous trees (BGC: 48–51), or even the armies of weed men that almost wipe out his entire party (BGC: 77, 175–85). It is almost as if the characters take decognition and anethical non-redemption as given, in other words as defining facts underpinning their struggles and hence fruitless to investigate or dispute. Such single-minded focus on the blow-by-blow narration of action is almost certainly what Hodgson meant when he wrote to Coulson Kernahan that he had "tried hard to be commonplace in [this novel]; but, I'm

---

[4] Valentinus' aphorism will also remind many readers of the couplet Lovecraft attributed to the "mad poet Abdul Alhazred" in both "The Nameless City" (1921) and "The Call of Cthulhu" (1928): "That is not dead which can eternal lie,/And with strange aeons even death may die" (Lovecraft 2015a vol.1: 232; Lovecraft 2015a vol.2: 40).

afraid, with but poor success. I cannot ride [sic] above that failing of mine which urges me to write original stuff" such as his previous novels (U: 34). The fact that this last-written novel was the first to be accepted for publication, ahead of his more formally and conceptually adventurous novels, no doubt also helped persuade Hodgson to focus on short, simpler narratives for the remainder of his career. Sam Gafford is not the only one of Hodgson's readers to wonder "what wonderfully imaginative excesses like *The Night Land* may have been lost because of an unappreciative public" (2013b: 26).

Perhaps the unresolved mystery that looms largest in *Boats* is what relationship, if any, links its two topographies: the Land of Lonesomeness (chapters I to IV) and the Sargasso Sea (chapters VI to XVII). The former appears as a broad plain made up of "vile mud" that, like the living derelict, "seemed veritably to have a fat, sluggish life of its own, so rich and viscid was it" (BGC: 12, 17). Strange low-hanging trees constitute the only living things visible, although unidentifiable sounds of sobbing and snarling mark the setting of the sun and the onset of night. The mud's omnipresence prevents the characters from making landfall until they row up a large creek and discover a marooned ship on which they stay briefly while replenishing their provisions. While aboard they discover the disordered pages of a handwritten log or diary kept by the ship's previous occupants, which offer information regarding an accessible water source as well as oblique and fragmentary warnings regarding nearby dangers. Interestingly, those dangers highlight the spatial challenges that the Land of Lonesomeness poses to the characters. No one ever actually sees the "Thing That Made Search" outside their cabin clearly, aside from one brief glimpse of a "reddish mass" through the stern window. However, in what may be an homage to the "Mad Trist" passage of Poe's "The Fall of the House of Usher" (1839), in which the unearthly scenes the narrator reads aloud from a novel in order to distract Roderick Usher from his fears are immediately acted out by his sister Madeline as she returns from her sepulcher (Poe 1984a: 332–5), the Thing attempts to break through the cabin door just as they are reciting aloud the diary entry that reads, "And now, beyond my door, I could hear that fearsome sound of the Thing searching—" (BGC: 38). The Thing never succeeds in doing the crew any harm, despite trying their door every night of their stay aboard the marooned ship, because it can never enter the space they have fortified. They come closer to harm once they go ashore to find the spring mentioned in the diary. Nearby they discover several bizarre trees, one of which has what appears to be a bird-shaped growth on its trunk that Winterstraw tries to take as a curio, but when he touches the tree, it feels pulpy like a mushroom (another of Alder's cryptogams) and he recoils. Another tree startles them by beginning to wail, and Winterstraw notices that there seems to be "a brown, human face peering at us" from among its branches. Closer inspection shows a second human face, a woman's, on the same tree. At that point, "the bo'sun cried out suddenly that he knew; though of what it was that he *knew* I had at that time no knowledge," and began slashing the tree with his cutlass, causing it to bleed (BGC: 50). Neither character ever shares that knowledge except obliquely, by quoting the diary pages again: "I hear my lover's voice wailing in the night, and I go to find him; for my loneliness is not to be borne" (BGC: 55). The reader is left to infer for herself that the marooned couple, like the couple in "The Voice in the Night" discussed above, abandoned the relative safety of the ship and was absorbed into or consumed by the fungal vegetation, becoming part of the landscape.

Having restocked their stores, the crew departs the Land of Lonesomeness for the open sea, where a titanic storm tosses them about for several days before depositing them in the midst of a "weed-choked sea" that can only be the Sargasso. In other words, they move from a swampy setting that may itself be alive to an even less stable one that most definitely is alive. They find themselves surrounded by great banks of weed that form "islets" and one great conglomeration that they label the "mainland" of the weed, although like the mud in the Land of Lonesomeness, these pseudo-lands lack "firm ground" (BGC: 13) over which people could efficiently travel or on which they could safely reside. In the distance they spy several trapped ships that appear unoccupied, and like the narrator of "The Call in the Dawn," they quickly discover that the weed supports a dense ecosystem dominated by giant octopi and enormous crabs. These threats pale into insignificance once they reach a small rocky island in the weed that proves to be the home of the weed men, bizarre, marginally anthropomorphic creatures with "great eyes, so big as crown pieces, the bill like to an inverted parrots, and the sluglike … white and slimy body" with "two short and stumpy arms" and legs that "divided into hateful and wriggling masses of small tentacles" (BGC: 176–7). These creatures represent the fullest flowering of what China Miéville calls the "tentacular novum" in Hodgson's fiction: "The spread of the tentacle—a limb-type with no Gothic or traditional precedents (in 'Western' aesthetics)—from a situation of near total absence in Euro-American teratoculture up to the nineteenth century, to one of being the default monstrous appendage of today, signals the epochal shift to a Weird culture" (Miéville 2008: 105). Whereas prior examples of the tentacle in Anglo-European fiction—the formless squid in Herman Melville's *Moby-Dick* (1851), the octopus in Victor Hugo's *Toilers of the Sea* (1866), the giant squid in Verne's *20,000 Leagues under the Seas*, and the swarm of squid in H.G. Wells's "The Sea Raiders" (1897)—constitute slight extrapolations from known animals, Hodgson's weed men introduce a far greater leap in teratology, one that prefigures the abandonment of folkloric threats like the ghost, vampire, or werewolf in favor of tentacled monstrosities in the work of Lovecraft and his circle and, through the latter's influence, the widespread use of cephalopod imagery as shorthand for the radically nonhuman today (see Wallen 2021: 117–21, 153–88).

As if to confirm the shift that this novel marks in the folkloric or mythological basis of fantastic fiction, Hodgson quite deliberately avoids Judeo-Christian references and terminology. The word "God" appears only six times in Winterstraw's narration, four times in stock phrases such as "the mercy of God," and twice in quotations of other characters' statements. When young Job, the ordinary seaman whose name evokes the most stubbornly faithful of the Christian God's believers and who is left to watch the longboat while the others explore the island, ultimately dies of the injuries he receives first from a devilfish (BGC: 86–91) and later from the weed men (BGC: 117–9), he is buried on the beach, but as Winterstraw pointedly observes, he and his comrades "made no prayer over him; but stood about the grave for a little space, in silence. Then, the bo'sun signed to us to fill in the sand; and, therewith, we covered up the poor lad, and left him to his sleep" (BGC: 126–7). Not only does Job die unshriven and go to his grave without funeral rites, but he is also deprived of his ultimate rest, and possibly even his bodily resurrection: following their nightlong battle with the weed men, the crew belatedly discovers that

> there had been something at Job's grave, ... and it was easy to see that it had been disturbed, and so we ran hastily to it, knowing not what to fear; thus we found it to be empty; for the monsters had digged down to the poor lad's body, and of it we could discover no sign. Upon this, we came to a greater horror of the weed men than ever; for we knew them now to be foul ghouls who could not let even the dead body rest in the grave.
>
> (BGC: 191)

Every experience the men have, from the "Thing That Made Search" to the weed men's assault, reinforces the notion that the Land of Lonesomeness and the Sargasso Sea are spaces not governed by divine law or protected by divine providence, but products of a very different material creation and subject to very different—and anethical—destinies.

As the novel draws to its unexpectedly upbeat end, Winterstraw candidly admits that he and his companions did not "discover more than the merest tithe of the mysteries which that great continent of weed holds in its silence" (BGC: 203). Instead of pondering those mysteries, he focuses his attention first on the ship trapped in the weed, which he and his comrades discover is inhabited, and later on Mistress Mary Madison, niece of the ship's deceased captain, who has grown up without experience of normal English everyday life. Perhaps his most reflective moment in the novel relates his growing sympathy, and love, for her:

> It was a strange and solemn time for her; for she, who had dreamed of the world as her childish eyes had seen it, was now, after many hopeless years, to go forth once more to it—to live in it, and to learn how much had been dreams, and how much real; and with all these thoughts I credited her; for they seemed such as would have come to me at such a time.
>
> (BGC: 236)

Living as she has within the weed's nightmare environment, she can only imagine England itself as a strange and distant dream, in a pointed inversion of Winterstraw's—and the reader's—perspective. Even long after their return to England and Winterstraw's predictable marriage to Mary, whenever he and his friend the bo'sun occasionally "let our talk drift to the desolate places of this earth, pondering upon that which we have seen—the weed-continent, where reigns desolation and the terror of its strange inhabitants," and "the land where God hath made monsters after the fashion of trees"—they quickly "change to other matters" when his children draw near, "for the little ones love not terror" (BGC: 252), and the older ones apparently feel no need to make their experiences manifest either cognitive mastery or moral redemption. They begin and end their adventures with an acceptance of the world's incomprehensibility and anethicality to which Hodgson's many other characters—and readers—only submit at the conclusion of his weird storytelling.

6

Familiar Land of Strangeness

The spaces of *The House on the Borderland*, like those of *The Night Land*, have been extensively investigated—and even mapped—by both scholars and fans, which is unsurprising given both the books' titles and their plots. Emily Alder goes so far as to deploy the title word "borderland" from Hodgson's second novel as an adjective to describe a broad array of experimental and investigative practices and perspectives during the late Victorian and Edwardian periods as "borderland science" (Alder 2020: 2, 16–26).[1] The geography of *House*, as described in the frame tale, provides the rationale for her borrowing: the Scandinavian vacationers Tonnison and Berreggnog quite intentionally seek a place of rest and relaxation far from the crowded cities and picturesque pastoral villages of Europe alike, with the result that they end up taking a fishing holiday in the isolated Irish village of Kraighten. Frame-tale narrator Berreggnog informs us at the start that "no map that I have hitherto consulted has shown either village or stream. They seem to have entirely escaped observation; indeed, they might never exist for all that the average guide tells one" (HB: 2). In this the setting clearly resembles the Sargasso Sea, which is always already displaced from any specific location. However, he goes on to situate the area as forty miles from Ardrahan in County Galway, where Hodgson's father had briefly served as a missionary among the Catholics during his childhood (E:3; M1, 15),[2] and the details he provides regarding the landscape—a "desert of stone" in which "the river we had followed so confidently came to an abrupt end" by "vanishing into the earth" (HB: 9)—allowed Joseph Hinton to identify it as part of the Burren, a broad glacial karst area in County Clare that is now an Irish national park as well as a UNESCO Global Geopark (Hinton 2016: 109–15). Amidst the arid and forbidding landscape, the visitors find an "oasis" of trees in a large depression that, although "disagreeably gloomy," shows "signs of a long departed cultivation" (HB: 10–11). This almost contradictory combination of normally distinct

---

[1] Alder does not coin this term solely on the basis of Hodgson's usage, however; she also links it to the establishment of a "new spiritualist and psychical research journal [titled] *Borderland*," which was published from 1893 to 1897 (Alder 2020: 16–17).

[2] Everts reports a disturbing recollection of Hodgson's sister Mary that may also help account for the choice of setting: "Some unfortunate happenings finally forced the family to leave Ardrahan—for the Catholics resented the presence of [Reverend] Hodgson, and spurred on by the local Catholic leaders, the peasants threatened the family several times. There was fear that the small children might be kidnapped by some of the locals; and one evening the Reverend Hodgson was struck seriously on the head by an anonymously tossed rock—while the orchards of the [Rectory] were stripped at the order of the local Catholic hierarchy" (E:3).

spaces again echoes the Sargasso Sea's liminal status between sea and land. Spray hanging in the air leads them to find the resurfacing point of their subterranean river in a tremendous, near-circular chasm into which it empties in a "monster cataract of frothing water" (HB: 13). Extended out over the chasm is a spur of rock on which the ruins of a building lie scattered, and buried among those ruins they find a handwritten book that contains the story related in the main narrative.

The area the fishermen investigate in the opening chapter presents a topographical anticipation of the climax to one strand of the main narrative, the one focused on the house itself, and it also lays the groundwork for the novel's most important set of literary allusions, to H.G. Wells's *The Time Machine* (1895), which has long been acknowledged as an influence on Hodgson. Like the covered "wells" in the distant future of Wells's novel, which eventually lead the Time Traveler to the lair of the Morlocks and thereby to a correct understanding of humanity's ultimate fate, the chasm in Hodgson's novel sets up a mystery that the reader, assisted by both the fishermen and the Recluse who narrates the central story, must solve, and in so doing glimpse the ultimate fate of the planet and the solar system. The connection between the two books is first made almost in passing: "The abyss was, as Tonnison put it, like nothing so much as a gigantic well or pit going sheer down into the bowels of the earth" (HB: 18). As a well it evokes Wells and his subterranean posthuman cannibals, and as a pit it evokes the more traditional terrors of Hell. Further Wellsian allusions appear throughout the main narrative.

Following a very brief and abstract description of himself and his house by the Recluse, the novel's main narrative begins practically *in medias res* with a three-chapter account of his first involuntary visionary journey across unmeasured but enormous stretches of space and time to an alien world lit by a black star with a shining red rim. This section of the novel contains no dramatic action in which the character takes part; his role is essentially that of a passive and bewildered witness to the spaces through which he is drawn, and those spaces constitute a sort of topographical overture to the rest of his story.[3] On the distant planet he is borne through a rift among towering mountains into an open space that he likens to an "enormous amphitheatre," in the center of which stands a gigantic simulacrum of his own house, "built apparently of green jade" (HB: 35). This curious structure calls to mind the spacious Palace of Green Porcelain in *The Time Machine*, the decrepit museum where the Time Traveler learns of humanity's ages-long loss of knowledge and control over its environment and destiny, but it also prefigures the massive Green Sun at the center of the cosmos, into which both the sun and the earth will be absorbed during the Recluse's second disembodied journey. Among the mountain peaks surrounding the amphitheatre, the Recluse sees what he first imagines are titanic sculptures of the "old gods of mythology," including Kali, the Hindu goddess of death, and Set, the Egyptian god of the underworld (HB: 38); these play a role not unlike that of the sphinx statue that is the first object the Time Traveler sees when he arrives in the year 802,701, which is to serve as a symbolic

---

[3] Based on a similar conviction that the various sections of the novel don't entirely cohere either formally or thematically, Brian Stableford has argued that "If Hodgson ever did sit down and write a version of the text from Introduction to Conclusion, then he must surely have incorporated into it new drafts of previously-written pieces. More likely, several pre-existent pieces may have been gathered together and then connected up with new material" (Stableford 1987: 29).

clue to the significance of the plot's central mystery. For Wells, the mystery involves the nature of humankind, which is the answer to the riddle the sphinx asks Oedipus, while for Hodgson, the mystery involves the meaning of death considered both personally and cosmologically. The Recluse soon recognizes, however, that these "old gods" give off "an indescribable sort of silent vitality, that suggested, to my broadening consciousness, a state of life-in-death—a something that was by no means life, as we understand it; but rather an inhuman form of existence, that well might be likened to a deathless trance" (HB: 40). They keep the jade house under constant, unblinking surveillance, giving "the impression of an eternal watchfulness—of having warded that dismal place, through unknown eternities" (HB: 37) just as the immense Watchers of the various directions keep the Last Redoubt under constant watch through ages of human time in *The Night Land*. And just as the Monstruwacans of the Redoubt guard it against smaller, more mobile, but equally deadly threats, so does the jade house face an enemy that seeks admission to its interior: the Recluse sees "a gigantic thing ... going almost upright, after the manner of a man ... Yet it was the face that attracted and frightened me the most. It was the face of a swine" (HB: 42). The swine-thing tries the doors and windows before approaching the Recluse, who is spirited away from it, up into the sky, and ultimately back to his study to puzzle over his experience. This overture, more than any other part of *House*, suggests that this novel and *The Night Land* take place in the same speculative universe and along the same timeline.

The Recluse first discovers the well or pit that the fishermen later find when trying to locate the origin of the smaller but still threatening swine-things that begin to besiege his house following his return. Like Wells's Morlocks, the swine-things are cannibalistic, as the Recluse learns when he watches one approach another that has been crushed under a heavy roofing stone: it uses its talons to tear off some flesh, "which it put to its mouth." Just as the Time Traveler doesn't realize that the Morlocks' meat is Eloi until he has returned to the surface, the Recluse initially "did not realise. Then, slowly, I comprehended" (HB: 87–8). Later, while investigating a loud explosion, he finds the nearby ravine has suffered a landslide that opens up a doorway-like hole in the ravine wall, while simultaneously damming the stream that flows at its bottom. Certain that this is "the place through which the Swine-things had made their exit, from some unholy place in the bowels of the world" (HB: 133), he must hurriedly explore the hole before it is submerged beneath the rising water. This tense episode parallels the Time Traveler's descent into the Morlocks' realm and its consequences. Upon entering the hole, he finds a tunnel that leads downward in the direction of his house, and at just the spot he infers must be beneath the house, his candle reveals the tunnel's terminus at a wide, cylindrical chasm. A stone he tosses into the chasm makes no sound of striking sides or bottom after a full minute, indicating tremendous depth (HB: 143–4). Returning to his house after almost being swept into the chasm by the torrent flowing into the tunnel from the rising water outside, he stumbles upon a trap door in the floor of his deepest cellar that opens onto thunderous noise and spray, and draws the only possible conclusion: "The great cellar was connected with the Pit, by means of the trap, which opened right above it; and the moisture was the spray, rising from the water, falling into the depths" (HB: 159). His house is built, or rather suspended, over the well or pit whence the swine-things come, just as the

Eloi's dwellings sit atop the Morlocks' warrens, and the landslide suggests just how precariously it is held up.

The Recluse spends most of his second, much longer and more complex involuntary voyage across time to the final demise of the solar system watching through the decomposing windows of the house, and it shelters his disembodied self until shortly before the earth falls into the dead sun. In this way, he paradoxically travels through interstellar space without leaving his room, and "lives" in a disembodied state through millions of centuries in the course of a single night. Somewhat like Wells's Time Traveler, who moves through time too quickly to be perceived, the Recluse perceives enormous scales of space and time without actually occupying them or experiencing them bodily. Time only slows to normal briefly near the end of his odyssey, so that he can watch the house collapse into the chasm beneath it after the swine-things, apparently the last living things on the planet, reappear to drive him out. "Then the ground seemed to cave in, suddenly, and the house, with its load of foul creatures, disappeared into the depths of the earth, sending a strange, blood-coloured cloud into the heights. I remembered the hell Pit under the house" (HB: 230–1). The passage of time then re-accelerates so that he can watch the earth fall into the dead sun and the sun fall into the Green Star at the center of the cosmos, leaving him a bodiless viewpoint hanging in space, unable to measure time's continuing passage in the absence of perceptible events.

In a short sequence that echoes the Time Traveler's poignant sense of human sympathy's devolutionary decline in his tragic relationship with the Eloi "woman" Weena, the Recluse is granted a brief, unsatisfying reunion with his lost beloved in one of the "Celestial Globes" that orbit the Green Star at the center of the cosmos (HB: 239–44). The brevity of this interval may also be a consequence of the temporal acceleration plaguing him. Thereafter he is drawn once more to the arena amidst the mountains that contains the giant jade replica of his now-vanished house. It shows signs of the very same depredations that his actual house underwent during the swine things' assault, which leads him to conclude that "this house, in which I live, was *en rapport*—to use a recognised term—with that other tremendous structure, away in the midst of that incomparable plain" (HB: 258).[4] This also explains how, when his spirit is drawn into the jade house through its great doors, he finds himself back in the study from which he originally departed, back in his body, and back at his departure point in time. What remains unexplained is how the reader is to square the second visionary sequence, in which the house remains almost completely intact while the earth on which it sits undergoes massive changes, including the freezing and precipitation of the atmosphere and the extinguishing of the sun, with the Scandinavian fishermen's account of finding the house collapsed into the chasm, with only part of its outer wall standing, in 1877, the year they discover the manuscript. How can the house be both intact until the end of the world, and fallen into near-total ruin more than a generation before the novel's publication?

---

[4] Alder (2009: 98) notes that Hodgson's use of "*en rapport*" "indicates a familiarity with *fin de siècle* theories of psychical connection. Alternatively, the two houses might be read as the same house, viewed from different dimensions, or existing in different dimensions but overlapping, just as occultists believed the astral realms overlapped with our own world."

The simplest explanation would undoubtedly be one that the text implicitly encourages at several points, but never explicitly confirms: the Recluse is merely hallucinating all the fantastic events in his narrative, none of which actually takes place. The main evidence for this interpretation is the behavior of his sister Mary with regard to the swine-things; since his visionary journeys are subjective, spiritual experiences, they leave no physical traces to be explained except the decomposition of his dog Pepper, which is apparently never mentioned to her. When the swine-things first appear and wound Pepper, Mary seems only "half satisfied" with the partial account the Recluse gives her (HB: 61), and a week later, when the creatures swarm the house and he hurries her indoors, he first attributes her fainting spell to terror of the monsters, but after she retreats from him, he wonders, "Could she be afraid of me? But no! Why should she? I could only conclude that her nerves were badly shaken, and that she was temporarily unhinged" (HB: 73). After a long night defending the house from the things, he awakens to the sound of his sister stealthily moving past his chamber, so he follows in order to see whether he "should have to take steps to restrain her." When she attempts to unbar the back door and flee into the arms of the things (or so he thinks), he stops her and then carries her, screaming, to her room and locks her inside (HB: 98–100), releasing her only when she promises not to attempt to leave the house or open the outer doors. Exhorting her to cheer up, he tells her, "I've seen none of the creatures since yesterday morning," but he is alarmed when "She looked at me, in a curiously puzzled manner; as though not comprehending. Then, intelligence swept into her eyes, and fear ... " (HB: 115). Thereafter he makes "a rule never to speak to her about the strange things that happen in this great, old house" (HB: 155), which may explain why she never displays any confusion about Pepper's whereabouts. These clues strongly imply that Mary sees nothing unusual in their surroundings and is disturbed instead by the Recluse's own erratic behavior. Iain Sinclair was perhaps the first to suggest that "The swine-things who rise from the pit to destroy him are of his own making: they are the breathing shape of his fear" (182).[5] If we adopt this perspective, then the incompatibility between the house's two fates is merely an unsurprising consequence of the logical inconsistency characterizing many hallucinations, or at most another telling symptom of the Recluse's underlying psychopathology, an uncertain figuration of his own recurring fear of death and loss.

Further inconsistencies involving Mary arise in the novel's final chapters, which narrate the Recluse's realization that the giant spectral swine-thing that sought entrance to the great jade house has somehow followed him back from the central suns and the end of time to his earthly dwelling and his present day. Most of these inconsistencies are relatively trivial, such as the attribution to Mary of a pet cat named Tip, which is never mentioned in the earlier sections (unless it is the unnamed cat that Pepper playfully chases before the exploration of the swine-things' underground tunnel [HB: 131]) but dies a shocking death that foreshadows the Recluse's own

---

[5] Sinclair ultimately concludes that the Recluse and Mary have rented the remote house to escape a scandal surrounding their incestuous relationship, which he further links to Hodgson's own parentage by noting his birth in 1877, the year the fishermen find the manuscript (1990: 186–7). Entertainingly lurid though this claim may be, it extrapolates far beyond the limited textual evidence to be found not only in this novel, but in Hodgson's fiction as a whole.

(HB: 267–9). The swine-thing also wounds the new dog, and the Recluse gets infected with a phosphorescent fungus when the dog licks his hand after licking its wound. Like the fungal infection in "The Voice in the Night," this one both visually evokes its source—glowing in the dark just like the spectral swine-thing—and rapidly takes over his body and mind. Just as that other fungus drove the couple to eat more of it despite its effects on their bodies, so this one drives the Recluse to open his barricaded door to the entity that is stalking him. He stops himself at the last possible instant, but as the infection spreads, his inner defenses weaken, although he abides by his rule never to tell Mary about such matters to the very end. On the last page of his narrative, he reports that the growth "has covered all my right arm and side, and is beginning to creep up my neck. Tomorrow, it will eat into my face. I shall become a terrible mass of living corruption." He contemplates using one of his guns to commit suicide, but before he can act on the thought, he loses consciousness and then awakens to the distant sound of "the opening of the great, oak trap" in the cellar, the one that covers the entrance to the chasm, followed by "strange padding steps, that come up and nearer" (HB: 289–91). His text ends mid-word, before he can confirm what is coming for him, but the reader is left with very few doubts or questions regarding his fate. The most relevant question for our purposes here is, what happens to Mary, the resident of the house who is unaccounted for? Are we to assume that she too has been absorbed or otherwise slain by the spectral monster, since she too is never seen again in the outside world? If on the other hand we proceed with our skeptical approach and infer that the Recluse's last moments represent more hallucinations that shock him to the point of death, why then doesn't Mary emerge from seclusion to seek help from the Irish villagers? The answer that renders both questions moot would be the immediate collapse of the house into the chasm beneath it, which carries away all the evidence that would allow us to choose between the possibilities, while at the same time contradicting the Recluse's vision of the house's unnatural lifespan. Like the Time Traveler's failure to return from his second trip through time, this conclusion leaves the reader, as it leaves Berreggnog and Tonnison, to wonder without hope of ever knowing the truth, but also without much of the comfort that Wells's narrator takes in believing that the future foretold may yet be changed.

While a rational demystification of the novel's horrors as psychological symptoms would conform to Hodgson's practice in several Carnacki the Ghost Finder stories, it does not account for all the details in the novel. Aside from Pepper's decomposition, already mentioned, there are the fishermen's initial reactions to the house's vicinity even before they discover the chasm or the ruins. As they approach, Berreggnog reports that "One could imagine things lurking in the tangled bushed; while in the very air of the place, there seemed something uncanny" (HB: 11). Their feeling of foreboding is confirmed after they find the book but before they have a chance to read it, when "there came a strange wailing noise out of the wood on our left ... It appeared to float through the trees, and there was a rustle of stirring leaves, and then silence." This clearly prefigures the skulking of the swine-things in the ravine, about which they have not yet read. Once they leave the region behind, Tonnison admits, "I would not spend the night in *that* place for all the wealth that the world holds. There is something unholy—diabolical about it ... It seemed to me that the woods were full of vile things" (HB: 19,

21). Their intuitions closely match those of the locals: "It was a place shunned by the people of the village, as it had been shunned by their fathers before them. There were many things said about it, and all were of evil. No one ever went near it, either by day or night. In the village it was a synonym of all that is unholy and dreadful" (HB: 298). However many of the fantastic events can be attributed to the Recluse's hallucinations, a stubborn residue of more intersubjective evidence clings to the space where the house once stood decades after it collapsed into the chasm. Even the rushing waters of the river can't scour it clean; Berreggnog concludes his frame narration by admitting how the pit haunts his dreams with harbingers of death: "And the noise of the water rises upwards, and blends—in my sleep—with other and lower noises; while, over all, hangs the eternal shroud of spray" (HB: 300). Such haunting undecidability situates *The House on the Borderland* as an explicit narrative of foreclosure and decognition.

In many ways, this chapter's discussion of fictional space up to this point has been little more than a prelude to the analysis of space in *The Night Land*, the most massive, convoluted, forbidding, and inventive of all Hodgson's works. If Gafford's analysis of the letters is correct, it was also among the first things, if not the very first thing, that he ever wrote, and in some ways, everything else he wrote derived from it. At several points we have emphasized the novel's unique features that challenge most readers' habits of interpretation and evaluation, especially its highly artificial syntax and baroquely ornate diction that make use of a simultaneously inventive and impoverished vocabulary, and the sentimentalized yet erotically perverse romantic relationship that drives its plot. Conversely, one of the novel's most attractive features for many readers is the evocative opacity of its spatio-temporal setting, which the narrator X nevertheless captures in such extraordinarily precise terms relative to the Great Redoubt itself that many fans have used them to draw remarkably congruent maps of the region. X sums up the paradoxical status of the landscape in an aside as he and Naani emerge from the eternal blackness of the Mighty Slope onto the open plain that is visible from the Great Redoubt: although he is not only relieved but exultant that he has led his beloved safely through the terrors of the unknown lands, he reminds both the reader and himself that "this familiar Land of Strangeness did be the last test and the greatest dreadfulness of our journey" (NL: 537). If the novel itself is considered a test of the greatest dreadfulness for some readers, then passing that test—as X does, at great personal cost, with regard to the landscape—earns them a pleasure and rest that parallel the "Love Days" that await Naani and X once their injuries are healed (NL: 580).

For many readers the quasi-oxymoron "familiar Land of Strangeness" might seem to imply Freud's uncanny, but my analysis follows China Miéville in interpreting Hodgson's vision as one that implies a different sort of "(monstrous) not canny" than Freud's returning but misrecognized repressed, and for which Miéville has proposed the term "abcanny": "The monsters of the abcanny are teratological expressions of that unrepresentable and unknowable, the evasive of meaning. Hence the enormous preponderance of shapeless, oozing gloopiness in the abcanny monstrous, the stress on formlessness, shapes that ostentatiously evade symbolic decoding by being all shapes and no shapes" (Miéville 2012: 381). In the terms used in this study, abcanny monsters are decognitive monsters, and the world they occupy is a decognitive one, which also means a psychically destructuring and anethical one. Its strangeness does not derive from any disavowed elements of the characters' unconscious that erupt into recognition, but from entities and forces that impinge upon human consciousness and bodies from an unthinkable outside, and its familiarity comes from the memories passed down by generations of constant watchfulness rather than recurrence of the threadbare theatrical tropes of psychoanalytic subjectivity.

Before we embark on an analysis of the Night Land's physical and symbolic geography, though, we must situate it as clearly as possible in relation to the spaces we as readers occupy in the present. In other words, we must somehow determine how to get from here to there and from now to then, just as X himself must. X depicts himself in the novel's opening chapter as a physically robust but rather reticent nobleman of an unspecified era preceding his author's by more than a century, a diegetic tactic that confuses readers almost as much as the artificial language used for narration. What purpose, if any, does this preliminary temporal displacement serve, aside from providing a rather flimsy rationale for the linguistic estrangement (and perhaps the sentimentality as well)? Which century Hodgson intends to suggest as X's era is impossible to determine; as Lovecraft and others have noted, X's writing does not correspond to any historical epoch of English. All that can be concluded with certainty is that his description of his natal era includes no instances of technologies that would have been commonplace in the nineteenth or twentieth centuries, such as motorized transportation or either gas or electric lighting. The characters ride horses, dine by candlelight, and hold outdoor events by torchlight and "lanthorn." Even significantly older technologies such as projectile weapons are absent—when X and the Lady Mirdath are attacked by "foot-pads," he defends her against the thieves' knives with a staff until her guardian's "footmen" arrive with cudgels (NL: 13–14). No doctor attends Mirdath as she slips toward death after giving birth to their child (NL: 30–2), so we can't infer anything from the medical practices either. Indeed, it seems as if Hodgson's aim is less to evoke a specific historical moment than to contrast X's original moment with that of his readers, as well as with the future in which he soon finds himself awakening. The artificial language is the most obvious marker of this contrast, but the absence of even the most quotidian technologies is also significant: it suggests that X first addresses us out of a time that is separated from his author's and our own by the accelerating feedback loop of the modern physical sciences, which constantly destabilizes our world but plays little if any role in his.

Extending this line of inference, we might then posit that X's initial unfamiliarity with science and technology constitutes a defining but generally overlooked aspect of his characterization, one that inflects or colors his reactions to the distant future in which most of his story takes place. To put it another way, he is almost as different from us, his readers, as the world of the distant future is. As inhabitants of a society that is both intensely mechanized and technologically literate, we might very well find the technologies that preserve and defend the Last Redoubt, as well as some of the unusual entities that besiege it, much more immediately intelligible if they were presented to us through the intermediary of a narrator who was our contemporary, or even a narrator who was Hodgson's contemporary, than we do when they are presented to us by this baroquely anachronistic narrator for whom everyday science and technology are as unusual as city-sized buildings, defensive force fields, ab-human monstrosities, and cosmic catastrophes.[6] Narration filtered through his perspective performs a secondary displacement upon the distant future's novel features, effectively decognizing them as evidence of a rational paradigm shift such as we would expect from science fiction but without translating them into the purely magical or mythic register associated with fantasy. The intervention of this often-exasperating narrator between the reader and the future world, then, contributes to the novel's essential weirdness, that is to say, its refusal to settle into a single, consistent explanatory mode or paradigm regarding the world it depicts. He compels us to take one step backward in history before we are allowed to take two giant steps forward in time.

X highlights this disjunction himself when he describes his own transition from the past to the future in terms of dreaming. After Mirdath's death, he reports that he regains hope only once he has, "at night in my sleep, waked into the future of this world, and seen strange things and utter marvels, and known once more the gladness of life; for I have learned the promise of the future, and have visited in my dreams those places where in the womb of Time, she and I shall come together" once again. Aware of the ambiguity of his terms, he further clarifies, "it was not as if I *dreamed*; but, as it were, that I *waked* there into the dark, *in the future of this world*," so that "to look back upon this, our Present Age, was to look back into dreams that my soul knew to be reality" (NL: 33–4). This reversibility of dream into reality and vice versa seems to make explicit the implications of a pre-existing harmony between the dreams of Mirdath and X that attracts them to one another at their first meeting. She reacts with shocked recognition when he mentions the recurring features of his dream landscape, admitting that she "thought that she was alone in the world with her knowledge of that strange land of her dreams; and now to find that [X] also had travelled in those dear, strange dream lands" excites her, and him as well. Their dream landscapes are not identical—"there was much that had been in my fancies that was foreign to her, and likewise much that was familiar to her, that was of no meaning to me"—but the overlap is considerable (NL: 16–17), and foreshadows their simultaneous connection and separation across the Night Land.

X's awakening in the far future is not "to ignorance; but to a full knowledge of those things which lit the Night Land; even as a man wakes from sleep each morning, and knows immediately he wakes, the names and knowledge of the Time which has bred him, and in which he lives" (NL: 34). Furthermore, he retains the memories of his prior life as a "sub-conscious" knowledge he can access, a reversal that lays the groundwork for the dialectic of knowing and unknowing that underpins both the romantic logic of reincarnation linking him to Mirdath/Naani across the ages and the dispersal of human knowledge and the mastery it enables over the course of time, which provides

---

[6] In this context it is important to remember that Hodgson himself was fascinated by many types of modern technology: he was a highly proficient amateur photographer (see WS 67–73, 119–31, 139–52) and prepared all his own manuscripts on the typewriter, while his non-fantastic stories often turn on cutting-edge technologies such as the phonograph ("Jem Binney and the Safe at Lockwood Hall," 1916), electrified vault security systems and the tools for defeating them ("The Getting Even of 'Parson' Guyles," 1914), and even swing-wing military aircraft ("The Plans of the Reefing Bi-Plane," posthumously published in 1996).

a dramatic backdrop to their personal story. But neither pole of this dialectic is sound or undamaged. During the enormous interval that lies between X's natal era (and our own) on the one hand and the Redoubt's far future on the other, human knowledge has at some point ceased to accumulate in accessible form, in large part because of the planetary calamities that have intervened (which we will discuss shortly). As a result, our era has been rendered quasi-mythical for the people of the future, and X's assured though sub-conscious knowledge of this era challenges their assumptions about us: "I had a dim knowledge—visionary, as it were, of the past, which confounded, whilst yet it angered, those who were the men of learning of that age" (NL: 37). As a "visionary of the past" he becomes renowned throughout the Redoubt, as his author hoped to be renowned in his own time, "for the stories that I told went downward through a thousand cities; and, presently, in the lowest tier of the Underground Fields, an hundred miles deep in the earth below the Redoubt, I found that the very ploughboys knew something concerning my tellings" (NL: 56). His "stories" are not exactly history but not entirely fiction either, and so constitute another "borderland" form that helps to establish the reciprocal weirdness of present and future.

The reversal of myth and knowledge also justifies X's recurring extra-diegetic queries as to the reader's understanding of his unusual mental state and acceptance of the marvels in his account. At one point his uncertainty regarding the clarity of his exposition becomes so great that he wonders whether the two distinct categories of information available to his consciousness (figured as future/present, history/fiction, and reality/dream) don't merely disagree with one another but actively interfere with one another, in what almost amounts to a direct statement of decognitive awareness, or at least an expression of cognitive distrust: "well it may be that the Reason of this age [the past] doth blind within me somewhat the Knowledge that I have concerning that [the future] ... I do the more distrust that Reason shall make foolish my Knowledge" by leading him to draw abstract conclusions without concrete evidence (NL: 209). Further frustrations of this sort ultimately lead him to insist on the need to

> modify Reason with heart-understanding; for, in verity, how shall that which we call Reason, bring any to the full and the great knowledge. And this doth be a power of holy things, and doth be a child that is born of Love and Reason, and in the one to hold the two, and to know all things is the gift of this power; so that no man may walk truly that hath only the first, neither any man do utter wise that hath only the second.
>
> (NL: 462)

He can appeal to the reader's reason as a shared repository of truth-procedures, but "heart-understanding" requires a leap of belief, confidence, or perhaps hope.

As noted, the fundamental strangeness of the Night Land coexists uneasily with its familiarity, at least to X and other inhabitants of the Great Redoubt. That familiarity derives in large part from the Redoubt's architecture, which is clearly designed to promote external observation: a slender metal pyramid of 1,320 floors, nearly eight miles high, crowned by a watchtower equipped with numerous devices for continuous surveillance (NL: 45). Many lower floors also have windows or other means—X calls them "spyglasses," "View-Tables," or "embrasures"—for viewing the landscape outside the Redoubt. The first and last of these are somewhat outmoded terms that seem intentionally chosen to highlight X's anachronistic perspective, while the second is explicitly likened to a camera obscura (NL: 86–7).[7] The vertices of the pyramid's base are aligned with the north-south and east-west axes, so its sides face northwest, southwest, southeast, and northeast. X reports that he fully "waked, or came, as it might be said, to myself" as an inhabitant of the Redoubt in one of the embrasures, from which he found himself gazing out upon "a landscape that I had looked upon and pored upon through all the years of that life, so that I knew how to name this thing and that thing, and give the very distance of each and every one from the 'Centre-Point' of the Pyramid," which serves to establish the geographical reference framework for the entire novel (NL: 34–6). His profound familiarity with the landscape is not at all unique, "For on none did it ever come with weariness to look out upon all the hideous mysteries; so that old and young watched, from early years to death, the black monstrosity of the Night Land" (NL: 38). For the next dozen pages he proceeds to give a meticulous verbal description of that inescapable "world of darkness, lit here and there with strange sights" (NL: 34).

Among the many mysterious and startling things visible, perhaps the most striking are the five Watchers, "mountains of living watchfulness and hideous and steadfast intelligence" (NL: 47) that stare unblinkingly back at the viewers inside the Redoubt. One Watcher gazes at each face of the building, and takes its name from that face: the Watcher of the North-West, illuminated by the Red Pit beneath its chin; the Watcher of the South-East, illuminated by two great Torches beside it; the Watcher of the South-West, lit by the Eye-Beam shining up from the ground into its right eye; and the Watcher of the North-East, lit from above by a luminous blue ring that casts its face in shadow. The fifth Watcher lies to the South, and it is the only one whose advent is remembered in the Redoubt's written histories: "A million years gone ... came it out from the blackness of the South, and grew steadily nearer through twenty thousand years; but so slow that in no one year could a man perceive that it had moved." Before it reached the Redoubt, however, a "Glowing Dome rose out of the ground before it ... which stayed the way of the Monster." If the Watchers, like the "old gods of mythology" that watch over the giant jade house in *The House on the Borderland*, are viewed as threats, the lights that impede them are interpreted as evidence "that there were other forces than evil at work in the Night Lands, about the Last Redoubt" (NL: 43).

Other visible elements of the external landscape are similarly grouped into categories, although the significance of those categories never becomes clear. Some categories are functional or associative, for example the sites related to the Giants, such as the Giants' Pit, the Giants' Kilns, and the Giants' Sea; and those somehow related to the mysterious Silent Ones, such as the long, winding Road Where the Silent Ones Walk, the Place Where the Silent Ones Kill, and the more puzzling Place Where the Silent Ones Are

---

[7] Mark Valentine notes that the Welsh university town of Aberystwyth, which is only seven miles from Hodgson's longtime hometown of Borth (where he wrote *The House on the Borderland* [HB: x] and other works), has since the nineteenth century had on its seafront a funicular railway that takes passengers up a cliffside to a camera obscura that is claimed to be the largest in the world by lens size (Valentine 2014: 88).

Never, which is presumably linked to the Silent Ones negatively as a site they absolutely avoid, although the rationale for this linkage is never given. However, the House of Silence, the location (immediately adjacent to the Road Where the Silent Ones Walk, at the northern edge of the Night Land) and name of which might seem to mark it as a member of this category, is actually *sui generis*: while the Silent Ones are largely indifferent to the other inhabitants of the Night Land, whether human or ab-human, and so cannot be classed as either definite threats or beneficent forces, the House of Silence is unequivocally "accounted the greatest danger of all those Lands" (NL: 40). That status is confirmed first when it swallows up the rash youths who embark on an unauthorized mission to succor the Lesser Redoubt (NL: 108–11), and later when it attacks Naani's spirit and nearly slays her (NL: 544–5). The Quiet City too appears to be unrelated to either the Silent Ones or the House of Silence. Other categories seem more arbitrary, like the topographical features distinguished by color, such as the Plain of Blue Fire, the Vale of Red Fire, the Pit of Red Smoke, the Silver Fire Holes, the Grey Dunes, the Black Hills, and the region containing the Black Mist. The Dark Palace may also belong in this category. Perhaps the most bizarre set of geographical features visible from the Redoubt are those named for their resemblances to forms of (mis)communication: the Country of Wailing, the Mountain of the Voice, the Country Whence Comes the Great Laughter, the Headland from Which Strange Things Peer, and the Thing That Nods. All these place names register an assignment of abstract or possible signification that nevertheless remains ambiguous and untranslatable in its details, like the writing of a long-dead civilization, a sophisticated cipher comparable to the *Voynich Manuscript* or the *Codex Seraphinianus*, or even the language of an alien species; as such, these sites may be related to the Place of the Ab-Humans that marks the western horizon seen from the Redoubt. In any case, these categories superficially—and perhaps even ironically—suggest a far greater understanding of the Night Land than its human inhabitants actually possess.

Only a small number of these landscape features play roles in the plot of *The Night Land*, as landmarks on X's journey to locate the Lesser Redoubt and rescue his reincarnated beloved Naani. Although his own intuition coincides with traditional belief and the telepathic testimony of Naani in placing the Lesser Redoubt somewhere to the north of the Great Redoubt, he decides to travel

> not direct towards the North; but to the North and West; and so in the end to mean to circle around to the back of the North-West Watcher, and thence to the North of the Plain of Blue Fire; and afterwards, as might be, have a true and straight way to the North; and by this planning come a long way clear of that House of Silence, which did put more fear upon me than all else that was horrid in the Land.
>
> (NL: 126)

He follows this route on the outbound leg, but is forced to depart from it on the inbound leg after Naani is stricken. Throughout his journey he reveals a distinctly topographic or cartographic turn of mind, discoursing learnedly on topics such as the variation of air density by elevation both within the Last Redoubt and outside in the Night Land (NL: 120–1, 208–11) and the geological history of the great rift valley in which both Redoubts are believed to be situated (NL: 127–9). Both these topics, to different degrees, clarify the future history that overthrew human mastery of the earth's surface and produced the nonhuman features of the Night Land. The rift valley, which was apparently not produced by tectonic catastrophe, came "out of the West, towards the South-East, and made turning thence Northwards, and was a thousand miles both ways. And the sides thereof were an hundred miles deep" (NL: 127–8). Over the course of millennia, the valley evolved into an exotic wilderness populated by great beasts. The Great Redoubt sits near the corner where the northern arm of the valley meets the western arm, but it was not built until after a titanic earthquake ruptured the planet's crust, vaporized the seas by releasing magma, and rendered the upper surface uninhabitable. Only then did humans gradually filter down into the valley over many generations, building a road to accompany them on their migration; that road would later be abandoned by humans to become the Road Where the Silent Ones Walk (NL: 40, 129–31). As the atmosphere gradually thinned, flight became impossible for both living things and machines, leaving only surface travel, open to attack by monsters, for human mobility (NL: 210).

The farther X travels from the Redoubt, however, the less reliable his geographical knowledge becomes. To avoid the highly visible and dangerous elements of the landscape, he must often travel through dark regions that no one in the pyramid has ever mapped, and even those that have been extensively mapped occupy space differently when one approaches them:

> so shall you have memory of me, there a-wander among those strange shapings and wonders of that grim Land, the which I had never but supposed to seem but as my memory did retain them, from the lookings of all my life within the Great Redoubt. And so it was; and ever there did this thing and that open out to a new view, and the Night Land take to itself a constant new aspect to mine eyes which had never until that time had but the one fixed vision of the same.
>
> (NL: 152–3)

Even the seemingly well-known landmarks contain hidden aspects that disorient him and keep him on his guard, and something similar happens to Naani when he finds her wandering terror-stricken in the second Night Land surrounding the Lesser Redoubt: "she was all adrift of her bearings, and was as a stranger, because that she had never lookt upon the Land from that place, before then" (NL: 346). The only fixed and comforting point in this unreliable landscape is the Great Redoubt itself, which serves both as a visual reference point and as the spot toward which X's compass points, as a consequence of the vital Earth-Current that powers the pyramid (NL: 76, 137–8). As the Redoubt dwindles in the distance, the compass provides only cold comfort to the anxious wayfarer, who likens his situation to that of a space traveler:

> It was borne in afresh upon my spirit how greatly I had wandered away, and how that I stood afar in the lonesomeness of that Land of Night; as it had been that a man of this age did wander amid the stars, and perceive a great comet to go by him very close; for then he should know in his heart how that he was far off in the Void.
>
> (NL: 182)

Past the House of Silence, he discovers that the Road Where the Silent Ones Walk ends in a boulder-strewn downward slope engulfed in darkness, through which he must navigate by touch while crawling on his hands and knees. The gigantic blue flame erupting from the ground, which he encounters halfway down the slope, allows him a brief interval of vision before he leaves it behind. Only at the bottom of the slope, at the end of the gorge that opens onto the comparatively lush Country of Seas, does he find sufficient light—generated by the glowing lava flowing from a multitude of volcanoes—to allow him to walk upright again, and equally crucially, to map out a route ahead of time. Indeed, he almost misses his chance: "I lookt about for a great while, and afterward did climb back into the Gorge, and called myself foolish, that I had not thought to map my way ere I came down" (NL: 226). Having learned his lesson, he makes another rough map when he emerges from the much narrower gorge that leads up from the Country of Seas to the second Night Land in which the Lesser Redoubt is located (NL: 269–70). Although he encounters unusual beasts, such as an odd creature with fourteen legs and gigantic carnivorous slugs, and primitive humanoids that he calls Humped (or Humpt) Men in these regions, they seem to him simply natural organisms that may consider him prey but do not otherwise threaten his existence or humanity's in general, as the forces of the Night Land do.

When he enters the second Night Land, however, he is immediately reminded of the differing threat levels even before he completes his mapping. In a nearby valley filled with shifting light he spots what looks like a monstrous head, which he cannot see clearly. Anticipating the Recluse's vision of the old gods on the Plain of Silence once again, he reflects, "whether it did be the shape of some utter monster of eternity—even as the Watchers about the Mighty Pyramid—or whether it did be no more than a carven mountain of rock, shaped unto the dire picturing of a Monster, I did have no knowing" (NL: 269). He avoids it anyway, and later learns from Naani that it was likely a Fixed Giant, which is the Lesser Redoubt's term for the great immobile Watchers (NL: 315). Thus the plain around the Lesser Redoubt takes shape as a "familiar Land of Strangeness" in a different way than X's natal Night Land: although he is unfamiliar with the layout of its geography, most of its dangers are analogous, if not identical, to those he knows from his previous education and experience. Recognition of this enables him to locate Naani as efficiently as possible and start back with her toward his home.

The beginning of the couple's return journey highlights the fundamental difference between X's quest and the cartographic travels characteristic of more positivist science fiction or redemptive fantasy: whereas science fictional travel constitutes voyages of discovery that will open up new territories, either for human occupation and exploitation or for human understanding, and fantasy travel restores order and value to lands that have been infected by evil, X's and Naani's weird journey constitutes what can only be called a voyage of renunciation or loss, much closer to a funeral procession than a celebration, despite their joy in reunion. Naani and X form not a vanguard but a rearguard, abandoning space to the ab-human and the alien rather than claiming it. When they reach the edge of the plain known to her, on which the now despoiled Lesser Redoubt stands,

> Naani said good-bye forever unto all that she had known of the world in all her life ... for in verity, there should no other human look upon that Land of terror all the quiet of eternity; and the Maid did lose all her young life into that blackness, and the Father that was her Father; and the grave of her Mother; and the friends of all her years.
>
> (NL: 347)

This farewell establishes a pattern, which X follows for much of their journey, of sentimental repetitions, final glances, and sorrowful reflections. Naani in particular is excited by the prospect of revisiting and even sleeping in the same spots X used on his outbound way, and occasionally takes souvenirs of them. X is more somber, as for example when they pass the Great Gas Fountain in the midst of the otherwise lightless upward gorge:

> And oft in the first hours did we turn about from our blind stumblings, and gaze downward out of that long height, unto the loom of the Flame, that did shudder far below in the night, and made a quaking light in that far darkness. And so did we leave it to dance forever through Eternity in that deep and lost place of the world; and we bent our will and our strength unto the climb.
>
> (NL: 531)

The Flame, shining alone in a lost place that it can do no more than fitfully illuminate, serves as a solemn figure for the Last Redoubt itself.

Even apparent exceptions to this elegiac attitude ultimately reinforce it. On his outbound journey, X finds the verdant and well-lighted Country of Seas to be comparatively benign, in that he is only threatened by natural organisms seeking to consume his body, not mysterious entities out to capture his soul, and the nonhumans there are apparently not ab-humans but prehumans (NL: 237–8). On the return journey, Naani too is struck by this region and the effect it has upon her state of mind:

> And she to turn constant this way and that, and to be never ceased of looking, and of deep breathings of the wide air; for never in that life had she been in a broad place of light ... And we to feel, both, that there did be no more need to talk husht, as we did alway in the gloom and narrow dark of the gorge.
>
> (NL: 404)

Both are similarly impressed with the extent to which the local geological activity has produced an area "truly like a great and wondrous park, that did be made of the skill and labour of godlike things," including a titanic geyser that balances a house-sized rock atop its blast (NL: 457–9). Naani's sense of pleasure and comfort in this lively landscape may help to explain why she allows her innate "naughtiness" freer rein than before, a choice that leads to the couple's most debilitating battle with the Humped Men followed by weeks of recuperation from near death on a fortuitously situated island. This reversal is foreshadowed in X's momentary fantasy that, "in some age that did be far after that time, the Humans to find some way to journey from the Pyramid, and to build a new Refuge in that deep Country; and mayhap the Humans thiswise to have a new space of life, after that all the Night Land did be dead and lost in the bitter frost of Eternity." Even as he articulates it, though, he knows it is to be impossible: "But this, indeed, to be no more than an odd thought; for how might any great multitude pass the Monsters; and I to ask you to take it for nothing of fact, but only as of my suppositions" (NL: 422).

The sense of resignation expressed here intensifies across the novel's penultimate chapters as X must carry the stricken Naani toward the Redoubt while simultaneously battling increasing numbers of monsters, only to be told upon arriving that she is dead, and "all the world did be quiet and emptied, and [his] task to have failed" (NL: 566). Even Naani's last-minute revival to life and consciousness just as her body is being consigned to the Earth Current can only temper but not erase this broader resignation, which is figured in the monument that the Redoubt's inhabitants erect to the couple: instead of a triumphalist tribute to their courage and strength, it is simply "a Statue of a man in broken armour, that did carry a maid forever" (NL: 582). The lovers' happy ending—what Tolkien would like to call the "eucatastrophe"—remains merely personal and affective, rather than cognitively objective or morally universal; it does not echo either the absolute and transcendent redemption promised by the revealed religion that Hodgson rejected or its secular and science-fictional equivalent, the successful voyage of discovery that opens up new lands for exploitation and new forces for mastery. Although the outcome here is cheerier than that of *The House on the Borderland*, it shares with the shorter work an ethos of humility, acceptance, and withdrawal in the face of the radically alien world beyond the dim pools of light that human understanding casts about itself. John Rieder (2008) argues that much early science fiction not only shares but universalizes the imperialist logic of colonial expansion and domination that characterized Anglo-European culture throughout the decades in which the genre was founded, while more recently David M. Higgins (2021) has shown how even reverse colonization narratives like Wells's *War of the Worlds*, in which readers are encouraged to imagine what it's like to be colonized rather than colonizers, can become vehicles for the preservation and reproduction of inequality and domination. While it would not be accurate to call *The Night Land* a decolonization narrative, which is a form used by the colonized to narrate their emancipation and the restoration of their autonomy, it's not a colonization narrative or a reverse colonization narrative either. In addition to being an entropic romance in terms of individual affect, in broader ideological terms it is essentially a withdrawal narrative that takes the reader through the experience of explicitly renouncing claims to knowledge, to value, to territory, to power, and to mastery over anything beyond our limited capacity to understand. While it may be true—though the particulars are lost in the abyss of time—that human control over the world outside the Redoubt was contested and overthrown by forces active in their own right, that overthrow is not the context or occasion for Hodgson's story. Neither the inhabitants in general nor X in particular is driven by resentment or a desire to restore the lost glory of a worldly empire, the possibility for which is never even suggested; X's instantaneously quashed fantasy of human settlement in the Country of Seas is the closest the tale comes to it. They aim only to survive by minimizing the conflicts they have with the entities outside the Electric Circle and the Air Clog. This is the only possible outcome of a narrative that aims not at cognitive mastery or ethical redemption of the spaces in which humans must live, but decognitive humility and anethical acceptance of those spaces' fundamental nonhumanity, which are the characteristics that Hodgson bequeaths to later weird fiction.

Part Three

Hope Out of Time

Among the most striking aspects of William Hope Hodgson's major weird fiction is its deployment of time shifts, which are present from early in his career: his first published novel, *The Boats of the "Glen Carrig"* (1907), takes the form of a first-person narrative of encounters with Sargasso Sea monstrosities written by a shipwrecked English gentleman in 1757. This relatively small historical displacement of a century and a half does little to prepare readers for the vast temporal shifts they find in his later, most innovative and important novels, *The House on the Borderland* (1908) and *The Night Land* (1912). The former takes its unnamed narrator on an involuntary, disembodied journey through time to the end not only of our world, but of the solar system, while the latter plucks its narrator's consciousness from his grief-stricken body in some earlier century and deposits it in a younger body, living in a titanic fortress on a dying earth, countless millions—perhaps billions—of years in the future. These novels, appearing early in the twentieth century, look both backward to the debates over geological and cosmological time that consumed scientists, theologians, and philosophers for the last half of the nineteenth century, and forward to the massively expanded time-scales of twentieth-century cosmology. In this Hodgson's vision converges with that of the distinguished Victorian geologist, friend and ally of modern geology's founder Charles Lyell, George Poulett Scrope, who wrote,

> The periods which to our narrow apprehension ... appear of incalculable duration, are in all probability but trifles in the calendar of Nature .... Every step that we take in its pursuit forces us to make almost unlimited drafts upon antiquity. The leading idea which is present in all our researches, and which accompanies every fresh observation, the sound which to the student of Nature seems continually echoed from every part of her works, is—
>
> Time!—Time!—Time! (Scrope, 1858, cited in Albritton 1980: 153)

Hodgson's depictions of inhuman timescales also beg the question, how did a sailor-turned-bodybuilder-turned-author like Hodgson, whose formal schooling ended at age thirteen, conceive and represent in print radical conceptions of time that the most distinguished scientists and writers of the nineteenth century dismissed as unthinkable?

Hodgson's novels mark one of the first appearances of what would become a powerful trope in science fiction: the abyss of time that makes almost unlimited drafts upon futurity and/or antiquity, a non- or anti-image that defies assimilation into human experience through measurement and only becomes accessible to reason through the disjunctive logic of the Kantian sublime. For Kant, our reason can calculate with large numbers, even infinity, but our imagination can't represent them. However, in Hodgson's work the abyss of time interrupts and undermines the process of cognitive assimilation and mastery that has come to define science fiction, in part by foreclosing the possibility of quantitative measurement that is essential to reason's power to produce conceptual unities (see Miéville 2009a: 510–1). By breaking the lines of historical and cultural continuity, the abyss of time also ungrounds the qualitative measures of social and ethical values that derive from those lines, rendering the prospect of redemption deeply ambiguous. With regard to genre, in his own time Hodgson's novels occupied the unstable space that was in the process of being defined as the triple border separating scientific romance (the precursor of science fiction), fantastic romance (the precursor of epic fantasy), and supernatural horror from one another, a space that would not be named "the weird" until after his death. As we have seen in previous chapters, the weird is a nonhuman mind- and body-space of non-knowledge, or even anti-knowledge, that the abyss of time reveals in all its unsettling power, and as such it participates in the decognitive dismantling of nineteenth-century scientific and intellectual certainties that marked the first decades of the twentieth century. As Hodgson's admirer H.P. Lovecraft, himself an exemplary artist of abyssal time in weird tales such as "The Nameless City" (1921), "The Call of Cthulhu" (1928), *At the Mountains of Madness* (1936), and *The Shadow Out of Time* (1936), once asserted, time "looms up in my mind as the most profoundly dramatic and grimly terrible thing in the universe. *Conflict with time* seems to me the most potent and fruitful theme in all human expression" (Lovecraft 2004b: 176). Following in the wake of these two writers, contemporary weird fiction continues to traffic in conflicts with time and travel through the abysses of time, on its way out of the world governed by humanity and into what Benjamin J. Robertson, discussing Jeff VanderMeer's work, calls "life after aftermath," that is, a world humans have helped to make impossible for ourselves to occupy or even think, but possibly home for something else:

> In this world of humanity's creation, individual humans can at best survive. The species can only disappear. This disappearance, however, is not cause for sadness. Rather, it is only a cause for human sadness. The life that shall inherit the broken places created by humans have their own affects, their own manner of living in the world, outside of the myths and other narratives that humanity tells itself about itself in order to make its own existence meaningful.
>
> (Robertson 2018: 144)

The question Hodgson sets before us, then, is how do we work through the horror of this transtemporal revelation so that we can find within ourselves the capacity to relinquish our mastery of the world to this posthuman life?

7

The Time That Is Left Us

If cognitive assimilation and mastery in a science-fictional mode, or moral redemption in a high fantasy mode, are neither its aim nor its means, either explicitly or implicitly, then what is the function or significance of abyssal time in Hodgson's work, and in weird fiction more generally? In order to answer these questions, we need a conception of time that focuses on its paradoxical foundation in the gap between the "now" of narrative engagement for both writer and reader and the distant "then" of the future, between time experienced as an unbroken sequence of moments in which we dwell and time running down to its endpoint. Giorgio Agamben's study of St. Paul, *The Time That Remains* (2005), might seem an odd place to look for elements of such a concept, but an attentive reading of Agamben's fourth chapter, which focuses on the word "apostolos" or "apostle"—meaning "emissary"—and gives his book its title, will justify this choice. There Agamben distinguishes the time of the apostle, which is defined by a messianic interval structurally unlike chronological or historical time, from on the one hand the time of the prophet, which is defined by the future he predicts, and on the other hand the time of the apocalypse, which is defined as the moment of time's end and, in monotheistic metaphysics, the advent of eternity. In Christianity, messianic time begins with Christ's resurrection, the event to which the apostle is faithful and on behalf of which he is an emissary, and the apocalypse will take place following Christ's second coming. In brief, the prophet announces the future messiah whose coming will one day bring time to an apocalyptic end, whereas the apostle attends the messiah during his liminal present, a present which is the interval between chronological/historical time and its abolition in eternity. As Agamben writes, "What interests the apostle is not the last day, it is not the instant in which time ends, but the time that contracts itself and begins to end ..., or if you prefer, the time that remains between time and its end" (Agamben 2005: 62). He provides a simplified visual representation of this:

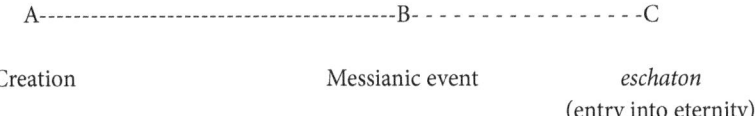

The line from A to B represents chronological or historical time, at some point in which the prophet predicts the coming of the messiah; B represents the appearance of the messiah, and the broken line from B to C represents the messianic time of the apostle that culminates in time's end.

In order to define the specificity of this messianic time, Agamben borrows from linguist Gustave Guillaume the concept of operational time, the time that the mind takes to realize or construct a time-image, such as the line above, to represent its experience of time. Reflection upon the time such an image takes to be constructed in and by the mind reveals what Guillaume calls the schema of chronogenesis, which Agamben says "allows us to grasp the time-image in its pure state of potentiality (time *in posse*), in its very process of formation (time *in fieri*), and, finally, in the state of having been constructed (time *in esse*) … " (Agamben 2005: 66). The result, for Agamben, is the realization that as thinking beings we produce another time in addition to chronological time, which is not

> a supplementary time added on from outside to chronological time. Rather, it is something like a time within time—not ulterior but interior—which only measures my disconnection with regard to it, my being out of synch and in non-coincidence with regard to my representation of time, but precisely because of this, allows for the possibility of my achieving and taking hold of it. We may now propose our first definition of messianic time: messianic time is *the time that time takes to come to an end*, or, more precisely, the time we take to bring to an end, to achieve our representation of time.
>
> (Agamben 2005: 67)

This kind of time is within us or of us as much as, or more than, it is before us or around us. Agamben continues:

> [Messianic time] is the time we need to make time end: *the time that is left us*. Whereas our representation of chronological time, as the time *in which* we are, separates us from ourselves and transforms us into impotent spectators of ourselves—spectators who look at the time that flies without any time left, continually missing themselves—messianic time, an operational time in which we take hold of and achieve our representation of time, is the time *that* we ourselves are, and for this very reason, is the only real time, the only time we have.
>
> (Agamben 2005: 68)

My claim, then, is that the narratives of abyssal time composed by Hodgson explore this messianic time *that* we ourselves are, the time we need to make time end, the only time we have to act, in order to determine *how* we might take responsibility for it, take hold of and achieve it.

Before we turn to the demonstration of this, we must forestall one misunderstanding that may seem implied by Agamben's frame of reference and nomenclature: the conclusion that, because his reading of Paul relies on explications of New Testament Greek to reveal the network of religious disputations operating in the biblical text, his conclusions are necessarily confined to the discipline of theology. Even if Agamben's book is taken in isolation, its final chapter on terminological and conceptual convergences between Paul and Marxist critic Walter Benjamin (Agamben 2005: 138–45) refutes this view. Indeed, Agamben's interest in Pauline messianism arises precisely from his lifelong project to understand Benjamin's messianic conceptions of classless society and the revolution that achieves it, which are expressed gnomically in his theses "On the Concept of History" (Benjamin 2003: 389–400) and their variants (Benjamin 2003: 401–11). In variant thesis XVIIa, Benjamin writes, "In the idea of a classless society, Marx secularized the idea of messianic time. And that was a good thing" (Benjamin 2003: 401) in that it also secularized the certainty that "there is not a moment that would not carry with it *its* revolutionary chance—provided only that it is defined in a specific way, namely as the chance for a completely new resolution of a completely new problem" (Benjamin 2003: 402). In thesis XIV, Benjamin renamed this revolutionary chance "*Jetztzeit*" or "now-time" (Benjamin 2003: 395), the present moment in which the historical materialist grasps the "constellation" that links his era to a specific history and "establishes a conception of the present as now-time shot through with splinters of messianic time" (Benjamin 2003: 397) that make successful revolutionary acts possible. Thus revolutionary agency can arise only in and from the *Jetztzeit* of messianic time, and indeed, for Benjamin revolution itself comes to occupy the position of the messiah who initiates the ending of time in Agamben's visual figure. However, reformist politics redefined the construction of classless society as an infinite task that must wait, through the bourgeoisie's homogeneous, empty time, for the impersonal arrival of its ideal revolutionary situation in order to be realized, thereby stripping the revolutionary subject of its material agency.

Hodgson's weird fiction confronts, interrogates, and ultimately inhabits a version of this secularized or atheist messianic time, "one that no longer looks for its decisive moment in a more or less remote future, but instead finds it in every minute of every day, in this world and in this life … " (de la Durantaye 2009: 120). In other words, it is "not the time while one waited for the coming of a Messiah but instead a manner of experiencing and acting on what is already here in the present … an attempt to grasp the potentialities of our present situation" (de la Durantaye 2009: 376). For Hodgson, then, we could say that the (non-)experience of the abyss of time itself comes to occupy the position of the messiah in Agamben's schema, thereby initiating the ending of time. In order to demonstrate this concretely, however, we need to contrast Hodgson's treatment of time's abyss with that of his better-known contemporary, H.G. Wells.

With few exceptions, Hodgson's short fiction shows no special concern for inquiry into or representation of time, and abyssal time only appears by allusion in the posthumously published tale "The Riven Night" (discussed in spatial terms in Chapter Six above), in which a sailing ship encounters an odd split or tear in the night sky through which it is drawn into a world of dead souls, who come to claim a murderous mate and a captain grieving the loss of his wife. The narrator, named Hodgson, senses that time passes differently there: "It seemed to me as though ages passed over my head and still I watched dreamily … Thus I stood, and the monotony of time passed over my head in silent aeons. Then, it might have been halfway through eternity," the ship is driven back to the everyday world by a great wave, and the crew tacitly agree to attribute their shipmates' demise to more conventional causes (CF 3: 516–8). This association of unmeasurable temporal acceleration and scale—"it might have been halfway through eternity"—with spatial or dimensional dislocation and with the "monotony" expressed through emptiness recurs in Hodgson's non-maritime novels, where he has the space to investigate it at length and, indeed, develop it into a logically consistent framework that implicitly links those novels. Schematically, we might say that *The House on the Borderland* (1908) presents a fantastically accelerated diachronic overview of deep cosmological time's abyss as Hodgson imagines it, a time-lapse narrative revelation of our world's terrifyingly nonhuman foundations that takes us from the (relatively) recent past to the distant end of time, the aftermath of human hopes, fears, plans, and unintended consequences. *The Night Land* (1912), then, offers us an in-depth synchronic experience of life on the thoroughly altered (and thus doubly alienated) earth as the end of time draws near—life after aftermath, a world "turning away from this [human] form of life to present opportunities for new forms of life to arise in the broken places, which are no longer broken but are whole places, the conditions of this new life" (Robertson 2018: 157–8).

As critics such as Andy Sawyer (2014: 174) have noted, the main narrative of *The House on the Borderland* is multiply framed: first, by a dedication "To My Father," which is accompanied by the poem "Shoon of the Dead" (HB: v); second, by an editorial introduction signed "William Hope Hodgson" that vouches for the authenticity of the story by evoking the materiality of the original manuscript (within the main narrative, this editorial voice points out contradictions, lacunae, and other anomalies by means of footnotes), and also proposes a metaphysical interpretation of the "simple, stiffly given account of weird and extraordinary matters" (HB: ix) which we shall discuss below; third, another poem, "Grief," described in a footnote as part of the original manuscript but written earlier (HB: xiv); and finally, the first numbered chapter, containing a first-hand account of the finding of the manuscript in the west of Ireland by the vacationers Tonnison and Berreggnog, which is mirrored by a closing chapter that records their reactions to the incredible story they (and we) have read. These two chapters are the only ones to make use of dialogue between characters; the main narrative offers only paraphrases of verbal exchanges. These framing paratexts multiply and complicate the temporality of the central story: the two poems are undated, but Tonnison and Berreggnog's account is dated 1877 (the year of Hodgson's birth), and Hodgson's introduction is dated 1907. The central narrative, told in first person by the unnamed Recluse, is also undated, but information provided by an elderly Irishman to the two discoverers in the closing chapter suggests that it must have taken place no more than eighty years earlier, around 1800 (HB: 297–300).

Cocooned within these layers of fictive time, the central tale begins abruptly: following a brief description of himself, his spinster sister, and his secluded house, reputedly built by the devil, the Recluse launches into an account of the first "real manifestation of the, so called, supernatural" (HB: 25) that he experienced there. While reading in his study, he has a sudden vision of a vast twilit plain, after which some force, which is never identified, draws his consciousness out of his body and takes it on a journey of undefinable duration "beyond the fixed stars" to the site of that vision, the Plain of Silence, on a planet orbiting a ring-shaped sun with black center (HB: 30–2). There he is confronted with a gigantic duplicate of his house, made of green jade, in the center of a natural arena formed by a ring of mountains, the peaks of which are occupied by "Beast-gods, and Horrors, so atrocious and bestial that possibility and decency deny any further attempt to describe them" (HB: 39). As we noted in Chapter Six, among the faces and quasi-faces staring fixedly at the house he recognizes Set, the

Egyptian god of chaos and the underworld, and Kali, the Hindu goddess of death and time, but many others are unrecognizable. At first he supposes them to be sculptures, but soon reconsiders: "There was something about them, an indescribable sort of silent vitality, that suggested, to my broadening consciousness, a state of life-in-death ... an inhuman form of existence, that well might be likened to a deathless trance—a condition in which it was possible to imagine their continuing, eternally" (HB: 40-1). The only movement he perceives is that of a giant biped that emerges from behind the house and tests all its entrances; when it turns toward him, he sees it has a humanlike body and the face of a swine, like a beast-god reanimated. As it rushes toward him, his viewpoint is suddenly drawn upward, into space, and he is brought back to his home, presumably by the same occult force, only after "A great time passed—ages" without event or stimuli (HB: 46).

This extraordinary experience serves as a kind of overture to the rest of the tale, foreshadowing the events that follow. When the Recluse looks back upon it from the vantage of his later transtemporal experience, he remembers most powerfully

> the sudden vision that had come to me, as I neared the Solar System, of the fast whirling planets about the sun—as though the governing quality of time had been held in abeyance, and the Machine of a Universe allowed to run down an eternity, in a few moments or hours. The memory passed, along with a, but partially comprehended, suggestion that I had been permitted a glimpse into further time spaces.
>
> (HB: 191)

The novel alternates, section by section, between two "time spaces" or narrative representations of time: the tremendously accelerated time of his visionary cosmic experiences and the frenetic but quotidian temporality of his life in the strange yet earthly house. Soon after his return the Recluse's house is besieged by swine-things, human-sized versions of the creature he saw on the Plain of Silence, that emerge from a newly opened cavern nearby, a cavern which leads to their ultimate lair, a bottomless chasm beneath the house. The next nine action-packed chapters focus on the siege and the Recluse's desperate efforts to keep the house secured, culminating in a flood that serves as a momentary *deus ex machina*, sealing up the nearby cavern and seemingly ending the threat of the swine-things. A break in the narrative tension finally occurs at this point when the Recluse pauses to explain why he could not leave the house, despite the danger: it is the only place from whence his disembodied consciousness, through dreams, can reach the Sea of Sleep, where he meets again the spirit of his previously unmentioned long-lost beloved (HB: 162-7).[1] A series of dreamlike fragments describing other journeys similar to his visit to the Plain of Silence reconnects this brief interlude to the main narrative; all of them emphasize the distortion of time involved in such visions: "It was as though time had been annihilated for me; so that a year was no more to my unfleshed spirit, than is a moment to an earth-bound soul" (HB: 168). This "annihilation" of time also prevents it from being quantified, measured, or otherwise grasped.

---

[1] On the question of narrative disjunctions in the novel, see note 3 in Chapter Six above.

The Recluse's narrative returns to diegetic continuity with a nine-chapter account of his most amazing "supernatural" experience, which many readers consider the most powerful and unique passage in the novel, and perhaps in Hodgson's work as a whole. Speaking for many others, Lovecraft writes, "The wanderings of the narrator's spirit through limitless light-years of cosmic space and kalpas of eternity, and its witnessing of the solar system's final destruction, constitute something almost unique in standard literature" (Lovecraft 2000: 59).[2] The Recluse prefaces his account by saying, "I have little doubt, but that, what I saw, was, in reality, the end of all things" (HB: 170), and thus the ultimate expression of Hodgson's abyssal vision of time. As many readers will recognize, its beginning takes the form of an homage to H.G. Wells's first novel, *The Time Machine* (1895), with a detailed, five-page depiction of temporal acceleration that Wells had described in two concise paragraphs. For example, Wells writes, "As I put on pace, night followed day like the flapping of a black wing ... Presently I noted that the sun-belt swayed up and down, from solstice to solstice, in a minute or less, and that, consequently, my pace was over a year a minute ... " (Wells 1934: 14–5). Hodgson echoes, somewhat less tersely,

> I can best describe the passage of day and night, at this period, as a sort of gigantic, ponderous flicker ... Quicker, and ever quicker, ran the flicker of day and night; and, suddenly it seemed, I was aware that the flicker had died out, and, instead, there reigned a comparatively steady light, which was shed upon all the world, from an eternal river of flame that swung up and down, North to South, in stupendous, mighty swings.
>
> (HB: 186–7)[3]

The more important difference between these passages, however, lies in the fact that Wells's Time Traveller travels through time of his own volition, using a machine of his own construction, and stops whenever he wishes, while Hodgson's Recluse is carried along involuntarily, by an external force that is never explained or even perceived, to a future far beyond the final day the Time Traveller reaches (Sawyer 2014: 173). Uncertainty wracks him as he struggles unsuccessfully to understand and categorize his experiences; throughout his journey he continually asks himself what is happening and why, but finds no answers even while his beloved dog Pepper expires and decays into dust. The Recluse later realizes that the same thing has happened to his own body, leaving him "a bodyless thing" (HB: 195) that can somehow still perceive.

The passage of time continues to accelerate, but unlike the Time Traveller's dwelling, which disintegrates shortly after he begins his journey (Wells 1934: 14), the Recluse's house stands firm through an "extraordinary space of time [that] was sufficient to have utterly pulverised the very stones of which it was built, had they been taken from any

---

[2] "Kalpa" is a unit of time in Buddhism and Hinduism that measures the duration of a universe from creation to destruction and re-creation; Hodgson uses the term in *The House on the Borderland* but not in *Night Land*.

[3] Jonathan Bignell (2004: 136–7) notes that Wells's description of time travel as primarily a visual spectacle closely resembles the experience of cinema spectatorship, and this applies even more accurately to Hodgson's description, since his narrator is unable to control his movement through time, as the Time Traveller is. Abyssal time is available to aesthetic experience only through the condensing mechanism of time lapse, whether in textual or filmic narrative.

earthly quarry" (HB: 196). "It might have been a million years later" (the subjunctive indicates that he still cannot actually measure time's passage) that he perceives the sun's light changing color, indicating its aging and impending death (HB: 200). He witnesses the earth's rotation slow to a stop (just as the Time Traveller does after he leaves the age of Eloi and Morlocks), but not before he sees, without fully understanding it, the freezing and precipitation of the earth's atmosphere like snow (HB: 208). While the inner planets are falling into the dying sun, it and the earth are drawn slowly toward a great green star, but before they reach it, the swine-things, unaffected by the absence of air, emerge from the shadows, frightening the disembodied Recluse into flight. From outside he sees "a vast column of blood-red flame" shoot up from the house and clash with the beams of the green star. As in his first vision of the Plain of Silence, he is suddenly carried upward into space to witness "the ground ... cave in, suddenly, and the house, with its load of foul creatures, [disappear] into the depths of the earth" from whence they came (HB: 229–30).

As we noted in Chapter Six, a discrepancy emerges here (though not one highlighted by the "editor" Hodgson): when this vision ends and he returns to the present, his house is intact, but not long thereafter (and presumably long before the destruction of the solar system) it collapses into the chasm beneath it, leaving only a bottomless abyss (and the swine-things it houses) for Tennison and Berreggnog to find. Does this call part or all of the vision into question, perhaps in the same way that the Recluse's sister's apparent inability to perceive the swine-things calls the siege sequence into question? The remainder of the novel offers no more answer to this question than it does to the Recluse's own questions, leaving the reader in a similar state of unknowing. Only a seeming moment after the future house disappears, "the earth appeared to shoot forward. In a moment it had traversed the space between it and the sun. I heard no sound; but, out from the sun's face, gushed an ever growing tongue of dazzling flame. [Then,] on the sun, glowed a vast splash of burning white—the grave of the earth" (HB: 231). The extinguished sun, in turn, shows "only as a dark blot on the face of the Green Sun. As I watched, I saw it grow smaller, steadily, as though rushing toward the superior orb, at an immense speed ... I was conscious of extraordinary emotions, as I realised that it would strike the Green Sun" (HB: 232–3), although his vision is cut off and he does not actually see the sun's end.

Upon realizing that he has witnessed "the final end of our [solar] System—that system which had borne the world through so many aeons, with its multitudinous sorrows and joys"—he wonders, is the Green Sun "the vast *Central* Sun—the great sun, round which our universe and countless others revolve[?] Do the dead stars make the Green Sun their grave? The idea appealed to me with no sense of grotesqueness ... " (HB: 233–4).[4] He has little time for grief once he notices that the Green Sun is garlanded

---

[4] Emily Alder traces this image to Theosophy, in which this sun is the source and endpoint of life (Alder 2009: 111). Stableford notes that this idea resembles the hypothesis of German astronomer Johann von Mädler that our solar system revolves around a "Central Sun" in the constellation Pleiades, but Stableford is at a loss to explain how Hodgson could have encountered it (1987: 35). A thorough discussion of Mädler's cosmological ideas appears in Poe's *Eureka: A Prose Poem* (1848), and since Poe is one of the few authors we know Hodgson venerated, that seems the most likely source for this image.

with glowing globes which make him feel "that I was less alone, than I had been for kalpas of years" (HB: 236). The Recluse is drawn to one globe in particular and passes into it, wherein he finds the Sea of Sleep and, on its shore, his lost beloved. He is granted an indefinite interval of peace with her before he must return to the Central Sun, which he discovers is accompanied by Dark or Dead Sun to form a double star (HB: 246). Around the Dark Sun orbits a dark nebula, in which he sees "ruddy-tinged spheres, similar, in size, to the luminous globes" among which he found the Sea of Sleep (HB: 252). He is drawn to one of the red globes as well, and when he passes into it finds himself once again on the Plain of Silence, carried toward the mountainous arena with its titanic house so like his own. The giant jade house has endured the same kind of damage from struggle against a siege as his own had, leading him to conclude that the "house, in which I live, was *en rapport*—to use a recognized term—with that other tremendous structure, away in the midst of that incomparable Plain" (HB: 258).[5] He wonders what material the giant green house is made of, just as he had wondered earlier (HB: 196) about the composition of his earthly house. He is suddenly drawn into the great green house on the Plain, but finds himself back at home in his study, physically intact, as if no time had passed since his departure—but Pepper is still dust, he will soon learn that the astral swine-thing from the arena is still hunting him, and he still has no idea what has happened to him or why. His house a temporal gateway between the swine-things' bestial origin and their final inheritance of the earth, he has no avenue of escape. Although the immaterial swine-thing can't compel him to come out of safety, it can infect his new dog with its corruption, and the dog in turn can infect the Recluse. The narrative ends even more abruptly than it began, with his pen trailing away down the page in reaction to something unnamed and undescribed entering his study.

Brett Davidson labels the Green and the Dark Sun "*metaphysical suns*," "meaning made visible, quasi-Manichean order manifested in the cosmos, radiating motive throughout the universe as they radiate light and gravitational force" (Davidson 2014: 186–8). Brian Stableford interprets the two Suns as allegorical representations of Growth and Decay, respectively, which he considers the metaphysical bases of Hodgson's worldview, "the former associated with love and ecstasy and the latter with emotional pain" (Stableford 1985: 95). If humanity aspires to continual Growth, then the swine-things embody the perpetual action of Decay. But Hodgson's "deep pessimism" means that, "In the end, man—individually and collectively—is bound to be consumed by the forces of decay, and so are the earth and the sun. Even the world of Ideas, it seems, must suffer dereliction" (Stableford 1985: 96). Certainly the two suns constitute what Hodgson describes in his "Introduction to the Manuscript" as "the shadowed picture and conception of that, to which one may well give the accepted titles of Heaven and Hell" (HB: ix), although he immediately qualifies this conventional theological interpretation by presenting

> the Celestial Globes as a striking illustration (how nearly had I said "proof"!) of the actuality of our thoughts and emotions among the Realities. For, without seeming to suggest the annihilation of the lasting reality of Matter, as the hub and

---

[5] See note 4 in Chapter Six above.

framework of the Machine of Eternity, it enlightens one with conceptions of the existence of worlds of thought and emotion, working in conjunction with, and duly subject to, the scheme of material creation.

(HB: ix-x)

This qualification situates the allegorical figuration within the framework of Hodgson's broader materialism, which was focused on finding a basis in matter for mental and affective forces that was consistent with the new physical forces of modernity such as electricity and radioactivity (see the Introduction above). As Emily Alder (2007 and 2009: chapter three) has demonstrated, Hodgson borrowed terminology and concepts from late Victorian spiritualism (such as the astral linkage expressed by the phrase *en rapport*) and Theosophy (such as the notion of the Central Sun as the source and end point of life) in order to express his cosmology, but the perspective adopted in his fiction, which is more materialistic but also more atheistic, anti-humanist, and Nietzschean than Blavatskian, does not conform to any specific school or sect, particularly with regard to the representation of time's abyss.[6]

In order to strengthen our grasp of the originality and consequences of this abyssal time in Hodgson's work, we now need to establish the broader intellectual and social context out of which it appeared. Although time has been acknowledged as an essential formal *condition* of every narrative since Aristotle, it has been uncommon as an explicit *subject or theme* of narrative, and even in most of those cases, the magnitude of the time in question is limited to human scales and materialized through human actions: the time of royal succession, in classical tragedy; the time of family genealogy, in the gothic; the time of national tradition, in the historical novel; the time of individual maturation, in the *Bildungsroman*; the inexorable countdown to destruction of the thriller. In most linguistic or cultural traditions, the representation of those superhuman intervals of time that we are calling abyssal time as subjects of narrative discourse has largely been the province of mythology and theology, in the form of creation stories and eschatological prophecies, at least until the advent of modernity in the West gave rise to experimental science, and consequently scientific romance and science fiction. For Christian Europe, the biblical narrative of creation and the descent of humanity, first from Adam and Eve and later from the children of Noah, had long constituted the privileged temporal foundation of secular storytelling. In 1650, the Irish Archbishop James Ussher published the first influential quantitative calculation of the time elapsed since creation, using biblical, classical, and astronomical

---

[6] Although this derivation might appear to imply that Hodgson's views were based in theology and/or the supernatural and hence non-scientific, Richard Noakes emphasizes that a more attentive and thorough attention to Victorian debates "challenges the use of natural and supernatural as unproblematic categories for analyzing disputes over Spiritualism, and prompts us to understand how boundaries between natural and supernatural emerged from disputes over spirit manifestations" and thus cannot be used to explain those disputes (Noakes 2004: 24–5). Alder concurs with respect to Hodgson's work: "if psychical ideas were ... at the cutting edge of modern scientific debates, so too was evolutionary science, and the two must be looked at in conjunction. Darwinism and the evolutionary history of humans cast doubts for many over the existence of God, heaven, or the immortal soul, but spiritualism, to an extent, allowed these same beliefs to be incorporated into a scientific and materialistic world view" (Alder 2007: 125).

sources to set the date of creation as October 22, 4004 BCE. This dating converged with popular belief that Christ would return in the year 2000 AD to give the world an overall lifespan of 6,000 years, an interval that was held to correspond typologically to the six days of creation according to 2 Peter 3:8: "one day is with the Lord as a thousand years, and a thousand years as one day."[7] With a few fascinating exceptions, such as French freethinker Benoît de Maillet's figure of 2 billion years (published in 1748, and derived from erroneous ideas about the shrinkage of the seas [Albritton 1980: 68–77]), Ussher's chronology for the cosmos was broadly accepted well into the nineteenth century, when the development of geology began to demand longer timescales.

Charles Lyell's *Principles of Geology* (first edition 1830-3) established *uniformitarianism* as a central tenet of geological science. This is the idea that the present physical state of the earth is most simply and logically explained by the continuous action of slow, small-scale processes operating over extremely long time periods (Albritton 1980: 137-47, Burchfield 1975: 66-71). Although Lyell never attempted to quantify the time necessary for his theory to operate, preferring instead to set the matter aside under the descriptor "indefinite," his allies (including Charles Darwin) were less cautious, and the numbers they produced were orders of magnitude greater than religious orthodoxy could accommodate. For example, in the first edition of *Origin of Species* (1859), Darwin crudely calculated the time necessary for the erosion of the Weald valley in southeast England at 300 million years, drawing a rebuke from the physicist William Thomson, later Lord Kelvin, co-discoverer of the laws of thermodynamics (Burchfield 1975: 71-3). In 1862 Thomson first calculated the lifespan of the sun, understood thermodynamically as a solid body heated by asteroid impacts that is gradually cooling, demonstrating that most probably, "the sun has not illuminated the earth for 100,000,000 years, and almost certain[ly] that he has not done so for 500,000,000 years" (Kelvin 1862: 368). Then he turned to the age of the earth, for which a similar calculation yielded a range of 20 million to 400 million years, with 98 million as the most likely precise figure (Kelvin 1863: 300). In 1868 he summed up his criticisms of geology in the essay "On Geological Time," concluding that

> Dynamical theory of the sun's heat renders it almost impossible that the earth's surface has been illuminated by the sun many times ten million years. And when finally we consider underground temperature we find ourselves driven to the conclusion in every way, that the existing state of things on the earth, life on the earth, all geological history showing continuity of life, must be limited within some period of past time as one hundred million years.
>
> (Kelvin 1868: 64; see also Burchfield 1975: 23-37)

Although geologists were certain that the geological record of superposed strata and their associated fossils required a much longer timeframe to be laid down, they were unable to dispute Kelvin's thermodynamic calculations, so the two camps took up the opposing positions they would occupy for the rest of the century, staking their claims in both specialist journals and popular magazines, until the discovery of radioactive

---

[7] For details regarding Ussher's methods and conclusions, see Barr 1984-5.

decay negated Kelvin's assumptions about both the earth and the sun and opened up the possibility of lengthier lifespans for both.[8]

This last third of the nineteenth century was the same period during which the genres of fantastika began to coalesce into those we know today, including the scientific romance that would first translate the Lyell-Kelvin debate into more popularly accessible terms. Most of the founding figures of fantastika do not deal with suprahuman intervals of time. For example, Jules Verne's extraordinary voyages travel no further than a century or two into the future, while William Morris's romances move no more than 1,500 years into the historical past; the fantastic works of George MacDonald, Lewis Carroll, Bram Stoker, and Robert Louis Stevenson all fit neatly into that same timeframe. The best-known exception to this tendency, and the most directly relevant to Hodgson's work, is H.G. Wells, as we have already noted.[9] In stark contrast to Hodgson, Wells's formal education in science, particularly biology, coincided with the final stage of the Lyell-Kelvin debate over the extent of geological time, and *The Time Machine* clearly reflects his understanding of Kelvin's ascendance. His acceptance of Kelvin's calculations, whether sincere or opportunistic, can be seen in the novel's penultimate section (Wells 1934: chapter 11, 58–62), a section that has generally been left out of the many media adaptations of the book that focus on the conflict between Eloi and Morlocks in the year 802,701.

Before going further, we should pause a moment over that number, because its faintly ludicrous precision arises from an aspect of Wells's novel that is absorbed and replicated by almost all later time-travel narrative, but not by Hodgson's. The Time Traveller announces it casually, in passing, at the conclusion of his first meeting with the Eloi: having impetuously "flung [himself] into futurity" (Wells 1934: 15), he has arrived in "the year Eight Hundred and Two Thousand Seven Hundred and One, A.D. For that, I should explain, was the date the little dials of my machine recorded" (Wells 1934: 21). The "little dials" are the readout of a temporal measuring device—clearly not a clock—that he never fully explains, even by analogy (as he does the time machine itself in the first chapter), although much later, when escaping the Morlocks, he describes it in slightly more detail: "One dial records days, another thousands of days, another millions of days, and another thousands of millions" (Wells 1934: 58). This instrument, which is taken for granted by the authors of later time-travel stories, is essential to Wells's progressive purpose in *The Time Machine*, for only by accurately measuring the temporal distance between the Time Traveller's listeners (and Wells's own readers) back in the 1890s and his adventures in the distant future can he rationally assimilate and thereby master the tragedy of "the human intellect" which "had committed suicide" (Wells 1934: 56) to produce the Eloi and the Morlocks, despite his earlier sense that

---

[8] For detailed accounts of Kelvin's criticisms, their reception and legacy, see Albritton 1980: chapters 14–16, and Burchfield 1975, *passim*. The source of the sun's energy, and hence its calculable lifespan, would not be determined accurately until 1939 when physicist Hans Bethe worked out the atomic fusion cycles for stellar nucleosynthesis.

[9] The other exception is Poe, whose late work *Eureka: A Prose Poem* (1848) is one of the very few in the nineteenth century to adopt a time-scale comparable to Hodgson's and the only one to present an eschatological model of cosmology that parallels Hodgson's in many ways. Its likely influence on Hodgson demands more attention than I can give it here, so I will defer its discussion to another forum.

his sympathy for and identification with them made him "perforce a sharer in their degradation and their Fear" (Wells 1934: 46). The paradox is no less sharp for being easily overlooked: only the objectifying, quantifying scientific reason that permitted the Time Traveller to construct his machine and its measuring devices can solve the Sphinx's riddle of that reason's undoing, even though the solution reveals scientific reason itself to be the cause of its own decay, as a consequence of its complicity with Victorian class hierarchy (Wells 1934: 57). The mathematician in Wells's tale "The Star" (1897) states this rationalist, indeed positivist faith bluntly when he addresses the planetary interloper that will soon pass close to earth: "You may kill me ... But I can hold you—and all the universe for that matter—in the grip of this little brain. I would not change. Even now" (Wells 1952: 684). A rational answer such as the Time Traveller's to the question of deep time's meaning, the certainty that human thought can master even its own extinction and replacement, is precisely what Hodgson's Recluse, and by extension his readers, never receive. The universe he confronts escapes the grip of our little brains, and there are no measurements of time's abyss in any of Hodgson's works; indeed, no mechanisms of any kind (except, of course, the mechanisms of narrative itself) are involved in his representations of time travel.

When the Time Traveller escapes the Morlocks by fleeing into the future, he glances at the instrument and notes that "the thousands hand was sweeping round as fast as the seconds hand of a watch" (Wells 1934: 59). Perhaps he really means the "thousands of millions" hand, since a thousand million (in US terms, a billion) days amounts to 2,740,000 years, and he is going farther into the future than that. Soon after this he observes the physical decline of the earth and sun:

> The alternations of night and day grew slower and slower, and so did the passage of the sun across the sky, until they seemed to stretch through centuries. At last a steady twilight brooded over the earth ... the sun had ceased to set—it simply rose and fell in the west, and grew ever broader and more red ... . At last, some time before I stopped, the sun, red and very large, halted motionless upon the horizon, a vast dome glowing with a dull heat, and now and then suffering a momentary extinction .... I perceived by this slowing down of its rising and setting that the work of the tidal drag was done. The earth had come to rest with one face to the sun, even as in our own time the moon faces the earth.
>
> (Wells 1934: 59)

Tidal drag is the phenomenon that Kelvin predicted would slow and ultimately stop the earth's rotation relative to the sun, and if the alternation of day and night is the unit measured by the Time Traveller's dials, they should cease to work at this point. However, it is the image of the sun "suffering a momentary extinction"—guttering like a candle or flickering like a failing incandescent bulb—that would become central not only to Hodgson's eschatological visions, as we have seen, but also to the fantastic subgenre of dying earth fiction, both of which extend the cosmological timeframe far beyond what Kelvin argued and Wells apparently believed was possible.

When the Time Traveller stops his machine, he discovers that the atmosphere has thinned; the only animal life he finds are giant butterflies and crabs from which he is again forced to flee futureward. He stops once more 30 million years into the future, a time in the middle of the range Kelvin calculated for the lifespan of the sun, when "the huge red-hot dome of the sun had come to obscure nearly a tenth part of the darkling heavens" (Wells 1934: 61). No explanation is given for how he determines this number. Although the atmosphere does not freeze and fall to earth as a kind of snow, as Hodgson's Recluse saw, the Time Traveller finds the ambient temperature has settled below freezing and the only life remaining is algal slime and some sort of primitive cephalopod. Although the stars still shine, to go further forward in time would only confirm the inevitability of solar and planetary demise, so as an eclipse shadow sweeps over him he is struck by "a horror of this great darkness" and "a deadly nausea" (Wells 1934: 62) which drive him backwards in time to the Victorian present, in which he tells his grammatically retrospective tale as a kind of prediction or prophecy. This momentary discomfort is the closest he comes to the continuous vertigo and confusion felt by Hodgson's Recluse.

The Time Machine is first and foremost a satire on class politics that uses evolutionary theory and geological time as its vehicles, but in its dying earth chapter it goes beyond such satire to stake a claim regarding anthropocentric reason and its consequences. Although the deaths of the earth and sun are the results of inexorable natural processes, the book's narrator links them to the self-destruction of class-divided humanity by reminding readers that the Time Traveller, like his creator, "thought but cheerlessly of the Advancement of Mankind, and saw in the growing pile of civilization only a foolish heaping that must inevitably fall back upon and destroy its makers in the end" (Wells 1934: 66). The question posed at the book's conclusion is whether or not the fate of organic life (including humanity) is to devolve and die out according to natural processes similar to those that will eventually "kill" the earth and sun. So long as scientific reason is subordinated to the irrationality of class domination, the answer appears to be yes, although the Time Traveller's story ultimately stands as an ambiguous prediction, explicitly challenging its readers when the narrator responds to the Time Traveller's pessimism: "If that is so, it remains for us to live as though it were not so" (Wells 1934: 66).

The fact that, despite Wells's disdain for conventional religion and preference for a humanistic philosophy, his tale corresponds well to Agamben's model of monotheistic messianic time will not surprise anyone who is aware of the Englishman's lifelong effort to reform human social and political institutions on the very largest scale, a project that *The Time Machine* arguably inaugurates and one that unites his scientific romances with his contemporary social satires like *Tono Bungay* (1909), his *Outline of History* (1920), his utopias and future histories such as *The Shape of Things to Come* (1933), and his writings on institutional reform such as *World Brain* (1938). In *The Time Machine*, the Time Traveller himself ultimately becomes a quasi-messiah, albeit a rationalist, scientific one, as his creator soon would. This transformation comes about not so much because of his implied self-sacrifice, his imitation of Christ, but rather because of the novel's adoption of his rational agency as a model for its concluding projection into the future. When the Time Traveller first departs into tomorrow, he expects to find what any Victorian gentleman would expect: continued progress along the lines of his own inventions and his era's self-image, resulting in "wonderful advances upon our rudimentary civilization" (Wells 1934: 15). What he finds is quite the reverse: the Victorian classes of capitalist and worker transformed into clades through nearly a million years of natural selection, neither capable of advancing civilization, or even of preventing the one they inherit from decomposing. Although the story he tells his friends upon his return echoes the jeremiads of the old prophets, he is not exactly predicting a future that will someday come to pass—rather, he is announcing that such a future is already in the process of beginning in their own present, and it leads ultimately but directly to that bleak, frozen, almost lifeless beach 30 million years hence. The time he has traveled, then, is the interval that human time, the time of our control over life on earth, will take to end; his trip ironically traces the steps in our achievement of the time image at work in class society—in other words, the time of capital's suicide machine. His knowledge makes his own machine possible, and his machine makes his messianism possible, with his narrator serving as his (first) apostle whose fidelity is implied in his remark "I must wait a lifetime" for the Time Traveller to return (Wells 1934: 66). This gives a slightly different meaning to the narrator's closing challenge: "If that is so, it remains for us to live as though it were not so" (Wells 1934: 66). On behalf of the vanished Time Traveller, to whom he remains faithful, the narrator is suggesting, or perhaps just hoping, that his readers act upon their own "non-coincidence" with their era's representation of time as endless mechanical progress predicated upon hereditary class status, that is to say they should perform the operational time they themselves are, and in so doing achieve a time image that may avoid the bleak destiny they have just read and allow their progeny to survive, if not eternally, at least indefinitely. As Agamben says, it is the only time they have to produce a different resolution.

Wells's messianism is not the messianism of faith or spirit, but the pragmatic or positivistic messianism of rational self-interest in the service of self-preservation, not the redemption of the soul or the resurrection of the flesh but the self-transcendence of the mind and the practical survival of the body. Hodgson's representation of time is quite different in both foundation and intent, and it emphasizes the most un- or even anti-theological implication of Agamben's reading of Paul and Benjamin: the possibility of an atheistic messianic time, one without an effective messiah as announcer, model and focus of its achievement, and thus without the *eschaton* of eternity as redemption or consolation for our achievement of it. In this version of the theory, the structure of messianic time would remain as a framework for agency and action, but both its center and its end would be emptied out into the unhuman abyss of time. Messianic history thus conceived "is not one in which we wait for the Messiah to come, end history, and redeem humanity, but instead is a paradigm for historical time in which we act as though the Messiah … has already come and gone" (de la Durantaye 2009: 120). In terms of the linear time-image noted earlier, from an atheist perspective point B would not be marked out by the arrival of eternity's agent, and, more importantly, point C would no longer correspond to the apocalyptic entry of the faithful into eternity, but simply the achievement of the time that remains, the end, in the double sense of aim and conclusion, of the time and world we are—our last chance to enact and conclude the human time-image on the threshold of its extinction and replacement by what Hodgson calls the ab-human, a neologistic category that resides at the intersection of the inhuman, the unhuman, and the posthuman and provides antagonists, witnesses, and heirs to the passing of the human.

We can evaluate this claim regarding messianic time without a messiah by considering the narrators and protagonists of Hodgson's abyssal narratives as apostles without a messiah, faithful not to the openly stated promise of a final transcendence of chronological time but rather to the belatedly recognized and achieved finality and disappearance of human time itself into the abyss. The Recluse of *The House on the Borderland* is granted—or compelled to acknowledge—an overwhelmingly powerful, indeed oppressive vision of that finality, but he has too little time left before the swine-thing and its infection silence him to make sense of that vision, to follow its contradictory clues out to their paradoxical endpoints, and to seize it as his own time-image. Even had he wanted to be an apostle, the opportunity would have been denied to him. The accomplishment of that task will be the aim of the quest undertaken by the protagonist in *The Night Land*, to which we will turn following an excursus into Hodgson's fantastic poetry that will allow us to clarify the conceptual context in which his notions of time find purchase.

8

That Song Past Human Tongue to Sing

In order to deepen our understanding of William Hope Hodgson's notions about abyssal time, we must take a detour through his posthumously published poetry. If we can accurately describe weird fiction's status within literary studies as marginal, despite its consistent popularity with general readers, then what adjective should we use to accurately describe the status of weird poetry, which doesn't seem to be popular with either academic or general readers—invisible? In Lovecraftian terms, unnamable? Although weird poetry may not have readers anymore, it does have a canon, or if you prefer a tradition, most of which predates the genre term itself: Samuel Taylor Coleridge's "Rime of the Ancient Mariner," John Keats's "La Belle Dame sans Merci" and "Lamia," Edgar Allan Poe's "City in the Sea," "Ulalume," and others, Algernon Charles Swinburne's "The Witch-Mother" and "Hymn to Proserpine," and several of Charles Baudelaire's *Fleurs du Mal* set the stage for the self-consciously weird or "cosmic" poetry of George Sterling, Clark Ashton Smith, H.P. Lovecraft, Frank Belknap Long, Leah Bodine Drake, Robert E. Howard, and Donald Wandrei. A sharp-eyed reader will have noted that all but one of the genre's precursors are Anglo-European, and that one American (Poe) is more highly venerated in Europe than at home, while all the later, self-styled weird poets are American. No doubt this disproportion can be explained in part by the fact that the precursors are considered members of the mainstream poetic canon that runs from Homer to Joy Harjo, despite their deplorable lapses into the fantastic, while the weird poets are mere "genre" poets just as weird fiction writers are mere "genre" writers, and their genre flourished more broadly in the United States than anywhere else.

And what of Hodgson, who composed perhaps the longest, most ambitious, and most formally striking weird poem of all at a time when the weird had not yet been constituted as a generic space? As such he can only have considered himself to be writing in the shadow of those mainstream precursors, whose readers took no notice of him, and his poetry remained unknown to the American weird poets by virtue of its extremely limited circulation. Nevertheless, Hodgson's contribution to weird poetry should be considered alongside that of Smith, Lovecraft, and their colleagues, since like them he is a member of one of the last generations of weird authors to dedicate itself systematically to the composition of verse as a twofold discipline essential to every writer's craft: first, in the conscious development of linguistic, sonorous, and rhythmic resources and the economy of their deployment, and second, in the articulation of thematic material in a lyric or reflective mode instead of a narrative or argumentative mode. Perhaps the fullest demonstration of any writer's command of this discipline lies in the composition of a long poem, which requires them to step outside the guardrails that had previously constrained them, whether these are defined by traditional short forms such as the sonnet, ballad, villanelle, or sestina, or (as with the high modernists) by haiku or Symbolist/Imagist linguistic compression.

Hodgson's long poem constitutes a virtual credo of his weird aesthetics and metaphysics, reflecting its author's aims and beliefs as expressed in his fiction, and thereby it provides important clarifications of his broader artistic practices. Like all early weird texts, it exists in a non-space between codified poetic spaces. Unlike many of the Victorian long poems that preceded it, *The Voice of the Ocean* is not a narrative, although it includes narrative elements; nor does it take history as its subject and the realist (re)production of factual truth as its goal, as the Victorian aesthetic ideologue Thomas Carlyle would have it do. Adam Roberts describes Carlyle as "less interested in the uses of the historiographic imagination in establishing the ideological vagaries of the present (for instance), and more interested in a single, monolithic, idealist notion of 'truth.' ... The reason why history was the proper subject for epic, said Carlyle, was that history was true, and that truth had the highest ethical value" (Roberts 1999: 11). Unlike the high modernist long poems that followed it, Hodgson's poem is neither engaged in a melancholy sifting through the ruins of tradition, nor does it propose self-consciously artificial replacements for those demolished myths, but this does not necessarily make it conservative in contrast to modernist innovation. Margaret Dickie notes at the conclusion of her study of T.S. Eliot, Hart Crane (whom Lovecraft knew), William Carlos Williams, and Ezra Pound that modernism

> is, at its most inclusive, a movement that started with a radical rejection of the conditions of modern life and developed into an awareness of its own limits, a nostalgic regret at such knowledge, and a retrospective appeal over it to a better knowledge. It was, from start to finish, conservative in the sense that it aimed to conserve and to destroy only in order to conserve.
> (Dickie 1986: 161; see also 1–17)

Like his weird fiction, we can best think of Hodgson's poetry not as Victorian or high modernist but as pulp modernist, an appropriate in-between space for an innovator of the weird.[1]

Hodgson's 940-line *Voice of the Ocean* was published posthumously in a tiny edition at his widow Bessie Farnsworth Hodgson's expense in 1921. Its precise date of composition is unknown, but according to Jane Frank, editor of Hodgson's *Lost Poetry*, manuscript evidence suggests that he "wrote most of his poetry between 1899, when he returned from his last tour of duty in the Merchant Navy, and 1906, whilst living in Blackburn" (LP: vi). Although at one point Hodgson considered "printing one volume of my verse, and sending it round to a lot of the big papers and critics" in order to "gain some little literary reputation" so that editors would "be less afraid of my stuff, and I might be able to sell some of my stories" (U: 40), he wrote far too

---

[1] See note 5 in Chapter One above.

much poetry for it to have been merely a means to an end, and a 940-line metaphysical phantasmagoria would have been unlikely to open the doors of magazine editors. Most of Hodgson's short verse, little of which is weird or cosmic, utilizes strict meters and relatively strict rhyme, although he rarely works in traditional forms other than the ballad.[2] Instead, he experiments with different mixtures of meter, rhyme scheme, and stanza pattern from poem to poem, probably as a consequence of his admiration for Poe (whose "Raven" stanza-form he uses to mock his own frustrations with publishers in "Nevermore" [1905]). His longer poems, most of which focus on the sea as either an arena for sublime experience or a symbol of death and immortality, are generally in blank verse. Hodgson spent a decade at sea during adolescence and early adulthood, an experience that his stories suggest left him ambivalent: although he loved being out at sea, where he felt himself to be transported beyond the trivialities of everyday life to a near-infinite expanse of space, time, and spirit, he loathed the brutality of tyrannical officers and the indignity of the common sailor's lot. His nautical verse, however, focuses almost exclusively on the experience of sublimity.

The Voice of the Ocean takes the overall form of a catechism in which various souls, some dead and others on the verge of death, question the ancient soul of the Sea about what they should expect in the next world, in the process expressing common misapprehensions regarding divine justice, time, and eternal life that the Sea corrects. Several of Hodgson's short, non-weird poems also personify the sea, addressing it as a protective parent who, at the speaker's death, will "encompass me,/And let thine arms, encompassing, avail/My shuddering soul until God's wrath abates" ("O Parent Sea!," LP: 89). In "Thou Living Sea," the wise parental sea counsels the poet "With many tongues … /With voices from the dead" (LP: 90), but in "The Calling of the Sea" he is compelled to ask, "What are the words said?/Has any caught them?/Are they the whisperings of the long dead?" (LP: 131). The lack of an answer to these questions unsettles the parental and pedagogical relationship:

> Yet none is able,
>   On the wide Ocean,
> O'er the great surface of the deep sea,
>   Tossed by the motion
>   Of its wild waters,
> Now, or forever, to tell unto me
>   What it is saying,
>   Jeering or praying,
>   Or whispering warnings
>   Unto its daughters
>   Of somber dawnings
>   Ushering mornings
> Pregnant with terrors the dead only see.
>
> (LP: 132)

---

[2] Aside from *The Voice of the Ocean*, Hodgson's only other clearly weird/cosmic poem is "Mors Deorum" (LP: 26–34), a dramatic monologue spoken by a dead hero restored to life in order to prevent Death from slaying the old pagan gods, a task at which he necessarily fails.

In these short lyrics, although the poet can address the sea, he cannot comprehend the reply it makes, perhaps because he is still living and thus unable to recognize the voices of the dead through which the sea speaks.

Surprisingly, in light of the very little we know about Hodgson's literary preferences, his personification of the sea as an inscrutable counsellor speaking in the voices of both a parent and the dead echoes Walt Whitman's colloquys with the sea in "Crossing Brooklyn Ferry" (1856–81) and the "Sea-Drift" poems, especially "Out of the Cradle Endlessly Rocking" and "As I Ebb'd with the Ocean of Life" (1859–81). "Crossing Brooklyn Ferry" opens with the direct address, "Flood-tide below me! I see you face to face!" (Whitman 1982: 307). Although the ferry in which Whitman rides is crossing not open sea but rather the East River to and from Manhattan, during flood tide the water of the Atlantic surges into the Upper Bay and from there into the East River, transforming it into a limb of the sea. The speaker's later address to "you that shall cross from shore to shore years hence" (Whitman 1982: 308), whom he confidently tells that "It avails not, time nor place—distance avails not,/I am with you, you men and women of a generation, or ever so many generations hence" (Whitman 1982: 308), directly anticipates Hodgson's imagined temporal leaps across cosmological timespans. In "Out of the Cradle," the speaker calls the sea "the savage old mother incessantly crying,/To the boy's soul's questions sullenly timing, some drown'd secret hissing,/To the outsetting bard" (Whitman 1982: 392), and in "As I Ebb'd" he admonishes the sea, "Cease not your moaning you fierce old mother,/Endlessly crying for your castaways, but fear not, deny not me,/Rustle not up so hoarse and angry against my feet as I touch you or gather from you" (Whitman 1982: 396). And the sea's answer to "outsetting bard" Whitman's entreaties in "Out of the Cradle," which was titled "A Word Out of the Sea" in an early draft, has become one of his defining passages:

> The word final, superior to all,
> Subtle, sent up—what is it?—I listen;
> Are you whispering it, and have been all the time, you sea-waves?
> Is that it from your liquid rims and wet sands?
> Whereto answering, the sea,
> Delaying not, hurrying not,
> Whisper'd me through the night, and very plainly before daybreak,
> Lisp'd to me the low and delicious word death,
> And again death, death, death, death.
>
> (Whitman 1982: 393)[3]

Whitman is granted this monosyllabic "key, the word up from the waves,/The word of the sweetest song and all songs" (Whitman 1982: 394), only at the end of "Out of the Cradle," but *The Voice of the Ocean* begins with it, and likewise with the unintelligible "whisperings of the long dead" that Hodgson heard in the ocean's voice, expanding

---

[3] Some scholars argue that "Out of the Cradle" alludes to stanzas fifteen and sixteen of Poe's "The Raven" ("'Prophet!' said I, 'thing of Evil! –prophet still, if bird or devil!'") when the mature Whitman who narrates reports, "Demon or bird! (said the boy's soul,)/Is it indeed toward your mate you sing? Or is it really to me?" (Whitman 1982: 392). See Killingsworth 2007: 53. This intertextuality increases the likelihood that Hodgson may have read Whitman's poem.

them into a colloquy of primally inhuman and no longer human speech that must be translated for us, the living, to read.

The poem is narrated in an unobtrusive, almost impersonal first person by one "who had been wise through dying soon" (VO: 8), an eerie premonition of Hodgson's own early death at age forty in the First World War. Hodgson's long poem is not only more exploratory in both form and content than his short poems, but it is also more formally varied than other major weird long poems such as Clark Ashton Smith's "The Hashish-Eater" (1920), which encloses a hallucinatory, galaxy-spanning battle in a blank-verse narrative, and H.P. Lovecraft's *Fungi from Yuggoth* (1929–30), which is a classical sonnet sequence on a range of weird themes. In contrast, Hodgson's narrator's framing reportage and many of the Sea's answers to questions are in blank verse, while most of the questions asked by the souls, as well as some of the Sea's answers, are set off in short lines (dimeter or trimeter) that rhyme in a variety of patterns, in order to individualize the speakers and their worries. Lord Byron's *Manfred* (1816–17), which alternates between the blank verse generally spoken by mortals and the variously rhymed stanza-forms spoken by the Spirits and Destinies, may be Hodgson's touchstone here, particularly in light of the overt defiance of Christian orthodoxy his predecessor's protagonist expresses in the face of death and damnation. Similarly, some of Hodgson's dead or dying souls express despair: "Thou Bodyless Thing in the sky,/Wherefore am I?/For why so alone?/Ah! Master of Death,/For why this mad breath?" (VO: 12). Others speak out of pride and a sense of joy that evoke William Blake's early lyrics: "Not even Thou, O God, canst rob/From me this hour of earthly joy,/And afterwards, Thou may'st destroy/My very soul—I care no jot/If in Thy Hell I lie and rot!" (VO: 26). Yet others speak out of scorn: "Get Thee to Thy kingdom, God!/I laugh at Thee!/Thou threatenest with a rod/That doth not frighten me" (VO: 28). In any case, all the narrative elements the poem contains are confined to brief episodes of discontinuous temporality that leap from the creation of the world to the end of time, and hence do not constitute an Aristotelian unity of action.

The poem begins with "small talk" among a ship's passengers, including "one of highest breed and leanest brain" who unknowingly goads the Sea into speech by stating, "'Tis foolishness this vain belief in God" (VO: 7). Speaking not to the oblivious living passengers but to the anxious dying souls, the Sea retorts, "I have seen God!" (VO: 8) and goes on to tell an intriguingly modified version of the creation story from Genesis in cosmological (VO: 9) and biogenetic terms (VO: 10). This story and all subsequent exchanges are "Heard and interpreted" (VO: 8) by the prematurely deceased narrator. In sharp contrast to the Bible's dark and formless void, the Sea asserts that "In the abyss of time, when God was young,/ ... heaven was one void of holy light/When the great stars slept in the future's womb,/And human atoms were undreamt of dust" (VO: 9). Then, as in Genesis, God spoke, "And at the sound the solemn light was gapped" (VO: 9) by the condensation of the galaxy ("The nebula of unformed suns," [VO: 9]), which "grew/Smaller, by aeons, casting off loose worlds,/Their flaming children, which in turn gave birth/To lesser worlds of fire, and so was born/The universe of suns and worlds, of which/This fireless world is part ... " (VO: 9). Note that God is described as "young," perhaps in the way that Olaf Stapledon's Star Maker is described as "a developing, an awakening spirit ... an infant deity, restless, eager, mighty, but without clear will ... limited also by his immaturity" (Stapledon 2004: 233–4). Since God, though young, is gendered male, it follows that the Sea is gendered female in this poem, although that only becomes clear when it describes its "wondrous task": "Pregnant I was" (VO: 10), convulsed with ages-long labor pains that ultimately result in "Ten-thousand times ten-thousand souls new born,/Like scarcely fallen snow-flakes on dark rocks" (VO: 11). These were not human souls, however, until "In his right time, man was evolved, and grew/ Into his present shape, with underneath/His heavier flesh, a soul such as was born/In that supremely distant time" (VO: 11). The verb "evolved" reminds us that a recurring aspect of Hodgson's writing is the attempt to re-interpret and reconcile human spiritual striving with scientific materialism, particularly Darwin's theory of evolution,[4] an attempt which anticipates Stapledon's similar project.[5]

Following this revisionary account of humanity's indirectly divine or spiritual origin, the souls of the dead and dying begin their questioning of the Sea. All told, a dozen human souls speak, seeking answers to their loneliness (VO: 12), their lack of success in spreading the word of "God's bounty" (VO: 13-4), the pain of last farewells and the fear of being forgotten (VO: 15, 16, 17), the exhaustion and despair of unvalued labor (VO: 37-8). To these the Sea responds sympathetically, consoling them with promises of future fellowship, remembrance, and the restoration of relationships. Later questioners ask or make assertions about immortality and redemption, to which the Sea responds more aggressively in correcting their errors, most importantly their dread of divine judgment and punishment after such short, confused lives (VO: 18, 20-1, 23-4). The Sea responds sharply to these fears: "There is no need for judgment. Thou shalt live/In many lives among thy deeds until/Thou shalt attain to the Last Life" (VO: 18-19). While the notion that the individual soul constructs the conditions of its eternal fate through its actions in life concurs with some versions of Christian doctrine, the rejection of judgment and the centrality of reincarnation in this description of the soul's fate are clearly heretical, as one soul frankly insists: "O, Sea,/I cannot e'er agree/With thy strange teachings, which seem blasphemy/To me!" (VO: 20). However, readers of Hodgson's novels *The House on the Borderland* (1908) and *The Night Land* (1912) will recognize the claims made for reincarnation as central to the metaphysics of eternal love that dictates the actions of the Recluse in the former book and those of the unnamed narrator X in the latter.

Thereafter the Sea takes pains to explain its claims in more detail, first by narrating a weird and grotesquely comic dream vision of the resurrection of the flesh on Judgment Day:

> from the heaving earth I saw drive up
> The misty forms of long forgotten dead.
> Forgotten now no longer, fast they came,
> Piecemeal and limbless—dreadful in their shrouds;
> But growing every moment into shape
> As flying limbs came jostling through the air
> In anxious haste to take a rightful place.
>
> (VO: 21)

---

[4] This attempt to synthesize Christian and Darwinist accounts of human origin conforms to those found in Hodgson's other works, for example, *The House on the Borderland*, as we noted in the previous chapter.

[5] See the Envoi for a discussion of this relationship.

Their clothes are not resurrected, however, so they stand naked, "Their manifold transgressions written large/Upon each others' naked breasts; so thus/Each man, each woman, knew the others' worth/At once, for all time, in a single glance" (VO: 22). In a phrase alluding to Matthew 8:22 and Luke 9:60, God commands, "Let the dead/Make haste their dead to bury from Mine eyes" (VO: 22), so each revenant tries to bury the others, with the result that all end up buried. Although God is saddened by this, he also "grasped/The grim, pathetic humour of it all" (VO: 23). In other words, God makes no explicit judgment of them; instead, He commands them to judge, condemn, and punish themselves, thereby continuing to act in all their later lives as they do in earlier ones, for example by terrifying themselves with the fear of hell.

At this point the poem indirectly confirms another deviation from Christian orthodoxy, perhaps the most shocking one of all, that has been implied all along. The most anguished of the dead souls addresses itself desperately, not to the Sea, but to Jesus Christ:

> My Jesu, hear my prayer;
> Turn not away; O Christ, turn not away!
> The fiend has me!—Jesu, my Christ, *assist*!
> Thou would'st not leave me, Christ—No! Jesu, No!
> Think of the PIT, my Christ! Think of the PIT!
> The gaping, hideous PIT!—God save my soul
> From this vast foulness!
>
> (VO: 23-4)

This passage contains the only references to Christ in the entire poem, which are not only attributed to a soul driven mad by fear of eternal punishment, but also implicitly dismissed when the Sea refutes the threat of a literal Hell, advising all the souls to "learn that heaven and hell/Are made up of thy deeds of good and harm" (VO: 30). The spiritual rebirth into Christ required especially by the stricter forms of Protestantism has no role to play in Hodgson's metaphysics, which may have set him at odds with his father, an Anglican minister.

The terrified soul's self-torture saddens the Sea, who points out, "How dreadful is religion that doth teach/Such terror to an erring soul!" (VO: 25). It then patiently restates and explicates its most audacious claim:

> Then know that every death thou diest leads on
> To a much fuller life, including all
> That thou hast thought and lived in those before.
> And as a fuller life implies more power
> To live, to understand, to suffer pain,
> So may'st thou comprehend that on each life
> Shall stand thy cause to suffer pain or joy
> When the Last Life be reached, and thou shalt live
> In culmination of all joy and grief
> That thou hast ever known in all thy lives.
>
> (VO: 26)

Although such reincarnation contradicts the Christian eschatology of a single ultimate resurrection of the immortal soul (with or without the body), it corresponds in a number of ways to ideas that spiritualist organizations such as the Theosophical Society had been investigating (or even promoting) in England since the 1880s.

Founder H.P. Blavatsky's first, rather disorganized articulation of Theosophical syncretism, *Isis Unveiled* (1877), includes brief passages that distinguish the Hindu and Buddhist concepts of reincarnation from the Greek concept of metempsychosis (Blavatsky 1877, I: 351–3) and describe the reincarnation of Buddhist lamas (Blavatsky 1877, I: 437–8, II: 598–602), but critics' attacks on the book's inconsistencies (e.g., the presumption on p.12 that metempsychosis and reincarnation are identical, contradicting her later differentiation) compelled her to clarify the doctrine in the 1886 article "Theories about Reincarnation and Spirits" (Blavatsky 1877: appendix, 31–44), where she writes:

> Like the revolutions of a wheel, there is a regular succession of death and birth, the moral cause of which is the cleaving to existing objects, while the instrumental cause is Karma (the power which controls the universe, prompting it to activity), merit and demerit. It is therefore, the great desire of all beings who would be released from the sorrows of successive birth, to seek the destruction of the moral cause, the cleaving to existing objects, or evil desire.
>
> (Blavatsky 1877: appendix 37)

Karmic "merit and demerit" apparently correspond to Hodgson's "good and harm" as the defining conditions of reincarnation. *Isis Unveiled* is doubly relevant as a source for Hodgson's ideas because it also introduces English readers to the vast temporalities of Hindu and Buddhist cosmology, including the term "kalpa," referring to an interval of 4.32 billion years, that Hodgson utilizes in *The House on the Borderland* (see Blavatsky 1877, 1: 32). Emily Alder asserts, apropos of *The Night Land*, that its "setting provides the vast temporal scope required to explore the Theosophical notion of a soul's successive reincarnations" (Alder 2007: 131), and *The Voice of the Ocean* similarly articulates Hodgson's variation on this notion across cosmological timescales and in explicitly eschatological terms.

I argued in the Introduction that Hodgson's phenomenology and epistemology of the weird, expressed in the final Carnacki story "The Hog," resemble Spinoza's conception of mind-body parallelism; here, it seems to me that Hodgson echoes both Spinoza's immanent ethics of seeking joyful encounters that increase the body's and mind's powers to act, to think, and to feel, and Nietzsche's Eternal Return in its ethical form as a principle of selection, which Gilles Deleuze paraphrases as follows: "*whatever you will, will it in such a way that you also will its eternal return*" (Deleuze 68). Further Spinozian and Nietzschean echoes follow: in response to a soul that cannot tell right from wrong as a result of both the disagreements among religions and the unreliability of culturally prejudiced conscience, the Sea declares (in language similar to Spinoza's critique of superstition in his *Theological-Political Treatise*),

> Reason in your religions had no place,
> Or if it had the place was out of sight.
> 	I know that to do right is hard enough;
> But harder far when there are diff'rent views,
> Holding that this is right, or that is wrong,
> Without the intervention of hard sense.
>
> (VO: 35–6)

It then proposes a simple ethical principle: "Ye want to know what's 'Right' and what is 'Wrong,'/Methinks 'tis all the same as 'Good' and 'Harm'" (VO: 37). This too seems comparable to Spinoza's ethics of composition, for which good is any encounter of bodies that increases the body's power of acting and/or the mind's power of thinking, and bad is any encounter that decreases them, as well as to Nietzsche's distinction between universal and abstract Good and Evil on the one hand, and concrete good and bad relative to specific forms of life on the other. The continuation of this passage, which contrasts the "active" performance of Good and Harm to inaction, supports this Nietzschean reading not only in defining the contrast in terms of active and reactive will but also in denigrating the latter as a "life so negative" (VO: 37), implying thereby that active will is the basis of affirmative life (and, contrary to strict Protestant dogma, that good deeds are essential to one's achievement of a joyous Last Life [VO: 40–1]).

The ethical doctrine propounded here further implies, in place of the monotheistic conception of time that comes to an end in eternity, the prospect of mastery over time as a consequence of affirmative life: "When thou art dead, time's space shall be thy road;/Thou shalt pass back or forward as thou wilt" (VO: 27–8). This freedom of time leads into the second unquestionably weird or cosmic interlude, when the sequence of human souls questioning the Sea is interrupted by the combined voices of many nonhuman souls, the long-dead inhabitants of an alien world whose time ran out long before ours began:

> 	because of length of days,
> *Our* time drew near for death. Our blazing suns
> Gave but a saddening light which dwindled on
> From red to deeper red, until in gloom
> We sank into vast graves of all that had
> Lived in our bosoms in the days of light.
>
> (VO: 31)

Like that of the dead aliens, the world of the Great Redoubt in *The Night Land* will experience a darkening prior to its invasion by the ab-humans, who will ultimately supplant humankind.

Attempting to mollify these extraterrestrials, the Sea asks for "Patience, thou deathly worlds!" (VO: 31), in the firm belief that

> A lonely universe of silent worlds,
> Dead aeons before thou had'st been nebula,

May on some orbit vast be nearing thee,
Though half eternity should pass ere they
Meet thee in full career. Ah! then the skies
Shall witness thy new birth, as in one bound
Dead world shall leap unto dead world, and each
Shall flash from death to life within one breath—
To life for some long age of mightier life.

(VO: 32)

Not only individuals, it seems, but entire species and civilizations will be tested by the cycle of reincarnations, no matter how far away in space and time they lie.[6]

The last voice to address the Sea may not be a dying soul, but rather a dreamer who dreams "of future times,/Of the most future times this world shall know" (VO: 42; in this he resembles X in *The Night Land*), allowing him to report how the Sea will face its own lingering and lonely death. This lengthy passage (VO: 42–5) abandons catechism for apocalyptic prophecy. At first sight, the Sea appears "Dead in the arms of Time, who once held me/Likewise when dead" (VO: 42), but then the speaker reports hearing "a sad, strange voice, despairingly/Come wailing o'er thy wastes" (VO: 42), which he realizes is the Sea's. The dead planet echoes its soul the Sea's dying song, which the speaker cannot reproduce because it is "past human tongue/To sing"; he is reduced to "conjur[ing] up its sense, though haltingly, and lacking all its power,/And all the sad'ning terror and the woe/Which trembled through its undertones" (VO: 43). This reflexive acknowledgment of the limits of human language (and understanding) reminds us that the entire poem is staged as an overheard conversation among entities that we cannot perceive, whose voices we can neither hear nor comprehend, and thereby it retroactively puts the entire poem under erasure, as a substitute or stand-in for itself.

This paradoxical—or even perverse—self-cancellation, coming as it does almost 900 lines into the poem, belatedly contests Whitman's relentlessly affirmative, "face to face" command to the flood-tide (Whitman 1982: 307) to "Receive the summer sky, you water, and faithfully hold it till all downcast eyes have time to take it from you!" (Whitman 1982: 313), an imperative that only the "strong and delicious word" death (Whitman 1982: 393) empowers the poet to utter. Hodgson's Sea is no Transcendentalist mirror of the human mind, to recognize and be recognized in turn, so it cannot address or be addressed, let alone commanded, in human language. But despite his rejection of an immediate communicative reciprocity between human and nonhuman or living and dead, Hodgson nevertheless suggests that the partial reciprocity of a pedagogical relationship between soul and Sea can be mediated by translation, understood in its etymological sense as a "carrying across" from the language of death to that of life, and

---

[6] The Sea's address to the dead alien world contains another possible allusion to Spinoza's metaphysics: on VO: 31–2, the Sea justifies that world's fate by asserting that "God's Might is right, because that self-same Might/Is governed and directed by a Mind/Born of the awful strength which lives in God." Although the terms used to recall Edmund Burke's conservative rejection of the French Revolution, they can more fittingly be read through Spinoza's gnomic argument that each thing has "*Tantum juris, quantum potentiae*" (as much right as it has power), and so God has infinite right because He has infinite power.

performed by one who, like Hodgson himself, lived and died in constant contact with the nonhuman sea. Like Whitman before him, he demonstrates that the poet is the only translator who can reveal that the sounds of wave and surf are actually speech and that the Sea is really a maternal "she."

Fifteen years after Hodgson's poem was published, however, Wallace Stevens's "The Idea of Order at Key West" (1936) would render such translation impossible:

> She sang beyond the genius of the sea.
> The water never formed to mind or voice,
> Like a body wholly body ...
>   ... yet its mimic motion
> Made constant cry, caused constantly a cry,
> That was not ours although we understood,
> Inhuman, of the veritable ocean.
>
> (Stevens 1997: 105)

This is not the inhumanity of a nonhuman intelligence, whether a maternal sea responsive to our concerns if we can but recognize it or a mystery akin to Stanislaw Lem's Solaris, but that of a nonintelligence, mere matter incapable of recognition: "It may be that in all her phrases stirred/The grinding water and the gasping wind;/But it was she and not the sea we heard" (Stevens 1997: 105). Despite their perceptible patterns of rhythm and sonority, the sounds of the sea are noise, not words. As Armin Paul Frank notes, for Stevens (and the modernists generally), "The intentional creative action of the poet and the materiality of matter are opposites. It is, therefore, not for nothing that right at the outset, 'she,' the maker of song, and the maker of physical noises, the 'sea,' are placed at the opposite ends of the [first] line" (Frank 1981: 86). Thus for Stevens, Hodgson's poetic ventriloquism, which makes the sea appear to speak, is illusory.

Stevens's critique lay in the future that Hodgson would not live to see, though. His abandoned, personified Sea bemoans its solitude and fear, "half-way between/The loneliness of two eternities" where it "brood[s] apart upon a dying world,/And pray[s] that I were something more, or less,/ Than what I am" (VO: 44), and following its plea "Haste thee, Death!" it falls silent for the last time. This drawn-out, entropic vision of the Sea's death echoes the devolution of life to primitive aquatic organisms that H.G. Wells's Time Traveller finds 30 million years in the future, and it differs radically from the oceans' spectacular fate in *The Night Land*:

> The Valley [in which the Redoubt lies] had come, as you shall mind, when the earth did split; and this thing was, in truth, like to be thought that same Ending of the World, which all Nations have been taught to believe shall come. For in verity, when the world did split and burst, and the oceans rushed downward into the earth, and there was fire, and storms, and a mighty chaos, surely it was proper to think that the End had come.
>
> (NL: 211–2)

The water of the seas flows through the cracks in the earth's crust down into the semi-molten mantle, where it turns instantaneously into steam, the pressure of which further shatters the crust, releasing even more subterranean fire. By the time X tells his tale, the only body of water left on earth that is large enough to be called a sea is found in the sheltered enclave called the Country of Seas, where it is bordered on one side by a wall of volcanoes and on the other by a revived primeval forest.

Following the Sea's last words in the poem, the final speaker awakens and falls silent as dawn breaks, drawing us back to the poem's present, uncounted millennia earlier. The concluding image, of daybreak transformed into a "sea of trembling hues" that casts its "beauteous sprays of light" upon the "dayless shore," echoes the "void of holy light" at the creation of the cosmos (l. 51) and at the same time absorbs the rest of the world—including the narrator and the reader—into the sea and into the sea's voice:

> And afar the world
> Reached up her sombre hills among the glow,
> Into the pure, ethereal waters of
> That sea of trembling hues which spumed and beat
> Softly upon the shore of night, and surged
> In beauteous sprays of foamy light above
> The gloomy cliffs that edge the dayless shore,
> And poured its living foam upon the world
> In cataracts of light ….
>
> (VO: 46)

The closing line's doubleness—cataracts can refer to large waterfalls or to the blurring of vision—restores the reader to a material world rendered double by the poem's own performative act. Thus the reader, like the dead narrator, has been guided by the Sea "beneath time's crust" and along a path that leads from the beginning of time, through repeated reincarnations, to a place that is both ethically and corporeally "near on the life which is to be" (VO: 41), a place that is metaphorically indistinguishable from the Sea itself.

In this, the culmination of his poetic effort, Hodgson has tried to make his readers figuratively see the sea's sublime spatial scale and temporal scope through his double's eyes, hear the sea's constantly calling yet indecipherable voice through his double's ears, and thereby learn the sea's metaphysical lesson as he himself has learned it. That lesson is essentially a vitalist one, as the parallels with Spinoza and Nietzsche have already implied, and it also resonates with Henri Bergson's conception of "creative evolution" in his 1907 book with that title, which Hodgson may well have encountered.[7] Hodgson's vitalism appears in expository form in several of his fictions, for example near the end of *The Night Land*, when X admits that

> [I]t not to offend me to suppose that there to be this inward force peculiar to each shaping of all bodies that do hold that wondrous quality of Life …. [I]t doth be

---

[7] On the resemblance between Hodgson's vitalism and Bergson's, see Alder 2020: 184.

reasonable to suppose that the Force or Spirit of the Human be peculiar to the Human, whether that it to be a Cause of Life, or the Result of that which hath been evolved out of a Condition. And whether it to be the one way or the other, you to know that where this Force or Spirit be found untainted, there is man; and I to be not opposed to think that Man doth be constant alway in matters of fundament, and neither to have been ever truly different; though something modified in the body and surely, in the first, all undeveloped in the lovely things of the spirit, because that there to be no call to these. Yet, presently, they likewise to come, and to act upon the flesh with refinings; and likewise, mayhap, there to be some act of the flesh upon the spirit …

(NL: 521)

That novel's faux-antiquarian style somewhat obscures the ideas; a more succinct and general version of this same doctrine appears at the beginning of the short story "The Derelict", as we noted in the Introduction: "Life is a thing, state, fact, or element, call-it-what-you-like, which requires the *Material* through which to manifest itself, and that given the *Material,* plus the Conditions, the result is Life. In other words, that Life is an evolved product, manifested through Matter and bred of Conditions … " (CF 3: 235). In his long poem, the Sea is the first living entity created by a developing God, its material body acting simultaneously as the mother and as the cradle of all subsequent life, but in sharp contrast to Whitman's unbounded future, Hodgson's thermodynamic pessimism demands that its rocking ultimately come to an end, along with human time itself.

9

Beautiful Things Hid in the Abyss of the Years

Like *The House on the Borderland*, *The Night Land* is multiply estranged, both formally and temporally, from its readers. After its title page (which also contains a subtitle, "A Love Tale"), readers find a page containing only the heading "The Dreams that are only Dreams." Is this a second subtitle to the book, a section title, or perhaps an epigraph? Following this mysterious interpolation comes a brief preface that defines "Human Love" as a relation in which "the Man to be an Hero and a Child before the Woman; and the Woman to be an Holy Light of the Spirit and an Utter Companion and in the same time a Glad Possession unto the Man." This preface turns out to be a condensation of two unapologetically idealized paeans to romantic love from chapter XIV, "On the Island," when the narrator X's wounds from battle compel him to depend upon the strength and resourcefulness of Naani, the Maid whom he has previously protected from harm (NL: 497, 510); although titled "Preface," this paratext functions more like an epigraph in its establishment of the fundamental values of reciprocal commitment and responsibility embodied in the "love tale." Following the table of contents is the first page of chapter one, "Mirdath the Beautiful," which opens with an untitled set of mournful verses: "And I cannot touch her face/And I cannot touch her hair,/And I kneel to empty shadows—" (NL: 11). The only other chapter to open thus is chapter four, "The Hushing of the Voice," which cites five lines of a poem that X wrote to his beloved Mirdath following her death in childbirth; in the first paragraphs of that chapter, the Maid Naani reads the lines in a dream of the past and recites one telepathically to X, confirming his sense that she is the reincarnation of Mirdath (NL: 71-2). Although these paratexts do not strictly parallel those of *The House on the Borderland*, the poems of grief clearly establish a similar existential dilemma for the narrators at each novel's outset.[1]

In their recursive sequence, these physical features of the book's layout reflect its temporal structure. The opening chapter is set in a past century, a fact that the reader must infer from both the language used and the customs displayed, but whether that century is supposed to be the eighteenth, the seventeenth, or (as Brian Stableford suggests [1985: 98]) some medieval epoch cannot be determined, for Hodgson has written it (and the rest of the novel, as we saw in Chapter One) in an alternative

---

[1] Jane Frank notes that, despite Hodgson's lifelong dedication to the writing of verse, he was unable to publish any poems on their own; "Those few [of his] poems that saw publication were insinuated into his novels and collections of short stories" (LP: v).

English as artificial as the faux medieval language that William Morris used in his romances, but less direct and elegant. The author's awareness of the difficulties his artifice entails is confirmed late in the book when X addresses the reader directly: "surely all this to be plain to you, and to be over-plain; for, in verity, I tell to you, and over-tell, until that I should be weary; and mayhap you to be the more so" (NL: 427). The word "over-tell" captures well the ambivalent literariness of Hodgson's style in this novel. The opening chapter tells of the gentleman X's first meeting with Lady Mirdath, his developing desire for her, her impudence that almost ends their romance, their marriage and her death in childbirth; these elements will be echoed in his later relationship with Naani, the Maid from the Lesser Redoubt. The second chapter, "The Last Redoubt," begins with his expression of anguished grief (not unlike that of the Recluse), the intensity of which is suddenly ameliorated by what seem to be strange dreams:

> I have, at night in my sleep, waked into the future of this world, and seen strange things and utter marvels, and known once more the gladness of life; for I have learned the promise of the future, and have visited in my dreams those places where in the womb of Time, she and I shall come together, and part, and again come together.
>
> (NL: 33)

Are these the "Dreams that are only Dreams" mentioned in the paratexts, or something more?

Whatever they are, they serve as his means of time travel: the tale he will tell is of his last "dream" of the earth's last millennia, which becomes as real, and ultimately more real, to him and to us than the ancient present from which he sets out. As in *The House on the Borderland*, no mechanism beyond narrative itself carries him to the far future, and this future is consistent with that depicted in the earlier novel, as we will see. X immediately confronts the problem of expressing the magnitude of the temporal abyss that separates the past from that far distant future:

> How shall you ever know, as I know in verity, of the greatness and reality and terror of the thing that I would tell plain to all; for we, with our puny span of recorded life must have great histories to tell, but the few bare details we know concerning years that are but a few thousand in all; and I must set out to you in the short pages of this my life there, a sufficiency of the life that had been, and the life that was, both within and without that mighty Pyramid, to make clear to those who may read, the truth of that which I would tell; and the histories of that great Redoubt dealt not with odd thousands of years; but with very millions; aye, away back into what they of that Age conceived to be the early days of the earth, when the sun, maybe, still gloomed dully in the night sky of the world. But of all that went before, nothing, save as myths …
>
> (NL: 38–9)

Just as we call "history" the interval of time past that is accessible through writing and symbolic artifacts, and we can only know what happened before, in the "prehistoric," in an abstract or general way through indirect signs, so do the people of the fortress-like Redoubt consider "true" only those records that date from the extinction of the sun; all that went before, all that we think of as the flowering of human civilization, is no more than a haphazard body of unreliable tales suspended between fact and fiction.

In further explanation of this predicament, X gives the example of the Road Where The Silent Ones Walk, which

> was, alone, the one [part of the Night Land] that was bred, long ages past, of healthy human labor. And on this point alone, had a thousand books, and more, been writ; and all contrary, and so to no end, as is ever the way in such matters. And as it was with the Road Where The Silent Ones Walk, so it was with all those other monstrous things ... whole libraries had there been made upon this and upon that; and many a thousand million mouldered into the forgotten dust of the earlier world.
>
> (NL: 40)

Much of the uncertain knowledge upon which he relies is drawn from an unusual metal book, a collection of first-hand accounts of the world's transformation into its future form, "that had lain forgot in a hid place in the Great Library through ten hundred thousand years, maybe, or less or more, for all that I had knowing" (NL: 126). X's situation (and therefore the reader's), in which knowledge has proliferated confusingly, been lost or mislaid, and then decayed into semi- or non-knowledge, echoes the alienated condition of modernity as Agamben interprets it through Benjamin:

> When a culture loses its means of transmission, man is deprived of reference points and finds himself wedged between, on the one hand, a past that incessantly accumulates behind him and oppresses him with the multiplicity of its now-indecipherable contents, and on the other hand a future that he does not yet possess and that does not throw any light on his struggle with the past.
>
> (Agamben 1999a: 108)

It is also practically the inverse of the Time Traveller's notion that the future would bring "wonderful advances upon our rudimentary civilization" (Wells 1934: 15): at least initially, he expected a continuous accumulation of human knowledge instead of radical discontinuity, and his final intellectual triumph is to incorporate the shocking dystopian future into knowledge, in other words, to transform nonhuman non-knowledge into human knowledge. This epistemological antinomy between the scientist's universe-enclosing "little brain" and the Redoubt's "monstrous archive" (Agamben 1999a: 108) marks the fundamental difference between science fiction and weird fiction.

X's first formulation of the temporal abyss in terms of (erosion or loss of) knowledge is later repeated, perhaps ironically, in terms of theological eschatology. As X descends the Mighty Slope that leads from the Night Land, past the Blue Flame, to the deeper plain where another, Lesser Redoubt is thought to stand, he reviews the history of geological catastrophe and human adaptation that produced the two Redoubts. Both sit on the floor of a vast valley, 100 to 150 miles deep (NL: 248), that was once part of the earth's mantle:

> The Valley had come, as you shall mind, when the earth did split; and this thing was, in truth, like to be thought that same Ending of the World, which all Nations have been taught to believe shall come. For in verity, when the world did split and burst, and the oceans rushed downward into the earth, and there was fire, and storms, and a mighty chaos, surely it was proper to think that the End had come. Yet was it, in truth, but the beginning of hope of a new Eternity of Life; so that out of the End came the Beginning, and Life out of Death, and Good out of that which did seem a dire matter.
>
> (NL: 211–2)

The old world ends in fire and fury, as so many religions and prophets have proclaimed, but that same fire gives birth to a new world unanticipated and virtually unimaginable by the old. The same event is also narrated in paleontological terms:

> Great Beasts were down there in that far depth ... And such there were in the Early World, and had now been bred in the Ending by those inward forces of Nature which did make the Valley a place of Good Warmth; so that there was, as it were, once more the Primal World born to give new birth unto such olden Monsters, and to others, new and Peculiar to that Age and Circumstance.
>
> (NL: 128–9)

This paradoxical space, simultaneously a new beginning and the final end, a theological eschaton and a prehuman fossil, is the setting for the two Redoubts and the entire action of the novel.

Not only have the spatial horizons of human control over the world shrunk to two edifices at the bottom of a deep vale, but much of humanity's accumulated knowledge has also been corroded and lost in time's abyss, while the objects of that knowledge have apparently vanished from the cosmos. As X notes, in a distant past still far in our future, the oceans infiltrated the earth's mantle and, flashing suddenly into steam, shattered the crust. All marine life is therefore extinct. The waning of the sun's light as it ages has darkened the sliver of sky that can be seen between the valley's walls, killed off most types of plants, and severely reduced the ambient temperature. The only light outside the Redoubts comes from volcanic fire-pits and chemical flames, strictly limiting the kinds of plants that can survive. Consequently, most herbivores and their predators have long gone extinct (except in small areas heated and illuminated by volcanoes, such as the verdant Country of Seas through which X passes on his mission to rescue Naani). Aside from arachnids, snakes, and rat-like mammals, only elaborately mutated animals such as the Night Hounds, monsters such as the Yellow Thing, and various human-monster hybrids, the "ab-humans," populate most of the chasm. The atmosphere has thinned, though in the Valley it remains dense enough for breathing (but not for flying machines, one of which X finds crashed in the Country of

Seas [NL: 208–11, 242–5]). No stars are visible in the sliver of sky, suggesting that the Recluse's vision from *The House on the Borderland* may have come true: not just our sun but all stars have been extinguished in the course of time, although whether they fell into the Green or the Dark Sun cannot be determined.

X awakens as a young man living in the Last Redoubt, which is described as a pyramidal metal fortress almost eight miles high, built to defend the last remnants of humanity from the bizarre and deadly creatures that control the rest of this narrow world. The Redoubt is powered by the Earth-Current, a non-renewable geophysical source of both mechanical and vital energy that not only runs the pyramid's utilities, labs, and defenses such as the Electric Circle (on the ground around the Redoubt) and the Air Clog ("an invisible Wall of Safety" like a force field [NL: 50]), but also generates the fertility of the titanic Underground Fields that extend miles beneath the fortress, where food is grown under artificial suns and reconstructed natural landscapes restore the human spirit.[2] Like the giant jade version of the Recluse's house on the Plain of Silence, the Last Redoubt is surrounded by immobile, immortal monstrosities which keep it under perpetual surveillance. As we noted in Chapter Six, these are the five Watchers, each identified by the compass point from which it watches the Redoubt and by the light source that illuminates it and separates it from the pyramid: the North-West Watcher, lit by the Red Pit of fire; the South-East Watcher, lit by the Torches; the South-West Watcher, lit by the Eye Beam; the North-East Watcher, lit by the blue ring above its head; and finally the Watcher of the South, the only watcher whose coming was witnessed by humans "A million years gone," when "came it out from the blackness of the South, and grew steadily nearer through twenty thousand years" before being blocked by the Glowing Dome (NL: 36–43). Some inhabitants of the Redoubt take these blockages to mean that "there were other forces than evil at work in the Night Lands" (NL: 43), a question to which we will return shortly.

As the names of the Watchers indicate, a certain impoverishment of language has accompanied the long, slow loss of the variegated material world we take for granted, and the concomitant loss of the knowledge humanity had begun to accumulate about it. Every item, object, and site in the Night Land has a descriptive phrase for a name: in addition to the Watchers, which are also called the Watching Things, the Redoubt is also surrounded by the Place of the Ab-Humans, the Thing that Nods, the Headland from which Strange Things Peer, the Country whence Comes the Great Laughter, and so on (NL: 40–2). Or perhaps the language is not actually impoverished, but instead the people have adopted a strict nominalism, abjuring the use of substantive categorizing or classifying terms for anything outside the Redoubt. Unlike scientific nomenclature, which attempts to encode signification into language by giving things distinct names that separate them into classes, species, or types, the language of the Night Land resists the classifying impulse as much as possible.

For example, anticipating Martin Heidegger's insistence that a thing is what emerges into presence or remains when we resist or lay aside the language and perspective of

---

[2] Alder describes the Underground Fields, and by extension the entire Redoubt, with the paradoxical Wellsian phrase "a defensively walled Eden" (from *A Modern Utopia*): "a safe garden in which the threat of the land outside is never quite forgotten" (Alder 2008: 125).

objectification, that is, the process by which subjects master objects (Heidegger 1971: 181–2), Hodgson's language here struggles to renounce both mastery and knowledge of its objects by using the word "thing" for most living, mobile entities other than bipeds: Watching Things, Yellow Thing, Bird-thing. To call them "things" is to say that we do not, and cannot, classify, know, control, or command them; for Heidegger, this also means that we cannot "secure" them and "follow them out" as objects of scientific classification:

> Entrapping representation, which secures everything in that objectness which is thus capable of being followed out, is the fundamental characteristic of the representing through which modern science corresponds to the real. But then the all-decisive work [*Arbeit*] that such representing performs in every science is that refining of the real which first in any way at all expressly works the real out into an objectness through which everything real is recast in advance into a diversity of objects for the entrapping securing.
>
> (Heidegger 1977: 168)

Instead of human thought "entrapping" things in scientific objectivity, things have entrapped humans within the Redoubt. Furthermore, the inhabitants of the Redoubt give bipedal entities names that highlight their most obvious difference from humankind, *Homo sapiens*, thus their distance from the one entity that can still be known (and mastered by the strict laws of the pyramid): Great Grey Men, Humped Men, Squat Men, Four-Armed Men, Beast-Men, and so on. There are a few exceptions to this, the most important of which are the Silent Ones, cloaked humanoid figures ten feet tall who move throughout the Night Land without fear of anything; their name, which connects them ambiguously to the most dangerous and unhuman site of all, the House of Silence, seems to imply a greater departure from human norms than other bipeds, although this is never clarified. Summing up this nominalist manner of speaking, Benjamin J. Robertson writes, "Hodgson's language suggests that things and their descriptions are utterly the same" (2018: 190n54).

When X "remembers" his future self, he recalls that he is a junior Monstruwacan, one of a group or caste of sentries who, in a perverse and almost certainly unconscious parody of Hegelianism, keep watch on the inscrutable Watchers and the other monsters and ab-humans who keep watch on the Redoubt, neither watcher finding recognition and hence subjectivity in the other's gaze. Just as the "things" evade objectification through their unknowability, they also evade subjectification by refusing reciprocal recognition; those correlative processes operate only within the pyramid, among the humans. The Monstruwacans' watchfulness is aided not only by mechanical technology such as the embrasures, View-Tables, and other machines, but also by two evolutionary developments of the human sensorium at odds with Well's vision of physical and mental decline: first, the Night Hearing, a form of telepathy that allows those who have it (including both X and Naani) to send and receive mental and emotional emanations, both human and otherwise, from afar; and second, the Master Word, a telepathic message that cannot be reproduced by nonhumans and so serves as an infallible password between human minds (NL: 52–4). These telepathic powers occur only rarely among the Redoubt's inhabitants, implying that they are natural results of evolution and not the products of eugenic breeding. Although the Monstruwacans possess "wondrous weapons ... that might slay without sound or flash at a full score miles and more" (NL: 93–4), those weapons waste the Earth-Current and attract attacks that would not otherwise take place, so the sentries "did very gladly keep a reasonable quietness, and refrained from aught that should wake that Land" (NL: 94). When anyone ventures outside the Redoubt, which rarely happens and should never happen without elaborate preparation (including not only training and research but also the implantation of a suicide capsule under the skin of the forearm [NL: 58]), he (and not she: women are not permitted to venture out into the Night Land, for fear that they will give birth to ab-human offspring) is armed only with the Diskos, a large, spinning circular saw mounted on an extendable handle and powered by the Earth-Current.

The reason such precautions are necessary can only be explained by reference to the aforementioned "myths" from the era preceding the death of the sun, which we first discussed in Chapter One above:

> The evil must surely have begun in the Days of the Darkening (which I might liken to a story which was believed doubtfully, much as we of this day believe the story of the Creation). A dim record there was of olden sciences (that are yet far off in our future) which, disturbing the unmeasurable Outward Powers, had allowed to pass the Barrier of Life some of those Monsters and ab-human creatures, which are so wondrously cushioned from us at this normal present. And thus there had materialised, and in other cases developed, grotesque and horrible Creatures, which now beset the humans of this world. And where there was no power to take on material form, there had been allowed to certain dreadful Forces to have power to affect the life of the human spirit. And this growing very dreadful, and the world full of lawlessness and degeneracy, there had banded together the sound millions, and built the Last Redoubt.
>
> (NL: 44–5)

In its hubris, humanity has the agency—acquired through its relentless application of scientific reason—to open up the world to the forces that will bring about its own ultimate extinction, but neither the prophetic foresight to predict the apocalyptic consequences of that action nor the messianic authority to redeem and eternalize itself. This is no *felix culpa*, no "fortunate fall" that holds out the gift of redemption as a divine intervention. Although the Redoubt has stood for millions or even billions of years by the time of the narrative, its end is pre-ordained: when the Earth-Current runs out, as it must according to the iron laws of Lord Kelvin's thermodynamics, the Redoubt will fall to its foes and life as we know it will cease on earth. This enormous interval, which I am calling messianic time, is what Brett Davidson calls a "long apocalypse," by which he means a slow-motion revelation or an unveiling by degrees: "nothing is revealed all at once; rather, they are worked out through the accumulation of knowledge over time" (2014: 185). This refers to an accumulation of knowledge on the part of the narrator and reader with respect to the radically transformed conditions of the far future, acquired through the time-lapse of dream projection and narrative compression and opening up the chance for X to seize a new time image; as we have already established, human knowledge as an archive of usable scientific information does not grow but rather shrinks as the cosmos to which it refers slowly decomposes and empties out over the course of aeons, so it can provide no basis for that new time image. In any case, nothing that X or we learn reveals the meaning of anything in the Night Land, nor provides any basis for expecting a messiah to come and show humanity the way to any eternity other than the self-evident one of heat death.

Even the successful completion of X's quest, which constitutes the central narrative of the novel and one of the most unusual events in the Redoubt's history, cannot change that ultimate fate of the world. When his Night Hearing puts him in contact with Naani, Mirdath's reincarnation who is an inhabitant of another, Lesser Redoubt, the defenses of which will soon be breached as a result of the failure of its Earth-Current, X must leave the security of the Great Redoubt to rescue her. His quest, "through death-haunted realms untrod by man for millions of years" (Lovecraft 2000: 60), bears apostolic witness to the ongoing passage of the messianic time that leads to the world's end, but without offering the chance of messianic salvation or an entry into eternity. X is no messiah: he goes not to bring truth to the world, nor to reclaim part of the world for human habitation, nor, as the Time Traveller does, to bring back its secrets for further exploitation, but to bring any survivors back to what is thereafter the only human space in the cosmos. He is no more than an emissary of the Redoubt's community, and an apostle faithful at first only to the transtemporal love that has drawn him across time's abyss. Just as the everyday time of the Recluse's battle with the swine-things clashed with the abyssal time of his visions, so does the far more exhaustively delineated temporality of X's journey through the Night Land contrast sharply with the incalculable temporal leap that brings him and his readers to the eve of time's end. He narrates every minute of every "day" (measured by a watch in hours, not relative solar motion, which no longer exists), every meal of food tablets and instant water powder (NL: 136–7), every interval of sleep, as well as the sudden excitement of his comparatively brief encounters with monsters such as Night Hounds, giant slugs, spiders, and several varieties of ab-humans including tusked swine-men (who recall the swine-things of *The House on the Borderland* [NL: 562–3]).

Although X describes most of the monsters and ab-humans he meets as "evil," they no more constitute an absolute, monotheistic conception of evil than the green and red globes orbiting the Central Suns in *The House on the Borderland* constitute simple allegories of heaven and hell. For example, once X finds Naani on the plain near the Lesser Redoubt, she tells him of its fall and her precarious survival: repeating the folly of their ancestors, her people, weakened by the failing of their Earth-Current, open their Redoubt's doors to the monsters, and in the ensuing confusion millions are slain trying to escape them (NL: 288–91). Shortly thereafter the couple witnesses another young woman, about Naani's age, slaughtered by a Squat Man (NL: 323–4). No force of good intervenes in either of these situations, but just a few pages later, when X and Naani are menaced by an invisible spinning thing described as "one of the great Evil Forces of the Land" (NL: 335), they are miraculously protected by a ring of light from "one of those sweet Powers of Goodness, that did strive ever to stand between the Forces of Evil and the spirit of man" (NL: 337). Andy Sawyer quite properly wonders,

> Why ... are only two saved and millions of others horribly killed? [O]ut of the episode comes a pervasive sense of doubt and despair which is at odds with any message that "Good" may be superior to "Evil." Such labels are inapplicable in *The Night Land*, where Humanity is the victim of contending forces and the "sweet Powers of Goodness" are unaffected by human notions of morality.
> (Sawyer 2014: 177)

Gradually it becomes clear that "Evil" in this context refers simply to those forces that seek to prey upon or otherwise destroy human life, and "Good" refers to the forces that sometimes, though not always, protect it; the morality here is Nietzschean, good versus bad relative to specific forms of life, rather than monotheistic, absolute Good versus absolute Evil. Such an immanent, anti-universalist conception of ethics corresponds to both the nominalist language of non-knowledge and the immanence of the emerging thermodynamic time image that promises no eternal salvation to follow its apostles' physical demise.

X arrives at a grasp of this time image gradually over the course of his quest, extracting it bit by bit from his transtemporal and intratemporal experiences. The catalyst for its crystallization, its arrival at completion so that it can be seized, is his passage through the Country of Seas, which he likens to the early earth in its restaging of biological evolution; even the ab-humans he finds there, the Humped Men, seem unlike the other ab-humans in being possibly still human, or rather teleologically prehuman—given time, X imagines they may develop into true humans (NL: 237–8). When he passes back through the Country of Seas with Naani, his perspective broadens further, to the point that he begins, quite unrealistically, to imagine the Country as potentially a "new Refuge" for the inhabitants of the pyramid (NL: 422), and ultimately the experience of unthreatening open space, light, seas, and forests burgeoning with life inspires the hypothesis "that maybe all diverse breeding not to be monstrous" (NL: 521). "Diverse breeding" functions as Hodgson's equivalent of the concept of hybridization or mutation, and in context refers to the origin of the ab-humans. X's words suggest that he is working through a momentous shift in attitude toward monstrosity or otherness, human and nonhuman alike, and thus a shift in time image as well:

> It not to offend me to suppose that there to be this inward force peculiar to each shaping of all bodies that do hold that wondrous quality of Life .... [I]t doth be reasonable to suppose that the Force or Spirit of the Human be peculiar to the Human, whether that it to be a Cause of Life, or the Result of that which hath been evolved out of a Condition. And whether it to be the one way or the other, you to know that where this Force or Spirit be found untainted, there is man; and I to be not opposed to think that Man doth be constant alway in matters of fundament, and neither to have been ever truly different; though something modified in the body and surely, in the first, all undeveloped in the lovely things of the spirit, because that there to be no call to these. Yet, presently, they likewise to come, and

to act upon the flesh with refinings; and likewise mayhap, there to be some act of the flesh upon the spirit; and so to the state of this Age of this our day, and to that far Age of which I do tell.

(NL: 521–2)

Here, in a passage that echoes the creation myth near the start of *The Voice of the Ocean*, X most extensively, almost dialectically articulates his own vision of subjectivity, transformation, and time, which is a vision of hesitant but genuine openness—he adds, "I do be ready to consider all matters, and do build no Walls about my Reason" (NL: 522)—that seems paradoxically at odds with the imminent (and also immanent) closure of his world, that is, the destruction of the Redoubt when the Earth-Current fails.

Naani helps bring about this shift in perspective and time image through performances of their transhistorical memories, performances that evoke the constellations of now-time and the past that Benjamin and Agamben insist can only take place in the enactment of messianic time. As they traverse the Country of Seas, she begins to sing an "olden love-song of the olden-world" (NL: 432) that brings her to tears, "but not to be cast down; but rather that she held her head upwise, as that she did walk in a glory" (NL: 433). There follows one of the most beautiful and evocative passages in the book, which is, perhaps surprisingly, made only the more powerful by the artifice of Hodgson's oft-lamented style:

And again the song to come full-remembered, and fresh, as that this Eternity did be but the yesterday of that moment. And Mine Own to be all in a sweet madness with those half-dreamed memories, and the wonder and pain of all that no man hath ever said, and that shall never be said; and of the utter lost years, and all that hath been lost, and all forgotten greatness and splendour, and the dreadfulness of parting, and the loveliness of beautiful things that do be hid in the abyss of the years.

(NL: 434)

This affirmation of the unmeasurable abyss of the years, which they have crossed in the course of many reincarnated lifetimes, as the singular place that hides—yet also holds—all that has *never* been said as well as everything ever lost and forgotten, deprives time's looming end of its pain for them. They don't understand why it is happening, they know only that they will not survive it and they cannot halt or delay it, and yet they do not mourn it as the Time Traveller does the suicide of human cognition. Only human time's final closure, its stopping short of eternity and turning away from an empty infinity toward a foreseeable endpoint, permits time's possibilities to permutate in such a way as to bring them together again and again after tearing them apart. This temporal involution offers one possible illustration of the paradox of redemption in Agamben's interpretation of messianic time: "Does this mean that redemption fails and that nothing is truly saved? Not exactly. What cannot be saved is what was, the past as such. But what is saved is what never was, something new … so in historical redemption what happens in the end is what never took place. This is what is saved"

(Agamben 1999b: 157–8). It is also a remarkable anticipation of Robertson's concluding description of life after aftermath: "There is no renewal here, only novelty. Human goals, motivations, desires, processes, techniques, narratives, meanings, histories, lives, environments—they pass and will not return. Nothing returns. Nonetheless, something always comes, but this coming does not mean anything. It involves no progress and no solution for nothing is broken for what comes. That is what life after aftermath is" (Robertson 2018: 157). And everywhere outside the Redoubt, the Night Land teems with that terrifying yet fitting life.

X tells Naani of Mirdath's death in childbirth, which she does not recall (NL: 494), and she tells him her memories of the intervening age of great cities rolling down the metal road that would later become the Road Where the Silent Ones Walk, which he does not remember (NL: 503–4). When X then asks her if she loved any other during her lives apart from him, she cannot answer with certainty; she says only, "there did be no surety in aught, but only that we did have been together before, and have borne a love so great that it did live through Eternity; and we to be now together, and maybe all else to be but dreams" (NL: 505). Dreams and reality, it seems, are what we make of them, so to our protagonists, their ages of separation are the "dreams that are only dreams" of the epigraph. Naani and X let go of knowing and measuring, of science and control, in order to seize the present time of their commitment to one another, and by extension to the other remnants of humanity within the great pyramid; they become apostles to its time image, for which there is no messiah to serve and no paradise to expect. Only in this way can connection and community fit into the shroud of unknowing that is the weird.

The weirdly intimate image of time's abyss they share here, and also later when X ponders the possibilities of life in the Country of Seas, lends X the physical, mental, and emotional strength to fight his way back to the Last Redoubt carrying Naani's body after her mind and spirit are attacked by an outside force from the House of Silence, and no "Power of Goodness" intervenes to block it (NL: 544–6). Although such a Power does later help X reach the pyramid safely with his burden (NL: 561), the Redoubt's Master Doctor sadly pronounces Naani dead, and X knows that he will only live long enough to witness her funeral (NL: 566–70). Since human time is nearing its end, have they lost their last chance to be reincarnated together? Miraculously, it appears, she is revivified when her body passes into the Earth-Current on its way along the Last Road to the Dome of the Dead in the Underground Fields (NL: 575–6), but the Doctors determine that she had not actually been dead but only "stunned and froze of the Spirit, and all her Being and Life suspend" (NL: 581).[3] Thus this resurrection encapsulates the whole pattern of the couple's lives across time's abyss; when she rises, their past is redeemed as new, and together they find a life after aftermath. The tale ends here, at the farthest possible remove from the Recluse's story in *The House on*

---

[3] Alder reads this death and resurrection as a necessary purification: born and raised in a failing Redoubt, Naani "is unclean, contaminated by the Night Land: her food has been 'the moss upon the rocks, and odd strange berries and growths' [NL: 290], and beneficent powers that protect the narrator shun her [NL: 544–6]. Ultimately, the dead woman has to be cleansed and revived by the 'luminous vapour of the Earth-Current' [NL: 574] in the Great Redoubt before she is worthy of taking her place in human society" (Alder 2007: 133).

the Borderland: although the lovers live in a world on the verge of annihilation and oblivion, the conclusion of their quest and their story is charged with the happiness of still-open possibility, while his, already receding into a dimming past after telling us of the most distant future, is tragically trapped by the very vision that takes him beyond his own—and humanity's—limits.

*****

Can such a conclusion really be possible—that the nihilism and negativity, the fear and unknowing, the maddening vertigo of unthinkable times, spaces, and things that define the weird could be reconciled, in a single tale, with the affirmation, the reciprocal acceptance and belonging, the hopeful anticipation of the future, that characterize the romance tradition? That humans could come to accept and affirm their world's end and the nonhuman one to come? Certainly this is not a result that could be deduced from the genre-defining weird fiction of Lovecraft, who denounced Hodgson's "artificial and nauseously sticky romantic sentimentality" even while praising his cosmic vision (Lovecraft 2000: 59). If so, then perhaps it is a mistake to read and analyze *The Night Land* solely in terms of weird fiction as a genre; perhaps instead of unintentionally founding that genre, Hodgson does what Walter Benjamin describes in his *Origin of German Tragic Drama*: "It is … precisely the more significant works, inasmuch as they are not the original and, so to speak, ideal embodiments of the genre, which fall outside the limits of genre. A major work will either establish the genre or abolish it; and the perfect work will do both" (Benjamin 1977: 44). Weirder even than the weird, *The Night Land* would then be the perfect work of an unknown, unnamed, fleeting genre it simultaneously invents and destroys (entropic romance?), leaving its readers with no option but to try and fit it into the more or less inadequate categories that remain.

Let's try another, less portentous way to end this chapter and the main argument of this book. The conclusion of *The Time Machine* imposes upon the reader a choice between mutually exclusive values and their correlative actions: either seize the moment to create a different time image along the lines indicated by the Time Traveller's messianic fable of rational survival, thereby taking humanity's agency and ultimately its destiny into their own hands, or close the book and do nothing, thereby submitting to the nihilistic closure of Victorian class hierarchy and the capitalism that corresponds to it. Hodgson's work, exemplified in *The House on the Borderland* and *The Night Land*, constructs no such opposition and imposes no such choice. Agency coexists with nihilism in a way that is unique in the history of weird fiction. As China Miéville, the leading contemporary advocate of Hodgson's literary importance (and as such the latest in a long line that goes back to H.C. Koenig and Lovecraft), recently wrote, Hodgson's fiction "is precisely great because it manages to ally the weird effect to an unbearably moving non-chauvinist humanism, *without* surrendering nihilism" (Miéville 2016: 207). The weird's well-known anti-humanism, which might more accurately be designated an ahumanism or, acknowledging Hodgson's contribution to the genre, an ab-humanism, is best measured not by its threats of mutation to the human body and madness to the human mind, but by its exposure of the limits of human knowledge and control over the world, limits transgressed by the extremity of time's abyss even as they continue to mark the interiority of the human subject. The weird's ecstatic nihilism is a function of those limits, which restrict agency but, for Hodgson at least, do not eliminate it the way many other weird writers do. In other words, Hodgson's disturbing synthesis of love story and weird tale may be one of the few narratives that can teach us how to keep living on the always already unhuman planet that is our earth, but also how to welcome our world's inevitable end, whether it arrives tomorrow or a million years later. The possibilities of the dark that he foresaw a century ago remain before us.

Envoi: Hope's Legacy

When Hodgson died, blown to bits at a forward observation post during the second Battle of Ypres in April 1918, his books were either out of print or sitting unsold in the publishers' warehouses; despite the strong impressions they made on reviewers, other writers, and a small number of readers, they sold poorly and earned him only a bare subsistence income. His prospects for posthumous acclaim at that moment were equally poor, but Sam Moskowitz's research has shown how crucial the efforts of Hodgson's widow, Bessie Farnsworth Hodgson, were to the belated revival of his reputation. Her dedication to the proposition that, in her words, "His name just must live!" (M2: 11) led her to undertake a quarter-century effort to restore his books and stories to print and to find publishers for his unpublished work, an effort that only ended with her own death in 1943, just three years before Arkham House published its landmark omnibus collection *The House on the Borderland and Other Novels*, which made Hodgson's major works available again and thereby jump-started his current reputation as a writer of weird fiction.

Indeed, we can trace much of Hodgson's twenty-first-century fame to a single one of the republications that Bessie arranged: in 1931 "The Voice in the Night" was included in an anthology of ghost stories, *They Walk Again,* edited by Colin de la Mare for Faber & Faber. Evidence suggests that it was read there by Dennis Wheatley, who was soon to become one of the world's bestselling authors of thrillers and occult fiction and who became perhaps the first dedicated Hodgson enthusiast outside his immediate family. Wheatley, who unlike Hodgson survived combat at Ypres during the First World War, is best remembered today for his second novel, *The Devil Rides Out* (1934), a tale of black magical combat later adapted into a film starring Christopher Lee (Hammer Productions, 1968), and for the influence his Gregory Sallust thrillers had on Ian Fleming's James Bond series. Wheatley acquired first editions of all Hodgson's books and, fifty years before Night Shade Books released their five-volume hardcover set, had them rebound in uniform cloth editions for his private library; he also promoted Hodgson's work by reprinting three stories (including "The Derelict") in the volume of supernatural fiction, *A Century of Horror Stories,* he edited for his own publisher, Hutchinson, in 1936. In his headnote to the stories, Wheatley describes *The Night Land* as Hodgson's "greatest achievement" which "contains a very beautiful love story and is a magnificent feat of imaginative writing. His other works deal almost entirely with the sea and with the occult, and there appears to be very little doubt that William Hope Hodgson's untimely death robbed us of a great master upon both those subjects" (cited in M2, 72–3). Wheatley would later republish *The Ghost Pirates* and *Carnacki the Ghost Finder* in "Dennis Wheatley's Library of the Occult" that he edited for Sphere Books between 1974 and his death in 1977. In the second volume of his memoirs, *The Time Has Come*, Wheatley confirms his opinion of Hodgson by including him in a list of favorite books and authors: "In occult spine-chillers M.R. James was excellent but William Hope Hodgson has never been surpassed" (Wheatley 1978: 149).

In addition to being the first stage of the bibliophile's relay that restored Hodgson's writings to later readers, Wheatley was also the first to take inspiration for his own work from his predecessor's fiction. Wheatley's biographer Phil Baker traces his use of a defensive pentagram in *The Devil Rides Out* and an "electric pentacle" in *To the Devil—A Daughter* (1953), as well as his stories of supernatural investigator Neils Orsen, back to Hodgson's Carnacki tales (Baker 2009: 282, 332, 492). Wheatley's 1938 novel *Uncharted Seas*, set aboard a smuggling vessel that gets trapped in the Sargasso Sea, constitutes a veritable coded homage to Hodgson, with chapter titles such as "The Thing That Came in the Night," "The Things That Tapped in the Night," and "The Silent Ship" that either echo or simply re-use Hodgson's own titles, repeated references to the "tideless sea," which is an allusion to the titles of Hodgson's earliest successful short stories, and even a few highly metaphorical uses of "redoubt." One wonders what Hodgson would have thought about that homage, however, for Wheatley's cast of flawed and unsavory characters is remarkable only for its consistent use of stereotypes, particularly racist ones. The plot ultimately degenerates into a tawdry and violent struggle between a community of the white descendants of shipwrecked mariners, some living on an island in the weed and others living aboard ancient sailing ships equipped with Hodgsonesque superstructures for protection against the giant octopus (or squid—no one in the book seems to know the difference) and crabs that infest the region, and the descendants of escaped African slaves, who live on nearby Satan Island. That struggle is eventually resolved by the smugglers' machine-gun massacre of the Black islanders in the course of their own escape from the islands. Baker notes that "The association between black people and evil runs deep in Wheatley's work, ultimately going beyond the obvious 'racism' of the period, and even beyond period ideas of primitive sexuality, to a more radical conflation of ethnic blackness and visual darkness, within Wheatley's Manichean and Gnostic split between light and dark" (Baker 2009: 570). Wheatley's racism is not limited to his treatment of Black characters, however: the smugglers' craft is also equipped with a simple-minded, pidgin-speaking Chinese chef for comic relief. In light of Hodgson's own, more sympathetic and nuanced portrayals of Black and Asian characters, we can infer that he may not have appreciated Wheatley's homage very much. If Wheatley's work in this novel has any value for twenty-first-century readers, that value lies in its demonstration that early twentieth-century popular fiction often manifested much cruder, more direct, and more vicious forms of racism than those for which writers such as Lovecraft have so often been criticized. Although the Hammer Films adaptation of Wheatley's novel, under the title *The Lost Continent* (1968), cannot be called progressive in its treatment of race—its cast is entirely white—at least its decision to replace the subplot involving savage people of color with one involving the brutal descendants of Spanish conquistadors results in a far less ludicrously racist climax.[1]

Even more influential on Hodgson's fortunes than Wheatley was American fantasy fan H.C. Koenig, who also read *They Walk Again* soon after publication and was so impressed with Hodgson's tale that he tracked down hard-to-find first editions of Hodgson's novels, which he later lent to his friends Clark Ashton Smith and H.P. Lovecraft (M2: 70–1). As discussed in the Preface, Lovecraft was shocked to discover a writer previously unknown to him who was nevertheless kindred in his aims, and he made a point of inserting a laudatory section on Hodgson into his tremendously influential essay *Supernatural Horror in Literature*, which devotees of weird fiction have long used as a reader's guide to the genre. Although Lovecraft was introduced to Hodgson's work in 1934, too late for it to influence most of his own major tales, John D. Haefele has argued that Lovecraft's reading of *The Night Land* in particular "served to inspire, motivate and perhaps re-energize him at a crucial time when he struggled to find his author's voice" while completing his 1936 masterpiece, "The Shadow Out of Time" (Haefele 2014: 196). Haefele draws attention not just to the enormous timescales the tales share, but also to the minutely described descents into ancient unknown spaces that the protagonists of both stories narrate. Lovecraft also shared Koenig's copies of Hodgson's books with his younger colleagues Fritz Leiber and Catherine L. Moore, the latter of whom had read "The Voice in the Night" already but did not connect it with Hodgson (Lovecraft 2017: 107–9).

Only a few years after Lovecraft's death, however, Moore and her husband Henry Kuttner (the couple had been introduced to one another by their late friend, and quickly matured into two of Golden Age science fiction's most beloved authors) collaborated on a short novel, *Earth's Last Citadel* (1943), which clearly shows *The Night Land*'s influence. Written and first published serially during the Second World War, this novel uses the device of a strange machine to transport two Axis agents and two Allied agents into earth's distant future, where they find a mutated humanity besieged in its delicate fortress-city Carcasilla, the citadel of the title, by monstrous forces under the control of a powerful extraterrestrial overlord called simply the Alien. The newcomers assist their descendants in defeating the Alien and its minions, but in the process Carcasilla itself is destroyed, its Earth Current-like "Source" relocated to humanity's new home on Venus in a happier, and more expansively science-fictional, ending than Hodgson gave to X and Naani. In a final nod to their precursor, however, Moore and Kuttner grant the few survivors left on the devastated earth a slim chance of resisting the slow, entropic decline of their world. Despite its rather crude framing device, *Earth's Last Citadel* displays all the strengths for which Moore and Kuttner were famous: swift, exciting plotting, balanced gender representation for the era, and sophisticated psychological characterization. One of the founding novels of science fiction's dying earth subgenre, it appeared just as Hodgson's novels *The Boats of the "Glen Carrig"* and *The Ghost Pirates* and his story "The Derelict" were being reprinted in the pulp magazine *Famous Fantastic Mysteries* (1943–5), and shortly before the Carnacki tale

---

[1] Wheatley himself was disappointed by this modification, writing in his memoir, "the story was entirely altered, with the result that it was less successful" (Wheatley 1979: 260).

"The Hog" was published for the first time in *Weird Tales* (1947). In recognition of its importance, *Earth's Last Citadel* was nominated for a 1944 Retro Hugo in 2019.

At several earlier points in this study, I have noted both formal and conceptual resemblances between Hodgson's most important novels, *The House on the Borderland* and *The Night Land*, and the work of English scientific romancer Olaf Stapledon. Not only the enormous timescales the latter utilizes (see the three progressively larger visual representations of time that Stapledon includes at the conclusion of *Star Maker*, which range from 100 billion years to a Spinozist view of eternity, Stapledon 2004: 265–9), but also the means by which his narrators traverse those scales—via telepathic communication from the future in *Last and First Men* (1930) and *Last Men in London* (1932) and via disembodied mental flight in *Star Maker* (1937)—are so similar to Hodgson's tales that critics such as Fritz Leiber have implied an influence (Berrutti, Joshi, & Gafford 2014: 42), while Sam Moskowitz has more forcefully stated that

> The evidence is very convincing that William Hope Hodgson was a possible inspiration for Olaf Stapledon's method as displayed in *Last and First Men, Last Men in London,* and *Star Maker,* those staggering speculative philosophical feats that tried to present the entire future history of mankind and the universe, and served as a major inspiration for a large part of modern science fiction.
>
> (M1: 13)

To these similarities I would add the authors' parallel metaphysical beliefs: despite their rejection of traditional religious faith, both maintained an attitude of open-minded spiritual wonder regarding the material cosmos, which seems to be what led them to take a serious interest in telepathy. Unfortunately, Moskowitz does not present any of the evidence he claims to have, and no explicit references to Hodgson appear in any of Stapledon's published books or Robert Crossley's biography of Stapledon, *Speaking for the Future* (1994). Thus this claim of influence that would indirectly make Hodgson one of the grandparents of modern science fiction must remain, like so many other aspects of his life and career, a matter of speculation until evidence appears.

Hodgson's Edwardian residues and peculiar personal theories about both art and gender might seem to stand in the way of any influence he might have on the vigorously forward-looking literary practices of the New Wave writers, and this holds true in the case of figures like J.G. Ballard and Brian Aldiss, despite the latter's admiration for Hodgson's depiction of spacetime abysses and inhuman landscapes (Aldiss and Wingrove 1986: 167–9). But several of the New Wave's standard-bearers have revealed longstanding fascinations with the fantastical visions of the Decadent writers and similar late Victorian and Edwardian dissidents, chief among them Michael Moorcock and M. John Harrison. Although his fiction shows few direct signs of Hodgson's influence—his comic *Dancers at the End of Time* sequence, for example, is decidedly un-Hodgsonesque—Moorcock expresses his respect for his predecessor repeatedly in his nonfiction. In their collaborative volume *Fantasy: The 100 Best Books,* Moorcock and his longtime friend and illustrator James Cawthorn include *The House on the Borderland* and *The Night Land* among the genre's classics, lauding their author's "unique vision" of "dizzying leaps through outer and inner space" as well as his tragic rigor: "There is no scientific miracle waiting in the wings, no hint of salvation. At best, the struggle will continue for so long as human resolution endures" (Cawthorn and Moorcock 1988: 54, 66). In his tendentious study of fantasy, *Wizardry and Wild Romance*, which is infamous for its dismissal of Tolkien's work as "Epic Pooh," Moorcock singles out for praise that aspect of Hodgson's style that most readers deride: the artificial diction of *The Night Land*. "All the nonsensical archaisms and meaningless sonority borrowed from Gothic and Pre-Raphaelite writers used, as often as not, to colour up an essentially lifeless and unimaginative narrative, tends to discredit those few writers, like William Hope Hodgson, who instil vigour and fresh meaning into their language" (Moorcock 2004: 51). Moorcock goes on to contrast Hodgson's artificial English favorably with the more widely admired modification of English practiced by William Morris.

Harrison's *Viriconium* sequence (1971–85) shows a more direct thematic influence from Hodgson in its baroque depiction of a far future earth saturated with decrepit, forgotten, yet still deadly technologies and inhabited by creatures both radically unhuman (such as the robotic *geteit chemosit* of *The Pastel City* or the insect swarm of *A Storm of Wings*) and subtly ab-human (such as the Reborn Men of both novels). Although Harrison's prose style is very different from Hodgson's and much closer to that of Mervyn Peake, his prologue to the first volume, *The Pastel City*, achieves an elegiac and incantatory tone in describing abyssal time that is surely akin to Hodgson's in *The Night Land*: describing the lordly Afternoon Cultures whose collapse left the earth poisoned and human civilization crippled, he writes,

> none of them lasted for less than a millennium, none for more than ten; ... each extracted such secrets and obtained such comforts as its nature (and the nature of the universe) enabled it to find; and ... each fell back from the universe in confusion, dwindled, and died. The last of them left its name written in the stars, but no one who came later could read it. More important, perhaps, it built enduringly despite its failing strength—leaving certain technologies that, for good or ill, retained their properties of operation for well over a thousand years. And more importantly still, it *was* the last of the Afternoon Cultures, and was followed by Evening, and by Viriconium.
>
> (Harrison 2005: 3)

Thematically, this establishing passage calls to mind the account of the "Days of the Darkening" that led to the construction of the Great Redoubt in *The Night Land* (NL: 44–5). Furthermore, the *Viriconium* sequence is the first of Harrison's works that can be classified as weird in their deployment of tropes and plot patterns from fantasy— especially sword and sorcery—to tell stories of a fundamentally rationalist nature characteristic of science fiction, stories that often produce effects of fear and anxiety most often associated with horror by marking the limits of rationalist understanding.

More recently, in his introduction to Jeff VanderMeer's *City of Saints and Madmen* (2002), Moorcock compares "Captain" VanderMeer's invented world of Ambergris to the milieux of his precursors using an extended metaphor drawn from Victorian travel writing; those precursors include "[Clark] Ashton Smith's *Zothique*, Jack Vance's *Dying Earth*, 'Crastinator Harrison's *Viriconium* or Lady [Leigh]

Brackett's *Old Mars* or ... the borderlands explored by the famous Hope Hodgson expedition" (Moorcock in VanderMeer 2006: 2–3). As narrated in Duncan Shriek's heavily footnoted pamphlet *The Hoegbotton Guide to the Early History of the City of Ambergris* (included in *City of Saints and Madmen*), Ambergris is a commercial city that is simultaneously growing and decaying, built on the site of a previous city, Cinsorium, that had served as a capital of sorts for the "gray caps" or "mushroom dwellers" (VanderMeer 2006: 109–13), whose fungal properties mark them as the literary descendants of the fungally infected couple in Hodgson's story "The Voice in the Night." Before Ambergris can be built, the gray caps must be displaced, so the city's founder, the rapacious Cappan Manzikert, orders their systematic slaughter (VanderMeer 2006: 122–4), and when Manzikert is rendered insane as a result of a mysterious encounter with the gray caps, his wife Sophia burns Cinsorium to the ground (VanderMeer 2006: 125–8). Ambergris prospers for a time following the gray caps' extermination, but the city is plagued by frightening and ineradicable fungal growths reminiscent of Hodgson's "The Derelict" (VanderMeer 2006: 140–2), as well as strange visitations culminating in the Silence, the name given to the inexplicable disappearance of the city's 25,000 inhabitants while its rulers and military were absent (VanderMeer 2006: 150–70). The escalating conflict between humans and gray caps that begins with these events provides the backdrop for the concluding volumes in VanderMeer's sequence, *Shriek: An Afterword* (2006) and *Finch* (2009).

Greg Bear's 2009 novel *City at the End of Time* goes one better than any previous tale in dialogue with Hodgson by all but name-checking him in its text. Bear's book, which starts with an epigraph from Moore and Kuttner's *Earth's Last Citadel* ("Time—gone out like a tide and left us stranded," Moore and Kuttner 1943: 15), offers readers an extraordinarily convoluted plot involving such Hodgsonesque features as: a pair of lovers whose minds leap forward from their present-day bodies in a decomposing Seattle into far-future, genetically-modified and artificially grown bodies living in a Great Redoubt-like fortress called the Kalpa, and back again; forbiddingly nonhuman watchers that keep the Kalpa and its occupants under unblinking surveillance and assault; mysterious creatures called Silent Ones that threaten the lovers when their quest takes them outside the Kalpa; and a large number of "easter egg" references to details in *The Night Land*. Four hundred pages into the novel, one of the secondary antagonists, a conflicted figure named Max Glaucous who hunts down "fate-shifters" like the lovers across time, reminisces about one of his failed hunts:

> I walked the trenches around Ypres, almost a hundred years ago, looking for a particular gent—a fine, strapping fellow and a poet. He dreamed, so I was led to believe, of a place he called the Last Redoubt. He'd written a book before shipping out, detailing his dreams ... But the war had already blown him to bits. Lean years for hunters, during wartime.
>
> (Bear 2008: 398)

In context, this anecdote implies that Hodgson himself was a "fate-shifter," whose uncannily accurate visions of the far future have to be blotted out along with all others so that the hostile entity Typhon can achieve retroactive non-existence by forcing a generalized quantum decoherence upon all possible versions of the multiverse. Bear's attempt to sum up and complete the entire dying earth subgenre by weaving elements of Hodgson's vision together with components from Wells's *Time Machine*, Lovecraft's "The Shadow Out of Time," Moore and Kuttner's novel, Arthur C. Clarke's *The City and the Stars* (1956), and the bibliophilic metafictions of Jorge Luis Borges is tremendously ambitious and attractive in its aims, so its serious weaknesses of characterization and muddled plotlines are all the more disappointing. Its comparatively upbeat ending, in which Typhon is defeated, the multiverse saved, and our protagonists can live wherever they wish throughout the time stream, highlights the fundamental incompatibility between Bear's technophilic ethos and Hodgson's darkly nihilist one.

Unquestionably the most vocal, committed, and systematic heir to Hodgson's version of weird fiction is China Miéville, who has drawn attention to Hodgson's work in numerous interviews, articles, and especially the introduction he contributed to Gollancz's 2002 reissue of the 1946 Arkham House omnibus *The House on the Borderland and Other Novels*. Miéville acknowledges the direct influence of Hodgson upon his own fiction by name before the epigraph to his 2010 novel *Kraken*, and that book's whimsical array of tentacular entities, ranging from the (real) preserved giant squid in the British Natural History Museum and Darwin Center to the (hopefully fictional) mutating teuthists of the underground Kraken cult, clearly owes a debt to Hodgson's devil-fish and weed men. However, his earlier novel *The Scar* (2002), the second in the Bas-Lag trilogy, presents a fuller range of Hodgsonian themes and imagery than any of his other books. Although tentacles are less often in evidence here than in *Kraken*, the setting of the entire plot either aboard ocean-going vessels or on isolated islands permits Miéville to pay tribute to many of his precursor's characteristic narrative patterns. Nonhuman sea monsters such as the avanc and the grindylow and ab-human hybrids such as the cactacae/cactus-men, the mosquito-like Anophelii, and the Remade abound, and the Armada itself, a floating city composed of hundreds of ships yoked together, evokes both Hodgson's efforts to invent new maritime settings for narrative such as the weed islands of the Sargasso and the tectonically raised seafloor on the one hand and, on the other, the immense artificial habitat that is *The Night Land*'s Last Redoubt. The novel's bravura concluding sequence, in which the cactus man Hedrigall tells the inhabitants of Armada how he witnessed their deaths and Armada's obliteration in the great Scar where reality itself splits open, leading to a rebellion that ends Armada's quest for the Scar and thus renders Hedrigall's story irreducibly paradoxical, raises the book to an even higher order of weird storytelling than that displayed in the other volumes of the trilogy (see Robertson 2016). In light of his many tales and essays denouncing the mistreatment and disrespect common sailors face from their superiors, Hodgson would no doubt have appreciated the success that crowns the common sailors' efforts to relieve Armada's self-mutilating captains, the Lovers, of command over their suicidal quest for the Scar. Of all the fictional tributes to Hodgson, *The Scar* is the most impressive both in style and in the variations it weaves upon typical Hodgsonian themes and tropes.

The most recent contributor to Hodgson's fictional legacy is in many ways the most unusual and unexpected: celebrated transgender author Charlie Jane Anders, who tips her hat to our subject obliquely in the short story "The Fermi Paradox Is Our Business

Model" (2010). The Fermi Paradox, which is named for physicist Enrico Fermi who first formulated it and which gives Anders's short story its title, consists in the observation that the universe as understood by contemporary cosmology is old enough and contains enough stars to have produced many technological civilizations more advanced than humanity, yet we have observed no clear signs of those civilizations' existence. The ongoing Search for Extraterrestrial Intelligence (SETI) project hopes someday to resolve the paradox, which continues to haunt astronomy and the speculative field of xenobiology. In the meantime, many science fiction writers, ranging from Arkady and Boris Strugatsky (*Definitely Maybe*, 1977) to Terry Bisson ("They're Made Out of Meat," 1991), have offered possible explanations for the paradox. Anders's story takes the resolution of the paradox as a given: the aliens who are the story's protagonists, the Falshi, imagine themselves to be members of the only species ever to survive the growing disproportion between its hyper-accelerating technological development gradient and its sluggish socio-economic evolution, and they have in fact made the apparent certainty of civilizational self-destruction the driving force of their economy. As one Falshi explains to the appalled humans they have unexpectedly discovered surviving on earth,

> Our employers seeded this galaxy with billions of life-seeding devices. It was just a wealth-creation schema ... We created you, along with countless other sentient creatures ... You dig up the metals, to make things. Right? You find the rare elements. You invent technology. Yes? And then you die, and leave it all behind. For us. We come and take it after you are gone. For profit.
>
> (Anders 2017: 26–7)

The Falshi are utterly pacifistic, unwilling to harm the humans even in self-defense, but their entire civilization paradoxically depends for its own survival on the self-immolation—which they call "Closure"—of all other civilizations.

This pointed satire of capitalist realism may seem rather distant from Hodgson's vision of human tenacity in the face of existential threats both radically alien and self-generated, but the means of human survival here is the same one Hodgson pioneered a century earlier and bequeathed to Moore, Kuttner, Bear, and others: when the Falshi arrive in earth orbit, their instruments locate amid the devastation "one spire, like a giant worship-spike, with millions of lights glowing on it. A single structure holding a city full of people, with a tip that glowed brighter than the rest. These people were as hierarchical as all the others, so the tip was probably where the leader (or leaders) lived" (Anders 2017: 19). Anders's version of the Last Redoubt was not built as a collective defense against ab-human invaders, however, but as the corporate headquarters of "a profit-making enterprise called 'Dorfco,'" so "everyone left alive on 'Earth' was the servant of someone called 'Jondorf'" (Anders 2017: 24). Capitalist competition and accumulation are thereby revealed to be the ultimate causes of this story's every feature, as well as the keys to resolving the Fermi Paradox: they all but guarantee the self-destruction of every civilization that develops the capitalist mode of production, allowing the sole surviving culture to maximize the efficiency of its own accumulation process, but capitalism's managerial requirements—humanity's creation of "a form of [wealth-accretion ideology] that was as strong as nationalism or religion" (Anders 2017: 29)—also enable humans to survive their Closure and perhaps offer a future competitive threat to the Falshi. The aliens depart for their base "hoping to hell the Tradestation isn't sporting a Dorfco logo when we show up there a few thousand years from now" (Anders 2017: 32). The narrator X's impossible dream in *The Night Land*—of humanity's emergence from the Redoubt to reclaim the earth's surface, revive an expansive human civilization, and perhaps more—is for the Falshi a nightmare of their own Closure that is all too possible.

In the decades since his death and belated revival, Hodgson's writings have gradually begun to inspire creative work in media other than literature as well. Oddly enough, despite his originality and increasing visibility as a writer of horror and science fiction, he has only rarely attracted the attention of cinema or television producers. Luckily, most of those who have been attracted were highly distinguished, indeed legendary. The first was Alfred Hitchcock, acting not as director but producer, who included an adaptation of "The Voice in the Night" in his US television anthology series *Suspicion* in 1958. Directed by Arthur Hiller from a screenplay by future Oscar-winner Stirling Silliphant (for *In the Heat of the Night*, 1967), it starred Barbara Rush (of *It Came from Outer Space*, 1953) and James Donald (famous for playing Theo Van Gogh in *Lust for Life* [1956] and Major Clipton in *The Bridge on the River Kwai* [1957]) as the fungus-infected couple, with Patrick Macnee (later John Steed of *The Avengers*) and a very young James Coburn as the seamen who listen to their woeful tale. Apart from a few minor changes, the episode follows the story closely up to the point of the couple's initial infections: instead of the parody of Adam's temptation by Eve that Hodgson narrates, the Hitchcock/Hiller version climaxes with the two becoming infected by unnoticed skin contact with the fungus, and then bravely resolving to die together on the island so as to avoid spreading the infection to other people. The black-and-white production design, by Robert Boyle, effectively generates a clammy, claustrophobic atmosphere aboard the derelict ship where the couple initially lodges and on the fungus-dominated island, although no trace of fully absorbed fungal victims ever appears.[2]

Only a few years later, in 1963, Japanese director Ishiro Honda, whose somber 1954 masterpiece *Gojira* (*Godzilla* in the Anglophone world) and its many sequels started one of the earliest and longest-lasting media franchises in history, made a second adaptation of "The Voice in the Night" for Toho Studios. The film's Japanese title is *Matango*, but it was released in the United States as *Attack of the Mushroom People* and as *Fungus of Terror* in the UK; designed by Shigekazu Ikuno, it stars a number of Toho contract players, including Kumi Mizuno, Yoshio Tsuchiya, Arika Kubo, and Kenji Sahara, who will be immediately recognizable to viewers of classic *kaiju* films. In it, the nautical frame tale of the story is replaced by one involving a man confined in a hospital who tells his doctors of his experiences as part of a group of alienated urban professionals—the narrator is a professor, and the group also includes his modest assistant, a selfish businessman, a hack writer, an opportunistic singer, and two disaffected sailors—who are shipwrecked on an apparently uninhabited island covered with strange fungus.

---

[2] This episode has never been officially released on videotape, DVD, or streaming, but a very low-resolution version can be viewed on YouTube (https://www.youtube.com/watch?v=ssi6_YWrrxc).

Taking shelter aboard a recently abandoned ship beached in the island's lagoon, the group swiftly begins to fracture as a result of class and gender antagonisms, distrust, and self-interest when their food supply starts to dwindle. Numerous clues, such as broken mirrors throughout the ship, ambiguous warnings in the damaged ship's log, and nocturnal visits by disfigured humanoid creatures, make them wary of eating the fungus, but one by one they each take that step, either voluntarily or as a last resort to stave off starvation. The first is the writer Yoshida, who peddles other people's stories as his own—in a self-reflexive flashback that Hodgson might have found amusing, he argues that plagiarism is the root of all literature—and looks forward to whatever hallucinations the mushrooms might bring, especially the "laughing mushrooms" that prefigure the mutated mushroom people who emerge at the film's climax. The last to succumb are the professor and his assistant, though as in the Hitchcock/Hiller adaptation, they don't do so in a parody of Adam and Eve's transgression; instead, the assistant Miss Akiko is carried off by the disfigured humanoids, and when Professor Murai finds her, she is feasting on the mushrooms and invites him to join her. The writer and the singer, whose bodies are visibly being taken over by the fungus, also entice him to partake, but when he retreats from them, several human-sized mushrooms detach themselves from the jungle foliage and try to trap him while laughing ominously. Murai escapes the island on a dismasted yacht, is picked up by a passing vessel, and concludes his story by revealing his own fungally infected face to his doctors and the audience. The film closes with his final assertion that the island isn't much different from Tokyo itself, which is being transformed into a similarly ab-human landscape by alienation, greed, and drugs. Honda and his writers Takeshi Kimura and Sakyo Komatsu succeed in turning Hodgson's oblique satire on religious faith into a direct satire on the negative consequences of Japan's postwar economic miracle.

Unfortunately, not all Hodgson dramatizations are as well made and interesting as Hitchcock's and Honda's. The first series of the British ITV television anthology program *The Rivals of Sherlock Holmes* (1971) included an adaptation of Hodgson's story "The Horse of the Invisible" (1910), starring veteran character actor Donald Pleasance (best known for playing the villain Blofeld in the 1967 James Bond film *You Only Live Twice* and the psychiatrist Dr. Loomis in *Halloween* [1978] and its sequels) as Carnacki the Ghost Finder, but Pleasance's performance is flat and perfunctory, and the series' drab videotape production values reflect the budgetary austerity which was a widely recognized constraint on much otherwise inventive British television at that time. Now that fantastic narrative has become a mainstream cinematic and television genre and CGI has reached a level of sophistication that allows it to depict fully realized fantastic worlds, Hodgson's most ambitious and original works may yet appear on screens big or small, but his admirers can only hope that any future adaptations follow the pattern established by Hitchcock and Honda and not that of ITV.

Perhaps surprisingly, very few creators of comics and graphic novels seem to have discovered Hodgson's work, and those few relatively late. In 2000, DC Comic's adult-oriented Vertigo imprint published an adaptation of *The House on the Borderland* by artist Richard Corben and writer Simon Revelstroke. Revelstroke's script dismantles, re-arranges, and supplements the components of Hodgson's novel so as to realize Iain Sinclair's exaggeratedly Gothic suggestion that the book's true source of horror is the unacknowledged incest that drove the Recluse and his sister Mary to the secluded house in the first place (Sinclair 1990: 185–7). Corben's art, which teeters disturbingly between the caricatural and the anatomically correct, intensifies the sensations of unpleasant surface textures and visceral depths that the characters' corporeal struggles with the swine-things and their immaterial astral counterpart inflict upon the reader; the effect is similar to the tactile volumes set into uncanny motion by stop-motion animation or claymation. Oddly, however, the adaptation ends in an inversion of the novel's foreboding conclusion: although the Recluse's journal trails off in mid-sentence as something comes through the door to take him, just as in the novel, he re-appears in the final pages as a kind of transcendental guardian, "the Watcher upon the Threshold … something less than immortal, something more than human" who will prevent future monstrous incursions in order to maintain "Balance—twixt Order and Chaos, Life and Death, Light and Dark" (Corben and Revelstroke 2000: 84). This decidedly un-Hodgsonian assignment of superhuman powers, responsibilities, and judgment to fallible human characters may explain why Alan Moore, in his preface to the adaptation, focuses entirely on praising the original novel and urging readers to seek it out, instead of assessing the significance of these changes to Hodgson's original vision.

In this envoi I have focused on Hodgson-inspired or -influenced works that have been published by recognizable presses in conventional formats such as print books, films, TV programs, and comics, but such works represent only a fraction of the stories, songs, and other artworks indebted to Hodgson that one can find circulating digitally across the internet. His own works are now largely out of copyright and many may be freely downloaded in multiple formats from Project Gutenberg and other repositories. Following the example of Andy Robertson's *Night Land* website and the story collections it shepherded to publication early in the twenty-first century, self-published pastiche sequels to Hodgson's works now abound in PDF, Kindle, Nook, and other formats. Carnacki the Ghostfinder has perhaps been the biggest recipient of this attention, with at least a dozen story collections and novels—including crossover fictions in which Carnacki joins forces with Captain Gault—currently available. High-quality, fan-generated visual art often accompanies these pastiches, or stands on its own on websites such as deviantart.com. Musicians, too, ranging from quirky chamber composers to metal bands and ambient sound artists, have produced imaginative soundtracks to Hodgson's tales. If Hodgson's work had trouble finding readers during the age of print, when a comparatively small number of commercial gatekeepers determined who and what was published, then perhaps these thriving online communities permit us to hope that his fame and audience have now found a medium that will enable them to grow faster than they ever have before. In January 1905, when he first set out to become a writer, Hodgson wrote to Coulson Kernahan that "I won't give in, not as long as I can sit at the typewriter" (U: 31), and even though success eluded him throughout his life, we don't have to speculate much to imagine that both he and Bessie, who worked so hard to keep her husband's writing in print, would be deeply gratified by the posthumous regard that has belatedly grown up around his still startling visions of hope and fear. Now it's our turn to embrace, expand, and realize those possibilities of the dark.

References

Agamben, G. (1999a), *The Man without Content*, trans. G. Albert, Stanford: Stanford University Press.
Agamben, G. (1999b), "Walter Benjamin and the Demonic: Happiness and Historical Redemption," in *Potentialities: Collected Essays in Philosophy*, ed. and trans. D. Heller-Roazen, Stanford: Stanford University Press. 138–59.
Agamben, G. (2005), *The Time That Remains: A Commentary on the Letter to the Romans*, trans. P. Dailey, Stanford: Stanford University Press.
Albritton, C. C. (1980), *The Abyss of Time: Changing Conceptions of the Earth's Antiquity after the Sixteenth Century*, San Francisco: Freeman, Cooper & Co.
Alder, E. (2007), "'Passing the Barrier of Life': Spiritualism, Psychical Research, and Boundaries in William Hope Hodgson's *The Night Land*," in *Boundaries*, ed. J. Ramone and G. Twitchen, Newcastle, UK: Cambridge Scholars Press. 120–39.
Alder, E. (2008), "'Buildings of the New Age': Dwellings and the Natural Environment in the Futuristic Fiction of H.G. Wells and William Hope Hodgson," in *H. G. Wells: Interdisciplinary Essays*, ed. S. McLean, Newcastle, UK: Cambridge Scholars Press. 114–29.
Alder, E. (2009), "William Hope Hodgson's Borderlands: Monstrosity, Other Worlds, and the Future at the Fin de siècle," PhD diss., Edinburgh Napier University.
Alder, E. (2013), "'Always Sea and Sea': *The Night Land* as Seascape," *Sargasso: The Journal of William Hope Hodgson Studies* 1 (2013): 89–101.
Alder, E. (2020), *Weird Fiction and Science at the Fin de siècle*, New York: Palgrave Macmillan.
Aldiss, B., with D. Wingrove (1986), *Trillion Year Spree: The History of Science Fiction*, New York: Avon.
Anders, C. J. (2017), "The Fermi Paradox Is Our Business Model," in Anders, *Six Months, Three Days, Five Others*, New York: Tor. 13–33.
Ashley, M. and R. A. W. Lowndes (2004), *The Gernsback Days: A Study of the Evolution of Modern Science Fiction from 1911 to 1936*, Holicong, PA: Wildside Press.
Baker, P. (2009), *The Devil Is a Gentleman: The Life and Times of Dennis Wheatley*, Sawtry, UK: Dedalus.
Barr, J. (1984–5), "Why the World Was Created in 4004 BC: Archbishop Ussher and Biblical Chronology," *Bulletin of the John Rylands University Library of Manchester* 67 (1984–5): 575–608.
Bear, G. (2008), *City at the End of Time*, New York: Ballantine.
Bell, I., ed. (1987), *William Hope Hodgson: Voyages and Visions*, Oxford: Bell & Sons.
Benjamin, W. (1977), *The Origin of German Tragic Drama*, trans. J. Osborne, New York: Verso.
Benjamin, W. (2003), *Selected Writings* volume 4, *1938–1940*, ed. H. Eiland and M. W. Jennings, Cambridge: Harvard University Press.
Berruti, M., S. T. Joshi, and S. Gafford, eds (2014), *William Hope Hodgson: Voices from the Borderland*, New York: Hippocampus Press.

Bignell, J. (2004), "Another Time, Another Space: Modernity, Subjectivity and *The Time Machine*," in *Liquid Metal: The Science Fiction Film Reader*, ed. S. Redmond, New York: Columbia University Press. 136–44.
Blackwood, A. (2002), "The Willows," in Blackwood, *Ancient Sorceries and Other Weird Stories*, New York: Penguin. 17–62.
Blavatsky, H. P. (1877), *Isis Unveiled: A Master-Key to the Mysteries of Ancient and Modern Science and Theology*, 2 vols, Pasadena: Theological University Press.
Bloch, E. (1972), *Atheism in Christianity: The Religion of the Exodus and the Kingdom*, trans. J. T. Swann, New York: Herder & Herder.
Bloch, E. (1986), *The Principle of Hope*, 3 vols, trans. N. Plaice, S. Plaice, and P. Knight, Cambridge: MIT Press.
Bloch, E. (1998), "Can Hope Be Disappointed?" in Bloch, *Literary Essays*, trans. A. Joron et al., Stanford: Stanford University Press. 339–45.
Bohr, N. (1963), "Quantum Physics and Philosophy—Causality and Complementarity," in Bohr, *Philosophical Writings* vol.III, *Essays 1958–1962 on Atomic Physics and Human Knowledge*, Woodbrige, CT: Ox Bow Press. 1–7.
Bourdieu, P. (1984), *Distinction: A Social Critique of the Judgement of Taste*, trans. R. Nice, Cambridge: Harvard University Press.
Budrys, A. (1960), *Rogue Moon*, London: Gollancz.
Burchfield, J. D. (1975), *Lord Kelvin and the Age of the Earth*, New York: Science History Publications.
Burkett, D. (1999), *The Son of Man Debate: A History and Evaluation*, Cambridge: Cambridge University Press.
Cawthorn, J. and M. Moorcock (1988), *Fantasy: The 100 Best Books*, New York: Carroll & Graf.
Comte, A. (1975), *Auguste Comte and Positivism: The Essential Writings*, ed. G. Lenzer, Chicago: University of Chicago Press.
Corben, R. and S. Revelstroke (2000), *William Hope Hodgson's The House on the Borderland*, New York: DC Comics/Vertigo.
Crossley, R. (1994), *Olaf Stapledon: Speaking for the Future*, Syracuse: Syracuse University Press.
Davidson, B. (2014), "The Long Apocalypse: The Experimental Eschatologies of H.G. Wells and William Hope Hodgson," in *William Hope Hodgson: Voices from the Borderland*, ed. M. Berruti, S. T. Joshi, and S. Gafford, New York: Hippocampus Press. 182–92.
Davidson, B. (2015), *Anima*, Brighton: Three Legged Fox Books.
De la Durantaye, L. (2009), *Giorgio Agamben: A Critical Introduction*, Stanford: Stanford University Press.
Deleuze, G. (1983), *Nietzsche and Philosophy*, trans. H. Tomlinson, New York: Columbia University Press.
Deleuze, G. (1988), *Spinoza: Practical Philosophy*, trans. R. Hurley, San Francisco: City Lights.
Derrida, J. (1978), "Structure, Sign and Play in the Discourse of the Human Sciences," in Derrida, *Writing and Diffference*, trans. A. Bass, Chicago: University of Chicago Press. 278–93.
Dickie, M. (1986), *On the Modernist Long Poem*, Iowa City: University of Iowa Press.
Ekman, S. (2013), *Here Be Dragons: Exploring Fantasy Maps and Settings*, Middletown: Wesleyan University Press.
Evans, A. B. (1988), *Jules Verne Rediscovered: Didacticism and the Scientific Novel*, New York: Greenwood P.

Evans, A. B. (1998), "Jules Verne," entry in *Encyclopedia Britannica*. Available online: https://www.britannica.com/biography/Jules-Verne

Finney, C. G. (1935), *The Circus of Dr. Lao*, New York: Avon.

Fisher, M. (2006), "Memorex for the Krakens: The Fall's Pulp Modernism Part 1," *K-punk* (blog), May 8, 2006. Available online: k-punk.abstractdynamics.org/archives/007759.html.

Foucault, M. (1988), *Technologies of the Self: A Seminar with Michel Foucault*, ed. L. H. Martin, H. Gutman, and P. H. Hutton, Amherst: University of Massachusetts Press.

Frank, A. P. (1981), "The Long Withdrawing Roar: 80 Years of the Ocean's Message in American Poetry," in *Forms and Functions of History in American Literature: Essays in Honor of Ursula Brumm*, ed. W. Fluck, J. Peper, and W. P. Adams, Berlin: Erich Schmidt Verlag. 71–90.

Freedman, C. (2000), *Critical Theory and Science Fiction*, Middletown, CT: Wesleyan University Press.

Freedman, C. (2013), "From Genre to Political Economy: Miéville's *The City & The City* and Uneven Development," *CR: The New Centennial Review* 13 (2): 13–30.

Gafford, S. (2013a), *Hodgson: A Collection of Essays*, Warren, RI: Ulthar Press.

Gafford, S. (2013b), "Writing Backwards: The Novels of William Hope Hodgson," in Gafford, *Hodgson: A Collection of Essays*, Warren, RI: Ulthar Press. 21–6.

Gafford, S. (2014), "Hodgson's Women," in *William Hope Hodgson: Voices from the Borderland*, ed. M. Berruti, S. T. Joshi, and S. Gafford, New York: Hippocampus Press. 117–28.

Gaskell, E. (2005), *Works* vol.2: *Novellas*, London: Pickering & Chatto.

Gifford, J. (2018), *A Modernist Fantasy: Modernism, Anarchism, & the Radical Fantastic*, Victoria, BC: ELS Editions.

Haefele, J. D. (2014), "Shadow out of Hodgson," in *William Hope Hodgson: Voices from the Borderland*, ed. M. Berruti, S. T. Joshi, and S. Gafford, New York: Hippocampus Press. 193–7.

Harrison, M. J. (2003), *Things That Never Happen*, San Francisco: Night Shade.

Harrison, M. J. (2005), *Viriconium*, New York: Del Rey.

Heidegger, M. (1971), "The Thing," in Heidegger, *Poetry, Language, Thought*, trans. A. Hofstadter, New York: Harper & Row. 165–86.

Heidegger, M. (1977), "Science and Reflection," in Heidegger, *The Question Concerning Technology and Other Essays*, trans. W. Lovitt, New York: Harper & Row. 155–82.

Heisenberg, W. (1927), "On the Perceptual Content of Quantum Theoretical Kinematics and Mechanics," in *Quantum Theory and Measurement*, ed. J. A. Wheeler and W. H. Zurek, Princeton, NJ: Princeton University Press, 1983. 62–84.

Higgins, D. M. (2021), *Reverse Colonization: Science Fiction, Imperial Fantasy, and Alt-victimhood*, Iowa City: University of Iowa Press.

Hinton, J. (2016), "The House on the Burren: The Physical and Psychological Foundations of *The House on the Borderland*," *Sargasso: The Journal of William Hope Hodgson Studies* 3: 109–21.

Horkheimer, M. (1972), "Notes on Science and the Crisis," in Horkheimer, *Critical Theory: Selected Essays*, trans. M. J. O'Connell, New York: Continuum. 3–9.

Houellebecq, M. (2005), *H.P. Lovecraft: Against the World, against Life*, trans. D. Khazeni, San Francisco: Believer Books.

Hurley, K. (2001), "The Modernist Abominations of William Hope Hodgson," in *Gothic Modernisms*, ed. A. Smith and J. Wallace, Basingstoke: Palgrave. 129–49.

Jameson, F. (1971), *Marxism and Form: Twentieth-Century Dialectical Theories of Literature*, Princeton: Princeton University Press.

Jameson, F. (1988), "Cognitive Mapping," in *Marxism and the Interpretation of Culture*, ed. C. Nelson and L. Grossberg, Urbana: University of Illinois Press. 347–57.

Jameson, F. (1991), *Postmodernism, or, The Cultural Logic of Late Capitalism*, Durham: Duke University Press.

Joshi, S. T. (1990), *The Weird Tale*, Austin: University of Texas Press.

Joshi, S. T. (2010), *I Am Providence: The Life and Times of H.P. Lovecraft*, 2 vols, New York: Hippocampus Press.

Kelvin, W. Thomson and First Baron (1862), "On the Age of the Sun's Heat," in Kelvin, *Popular Lectures and Addresses* vol.I: *Constitution of Matter*, London: Macmillan & Co., 1889. 349–68.

Kelvin, W. Thomson and First Baron (1863), "On the Secular Cooling of the Earth," in Kelvin, *Mathematical and Physical Papers* vol.III: *Elasticity, Heat, Electromagnetism*, London: C. J. Clay & Sons, 1890. 295–311.

Kelvin, W. Thomson and First Baron (1868), "On Geological Time," in Kelvin, *Popular Lectures and Addresses* vol.II: *Geology and General Physics*, London: Macmillan, 1894. 10–72.

Kelvin, W. Thomson and First Baron (1902), "Nineteenth Century Clouds over the Dynamical Theory of Heat and Light," in *Notices of the Proceedings at the Meetings of the Members of the Royal Institution of Great Britain, with the Abstracts of the Discourses Delivered at the Evening Meetings vol.XVI, 1899–1901*, London: William Clowes & Sons. 363–97.

Killingsworth, M. J. (2007), *The Cambridge Introduction to Walt Whitman*, New York: Cambridge University Press.

Kolakowski, L. (1968), *The Alienation of Reason: A History of Positivist Thought*, trans. N. Guterman, Garden City: Doubleday.

Lefebvre, M. (2016), "Between Setting and Landscape in the Cinema," in *Landscape and Film*, ed. Lefebvre, New York: Routledge. 19–59.

Leiber, F. (1966), "Through Hyperspace with Brown Jenkin: Lovecraft's Contribution to Speculative Fiction," in *H.P. Lovecraft: Four Decades of Criticism*, ed. S. T. Joshi, Athens: Ohio University Press, 1980. 140–52.

Lem, S. (1961), *Solaris*, trans. J. Kilmartin and S. Cox, New York: HBJ, 1970.

Lem, S. (1968), *His Master's Voice*, trans. M. Kandel, Evanston: Northwestern University Press, 1999.

Lenin, V. I. (1916), "Imperialism, the Highest Stage of Capitalism," in Lenin, *Selected Works in Three Volumes* vol.1, New York: International Publishers, 1967. 677–777.

Lenzer, G. (1975), "Introduction: Auguste Comte and Positivism," in Comte, *Auguste Comte and Positivism: The Essential Writings*, ed. G. Lenzer, Chicago: University of Chicago Press. xvii–lxviii.

Lewis, C. S. (1966), "On Science Fiction," in Lewis, *Of Other Worlds: Essay & Stories*, ed. W. Hooper, New York: HBJ. 59–73.

Lovecraft, H. P. (1968), *Selected Letters* vol.2, ed. A. Derleth and D. Wandrei, Sauk City, WI: Arkham House.

Lovecraft, H. P. (1971), *Selected Letters* vol.3, *1929–1931*, ed. A. Derleth and D. Wandrei, Sauk City, WI: Arkham House.

Lovecraft, H. P. (1976), *Selected Letters* vol.5, ed. A. Derleth and J. Turner. Sauk City, WI: Arkham House, 1976.

Lovecraft, H. P. (2000), *The Annotated Supernatural Horror in Literature*, ed. S. T. Joshi, New York: Hippocampus Press.

Lovecraft, H. P. (2003), *Letters to Alfred Galpin*, ed. S. T. Joshi and D. E. Schultz, New York: Hippocampus Press.
Lovecraft, H. P. (2004a), *Collected Essays* vol.2: *Literary Criticism*, ed. S. T. Joshi, New York: Hippocampus Press.
Lovecraft, H. P. (2004b), "Notes on Writing Weird Fiction," in *Collected Essays* vol.2: *Literary Criticism*, ed. S. T. Joshi, New York: Hippocampus Press. 175–8.
Lovecraft, H. P. (2005), *At the Mountains of Madness: The Definitive Edition*, New York: Modern Library.
Lovecraft, H. P. (2006), *Collected Essays* vol.5: *Philosophy, Autobiography & Miscellany*, ed. S. T. Joshi, New York: Hippocampus Press.
Lovecraft, H. P. (2011), *Letters to James F. Morton*, ed. D. E. Schultz and S. T. Joshi, New York: Hippocampus Press.
Lovecraft, H. P. (2013), *The Ancient Track: The Complete Poetical Works*, ed. S. T. Joshi, New York: Hippocampus Press.
Lovecraft, H. P. (2014), *Letters to Elizabeth Toldridge & Anne Tillery Renshaw*, ed. D. E. Schultz and S. T. Joshi, New York: Hippocampus Press.
Lovecraft, H. P. (2015a), *Collected Fiction: A Variorum Edition*, ed. S. T. Joshi, 4 vols, New York: Hippocampus Press.
Lovecraft, H. P. (2015b), *Letters to Robert Bloch and Others*, ed. D. E. Schultz and S. T. Joshi, New York: Hippocampus Press.
Lovecraft, H. P. (2016), *Letters to F. Lee Baldwin, Duane W. Rimel, and Nils Frome*, ed. D. E. Schultz and S. T. Joshi, New York: Hippocampus Press.
Lovecraft, H. P. (2017), *Letters to C. L. Moore and Others*, ed. D. E. Schultz and S. T. Joshi, New York: Hippocampus Press.
Lovecraft, H. P. (2020), *Letters to Rheinhart Kleiner and Others*, ed. S. T. Joshi and D. E. Schulz, New York: Hippocampus Press.
Lovecraft, H. P. and C. A. Smith (2017), *Dawnward Spire, Lonely Hill: The Letters of H.P. Lovecraft and Clark Ashton Smith*, ed. D. E. Schultz and S. T. Joshi, New York: Hippocampus Press.
Luxemburg, R. (2003), *The Accumulation of Capital*, trans. A. Schwartzchild, New York: Routledge.
Machen, A. (2011), *The White People and Other Weird Stories*, ed. S. T. Joshi, New York: Penguin.
Marx, K. (1973), *The Revolutions of 1848: Political Writings Volume 1*, trans. D. Fernbach, New York: Penguin.
Marx, K. (1974), *Early Writings*, trans. R. Livingston and G. Benton, New York: Penguin.
Melville, H. (1983), *Pierre, Israel Potter, the Piazza Tales, the Confidence-Man, Billy Budd*, ed. H. Hayford, New York: Library of America.
Mencken, H. L. (1913), *Friedrich Nietzsche*, New York: Routledge, 1993.
Michelson, A. A. (1896), "Schools of Arts, Literature and Sciences—Courses of Instruction: Department of Physics," in The University of Chicago's *Annual Register July 1895–July 1896*, Chicago: University of Chicago Press. 159–62.
Miéville, C. (2002a), "And Yet: The Antinomies of William Hope Hodgson," in Hodgson, *The House on the Borderland and Other Novels*, London: Gollancz. vii–ix.
Miéville, C. (2002b), *The Scar*, New York: Ballantine.
Miéville, C. (2005), Introduction to H.P. Lovecraft, *At the Mountains of Madness: The Definitive Edition*, New York: Modern Library. xi–xxv.
Miéville, C. (2008), "M.R. James and the Quantum Vampire: Weird; Hauntological: Versus and/or and and/or or?" *Collapse* IV (May): 105–28.

Miéville, C. (2009a), "Weird Fiction," in *The Routledge Companion to Science Fiction*, ed. M. Bould, A. M. Butler, A. Roberts, and S. Vint, New York: Routledge. 510–15.
Miéville, C. (2009b), "Afterword: Cognition as Ideology, a Dialectic of SF Theory," in *Red Planets: Marxism and Science Fiction*, ed. M. Bould and Miéville, Middletown, CT: Wesleyan University Press. 231–48.
Miéville, C. (2012), "On Monsters: Or, Nine or More (Monstrous) Not Cannies," *Journal of the Fantastic in the Arts* 23 (3): 377–92.
Miéville, C. (2016), "Morbid Symptoms: An Interview with China Miéville," by B. Noys and T. S. Murphy, *Genre: Forms of Discourse and Culture* 49 (2) (July), special issue on *Old and New Weird*: 199–211.
Milner, A. (2009), "Utopia and Science Fiction Revisited," in *Red Planets: Marxism and Science Fiction*, ed. M. Bould and C. Miéville, Middletown: Wesleyan University Press. 213–30.
Moorcock, M. (2004), *Wizardry and Wild Romance: A Study of Epic Fantasy*, Austin, TX: MonkeyBrain.
Moorcock, M. (2008), *Elric: The Stealer of Souls*, New York: Del Rey.
Moorcock, M. (2013), *Hawkmoon: Count Brass*, London: Gollancz.
Moore, C. L. and H. Kuttner (1943), *Earth's Last Citadel*, New York: Ace Books, 1964. Originally published in *Argosy*.
Moskowitz, S., ed. (1996), *Terrors of the Sea: Unpublished Fantasies by William Hope Hodgson*, Hampton Falls, NH: Donald M. Grant.
Murphy, T. S. (2009), "Random Insect Doom: The Pulp Science Fiction of *Naked Lunch*," in *Naked Lunch@50: Anniversary Essays*, ed. O. Harris and I. MacFadyen, Carbondale: Southern Illinois University Press. 223–32.
Murphy, T. S. (2019), "William Morris and the Counter-Tradition of Materialist Fantasy," *Journal of the Fantastic in the Arts* 30 (#3): 312–30.
Nagel, E. and J. R. Newman (1958), *Gödel's Proof*, New York: New York University Press.
Nevala-Lee, A. (2018), *Astounding: John W. Campbell, Isaac Asimov, Robert A. Heinlein, L. Ron Hubbard, and the Golden Age of Science Fiction*, New York: Dey St.
Newell, J. (2020), *A Century of Weird Fiction 1832–1937: Disgust, Metaphysics and the Aesthetics of Cosmic Horror*, Cardiff: University of Wales Press.
Nietzsche, F. (1968), *Basic Writings*, ed. and trans. W. Kaufmann, New York: Random House.
Nietzsche, F. (1969), *Selected Letters*, ed. and trans. C. Middleton, New York: Hackett.
Nietzsche, F. (1983), *Untimely Meditations*, trans. R. J. Hollingdale, Cambridge: Cambridge University Press.
Noakes, R. (2004), "Spiritualism, Science and the Supernatural in Mid-Victorian Britain," in *The Victorian Supernatural*, ed. N. Brown, C. Burdett, and P. Thurschwell, Cambridge: Cambridge University Press. 23–43.
Noys, B., and T. S. Murphy (2016), "Introduction: Old and New Weird," *Genre: Forms of Discourse and Culture* 49 (2) (July), special issue on *Old and New Weird*: 117–34.
Pater, W. (1980), *The Renaissance: Studies in Art and Poetry: The 1893 Text*, ed. D. L. Hill, Berkeley: University of California Press.
Poe, E. (1984a), *Poetry and Tales*, ed. P. F. Quinn, New York: Library of America.
Poe, E. (1984b), *Essays and Reviews*, ed. G. R. Thompson, New York: Library of America.
Popper, K. R. (1959), *The Logic of Scientific Discovery*, New York: Routledge. German edition 1934.
Rabinowitz, P. (2002), *Black and White Noir: America's Pulp Modernism*, New York: Columbia University Press.

Rieder, J. (2008), *Colonialism and the Emergence of Science Fiction*, Middletown: Wesleyan University Press.
Roberts, A. (1999), *Romantic and Victorian Long Poems: A Guide*, Brookfield: Ashgate.
Roberts, A. (2005), *The History of Science Fiction*, New York: Palgrave.
Robertson, A., ed. (2003), *Night Lands* Volume I: *Eternal Love*, Doylestown, PA: Betancourt & Co.
Robertson, A., ed. (2007), *Night Lands* Volume II: *Nightmares of the Fall*, Brighton: Three Legged Fox Books.
Robertson, B. J. (2016), "*A Place I Have Never Seen*: Possibilities and Impossibilities, Genre and Politics in China Miéville's *The Scar*," *Journal of the Fantastic in the Arts* 27 (#1): 68–88.
Robertson, B. J. (2018), *None of This Is Normal: The Fiction of Jeff VanderMeer*, Minneapolis: University of Minnesota Press.
Roskill, M. (1997), *The Languages of Landscape*, University Park: Penn State University Press.
Sapir, E. (1968), "The Status of Linguistics as a Science," in *Selected Writings of Edward Sapir in Language, Culture and Personality*, ed. D. G. Mandelbaum, Berkeley: University of California Press. 160–6.
Sawyer, A. (2014), "Time Machines Go Both Ways: Past and Future in H.G. Wells and W.H. Hodgson," in *William Hope Hodgson: Voices from the Borderland*, ed. M. Berutti, S. T. Joshi, and S. Gafford, New York: Hippocampus Press. 169–81.
Serres, M. (1974), *Jouvences sur Jules Verne*, Paris: Editions du Minuit.
Shaviro, S. (2015), *Discognition*, London: Repeater Books.
Shiel, M. P. (2012), *The Purple Cloud*, ed. J. Sutherland, New York: Penguin.
Shklovsky, V. (1965), "Art as Technique," in *Russian Formalist Criticism: Four Essays*, trans. L. T. Lemon and M. J. Reis, Lincoln: University of Nebraska Press. 3–24.
Sinclair, I. (1990), "An Aberrant Afterword: Blowing Dust in the House of Incest," in Hodgson, *The House on the Borderland*, London: Grafton. 179–88.
Sorensen, L. (2010), "A Weird Modernist Archive: Pulp Fiction, Pseudobiblia, H.P. Lovecraft," *Modernism/Modernity* 17 (#3): 501–22.
Spinoza, B. (1985, 2016), *Collected Works*, 2 vols, ed. and trans. Edwin Curley, Princeton: Princeton University Press.
Stableford, B. (1985), *Scientific Romance in Britain 1850–1950*, New York: St. Martin's Press.
Stableford, B. (1987), "The Composition of *The House on the Borderland*," in *William Hope Hodgson: Voyages and Visions*, ed. I. Bell, Oxford: Bell & Sons. 29–36.
Stapledon, O. (2004), *Star Maker*, ed. P. A. McCarthy, Middletown: Wesleyan University Press.
"Sterling, Bruce," entry in *The Encyclopedia of Science Fiction*. Available online: https://www.sf-encyclopedia.com/entry/sterling_bruce.
Stevens, W. (1997), *Collected Poetry and Prose*, ed. F. Kermode and J. Richardson, New York: Library of America.
Stoddard, J. (1998), *The High House*, London: Earthlight.
Stoddard, J. (2000), *The False House*, New York: Warner Books.
Stoddard, J. (2011), *The Night Land: A Story Retold*, Petersfield: Ransom House.
Stoddard, J. (2015), *Evenmere*, Petersfield: Ransom House.
Strugatsky, A. and B. (2012), *Roadside Picnic*, trans. O. Bormashenko, Chicago: Chicago Review Press.
Suvin, D. (1979), *Metamorphoses of Science Fiction: On the Poetics and History of a Literary Genre*, New Haven: Yale University Press.

Suvin, D. (1988), *Positions and Presuppositions in Science Fiction*, Kent, OH: Kent State University Press.
Tauber, A. I. (2009), "Freud's Philosophical Path: From a Science of Mind to a Philosophy of Human Being," *Scandinavian Psychoanalytic Review* 32: 32–43.
Thacker, E. (2011), *In the Dust of This Planet: Horror of Philosophy*, vol.1, Winchester, UK: Zero Books.
Tolkien, J. R. R. (1954), *The Lord of the Rings*, Boston: Houghton Mifflin.
Tolkien, J. R. R. (1966), "On Fairy Stories," in *The Tolkien Reader*, New York: Ballantine. 33–99.
Tolkien, J. R. R. (1977), *The Silmarillion*, Boston: Houghton Mifflin.
Valentine, M. (2014), "A Home on the Borderlands: William Hope Hodgson and Borth," *Sargasso: The Journal of William Hope Hodgson Studies* 2: 79–89.
VanderMeer, J. (2006), *City of Saints and Madmen*, New York: Bantam/Spectra. Introduction by M. Moorcock.
VanderMeer, J. (2014), *Area X: The Southern Reach*, New York: Farrar, Straus & Giroux.
Wallen, M. (2021), *Squid*, London: Reaktion Books.
Wellmer, A. (1971), "The Latent Positivism of Marx's Philosophy of History," in Wellmer, *Critical Theory of Society*, trans. J. Cumming, New York: Seabury Press. 67–119.
Wells, H. G. (1907), "The So-Called Science of Sociology," *Sociological Papers* 3: 357–69.
Wells, H. G. (1934), *The Time Machine* in *Seven Famous Novels*, New York: Alfred A. Knopf.
Wells, H. G. (1952), "The Star," in Wells, *28 Science Fiction Stories*, New York: Dover. 680–91.
Wells, H. G. (2005), *The Shape of Things to Come*, New York: Penguin.
Wheatley, D. (1938), *Uncharted Seas*, London: Hutchinson.
Wheatley, D. (1978), *The Time Has Come: The Memoirs of Dennis Wheatley* vol.2: *Officer and Temporary Gentleman 1914–1919*, London: Hutchinson.
Wheatley, D. (1979), *The Time Has Come: The Memoirs of Dennis Wheatley* vol.3: *Drink and Ink 1919-1977*, London: Hutchinson.
Whitehead, A. N. (1978), *Process and Reality*, corrected edition, ed. D. R. Griffin and D. W. Sherburne, New York: Free Press.
Whitman, W. (1982), *Poetry and Prose*, ed. J. Kaplan, New York: Library of America.
Whorf, B. L. (1956), *Language, Thought & Reality: Selected Writings*, ed. J. B. Carroll, Cambridge: MIT Press.
Wilson, E. (1950), *Classics and Commercials: A Literary Chronicle of the Forties*, London: Allen.
Wright, J. C. (2014), *Awake in the Night Land*, Kouvala, Finland: Castalia House.

Index

ab-human 22, 25, 27–8, 42, 46–8, 95, 118, 121, 123–4, 142–3, 152, 160–5, 168, 174, 176, 179
abyssal time xxvii–xxviii, 102, 125, 128, 129–32, 134, 137, 140, 142–3, 144, 148, 158–60, 164, 166–7, 169, 173–4
aesthetics xx, 2–4, 6, 18, 49, 72, 81, 89–90, 108, 134, 145
Agamben, Giorgio xxvii, 129–31, 141–2, 159, 166–7
Albritton, Claude C. 127, 138–9
Alder, Emily xiv, 5, 20, 25, 89, 99–100, 107, 110, 113, 135–7, 151, 155, 161, 167
Aldiss, Brian 173
Anders, Charlie Jane xxviii, 176–8
anethical 14, 16, 18, 20, 86–7, 92, 95, 106, 109, 117, 126
anthropocentrism xx, xxvi, 13, 16, 84, 141
apocalypse 13, 85, 96, 105–6, 129, 142, 153, 163
apostle 129, 142–3, 164–5, 167
Aristotle xxiv, 137
astronomy 2, 7, 83, 137–8, 177
atheism 1, 14, 20, 65, 92, 100–1, 105, 131, 137, 142

Baker, Phil 171
Ballard, J. G. 49, 173
Bear, Greg xxviii, 175–7
Bell, Ian 43
Benjamin, Walter 130–1, 142, 159, 166, 168
Bergson, Henri 6, 155
Bierce, Ambrose xv–xvi
Bignell, Jonathan 134
biology 2, 5, 20, 22, 24, 32, 99, 139, 165, 177
Blackness xvii, 31–2, 39, 51, 60–2, 171. *See also* ethnicity, race

Blackwood, Algernon xv–xvii, xx, 1, 5, 17–19, 86
Blavatsky, H.P. 151. *See also* Theosophy
Bloch, Ernst xxi–xxv, 63, 105–6
Bloch, Robert xv–xvi, 32
body building. *See* physical culture
Bohr, Niels 10–11, 19
Bourdieu, Pierre xix
Brontë, Emily 33, 37
Buddhism 134, 151
Budrys, Algis 82
Burchfield, Joe D. 138–9
Burke, Edmund 43, 153
Burkett, Delbert 105
Butler, Judith 77
Byron, George Gordon (Lord) 75, 148

Campbell, John W. 4, 6
capitalism xx, 4, 12, 15, 28, 142, 168, 177
Carter, Lin 45, 47
cartography 81–2, 102, 121, 123
Cawthorn, James 43, 173–4
chemistry 7, 9, 20, 57, 98
China 58–60, 171
Christianity xiv, 13–17, 32, 53–4, 92–3, 99–101, 105, 108, 129, 137, 148–51
Clarke, Arthur C. 82, 176
class xviii–xx, xxvii, 29, 33, 37–8, 41, 42, 49, 55, 65, 131, 140–2, 168, 179
cognition xxvi, 3–7, 10, 12–14, 16–18, 28, 42, 50, 82–3, 85–7, 109, 119, 125–6, 128, 129, 166
cognitive mapping xxvii, 82, 87
Coleridge, Samuel Taylor xiv, 144
Comte, Auguste 7–9, 11–12, 18
copyright xviii, 180
Corben, Richard 179–80
cosmology xxvii, 2, 12, 22, 24, 112, 127, 132, 135, 137, 139–40, 148, 151, 177

crossdressing 24, 75–7
Crossley, Robert 173
cryptogams 99, 107

Da Vinci, Leonardo 68–71
Darwin, Charles 138, 149
Darwinism 8, 25, 137, 149
Davidson, Brett 48, 136, 163
decognition xxvi–xxvii, 3–5, 8, 11–14, 16, 18, 20, 87, 99, 106, 116, 119, 126, 128
    decognitive mapping xxvii, 82–3, 86, 95
de la Durantaye, Leland 131, 142
de la Mare, Walter xv–xvi
Delany, Samuel R. 14, 29
Deleuze, Gilles 6, 13–14, 16, 83, 151
Derleth, August xvi, 43, 47
Derrida, Jacques 12
determinism 6, 10–11
dialect 36–8, 49, 55, 65
dialectic xxiv, 17, 37, 118–19, 166
Dickie, Margaret 145
Doyle, Arthur Conan xix, 54
Dunsany, Lord (Edward John Moreton Drax Plunkett) xv–xvi, xix, 19
dystopia 9, 159

Eden 100–1, 106, 161
education xiv, xviii–xix, 31, 35–8, 139
Einstein, Albert 10, 19
Ekman, Stefan 83
Engels, Friedrich 14–16
England 13, 17, 25, 31, 37–8, 52–7, 58–9, 67, 75, 109, 138, 141, 151
entropy 23, 125, 154, 168, 172
epistemology xx, 11–13, 18, 23, 28, 82–3, 85–7, 151, 159
eschatology 14, 19, 93, 137, 139–40, 151, 159
ethics xxvii, 3, 6–7, 13–14, 16–17, 33, 36–7, 39, 41, 67–8, 83–7, 91, 126, 128, 145, 151–2, 155, 165. *See also* anethical, morality
ethnicity xxvii, 28–9, 51–2, 56, 62, 171. *See also* Blackness, race
eucatastrophe 13, 84, 125. *See also* redemption
Evans, Arthur B. 8–9

Everts, R. Alain xxi, xxiii, 66, 110
evolution xxvii, 2, 20, 22, 25, 86, 113, 137, 141, 149, 154–5, 162–3, 165. *See also* Darwinism

fantastika 4, 18–19, 35, 139
fantasy xiv, xix, xxvi, 1–4, 7, 13–18, 29, 65, 72–4, 81, 83–6, 118, 123, 128, 174
fear xv, xxi–xxii, xxiv, 2, 15, 17, 32, 36, 53, 92, 105, 107, 114, 121, 140, 149–50, 154, 168, 174, 180
femininity 64, 66–7, 69, 77, 79. *See also* gender, women
Fermi Paradox 176–7
film 81, 134, 170–1, 178–9
Finney, Charles Grandison 84–5
First World War, the xiv, xix, 4, 28, 32, 148, 170, 175
Fisher, Mark 49
Foucault, Michel 27
Frank, Armin Paul 154
Frank, Jane 28, 64, 90, 145, 157
Freedman, Carl xxiv, 2, 4, 9, 82
Freud, Sigmund 8, 116
future xxi–xxii, xxiv–xxv, 8–10, 17, 21, 25, 34, 35, 85–7, 89, 105, 115, 117–19, 122, 127, 129, 131, 134, 139–42, 149, 153–4, 158–60, 163, 168, 172–5

Gafford, Sam xiv, xviii, xxi, 44, 64–7, 72, 89, 107, 116, 173
Gaskell, Elizabeth 75–6
gender xvii, xxvii, 31, 33, 64–70, 73–9, 148, 172, 173, 176, 179. *See also* femininity, masculinity, sexuality
genre xiv–xv, xvii, xix, xxvi, 3, 6, 8, 13, 18, 24, 31, 49, 69, 81–3, 86–7, 93, 97, 125, 128, 139–40, 144, 168, 172–3, 176, 179
geography xxiii–xxiv, xxvii, 82, 84–7, 110, 117, 120–3
geology xxiv, 2, 121, 124, 127, 138–9, 141, 160
Gernsback, Hugo 4, 6
Gödel, Kurt 11
gothic xv, 3–4, 13, 17–18, 108, 137, 179

Haefele, John D. 172
Harrison, M. John xxv, xxviii, 173–5
heat death 24, 164
Heidegger, Martin 161–2
Heisenberg, Werner 10–11, 19
Hetzel, Pierre-Jules 9
Higgins, David M. 125
Hinduism 53, 111, 133, 134, 151
Hinton, Joseph 110
history xiv, xvi–xviii, xx, xxii, xxiv, xxvii, 1–2, 4–5, 6–7, 13–18, 29, 31–2, 34, 47, 75, 81, 83, 86, 117–22, 127–9, 131, 138–9, 141–2, 145, 158–9, 166–7
Hitchcock, Alfred 178
Hodgson, Bessie Farnsworth (wife) xxi, 74, 79, 145, 170, 180
Hodgson, Lissie (mother) xviii, xix, xxi, 65, 93
Hodgson, Samuel (father) xviii, xxi, 66, 76, 90, 101, 105–6, 110, 132, 150
Hodgson, William (grandfather) xxi, 101, 105
Hodgson, William Hope
　death xix, 11, 93, 148, 170, 175
　early life xviii–xix, xxi, 61, 76, 105, 110, 114
　sailing career xix, xxiii, 26–7, 40, 90, 146
　writing career xix, xxi, xxv, 44, 47, 52, 64–6, 71–4, 79, 102, 111, 118, 120, 127, 137, 144–5, 157, 170, 180
　works:
　　The Boats of the "Glen Carrig" xxi, xxvii, 45, 62, 78, 89, 100, 102, 106–9, 127, 172
　　Captain Gault stories 58–60, 64, 67–72, 90, 180
　　Carnacki the Ghostfinder stories xix, 20–4, 53, 58, 91, 94, 97, 115, 171–3, 179–80
　　"The Derelict" 20, 22, 24, 97–101, 156, 170, 172, 175
　　The Ghost Pirates xxi, 25–7, 39, 44, 64, 89, 93–6, 106, 171–2
　　The House on the Borderland xiv, xvi, xxi, xxvii, 19, 22, 24, 44, 46, 51–2, 66, 72, 78, 89, 102, 106, 110–16, 120, 125, 127, 132–7, 143, 149, 151, 156–68, 170, 173–4, 176, 179
　　The Night Land xiv, xix, xxi, xxvii, 19, 21–2, 25, 35–6, 42–5, 47–8, 56, 64, 71–2, 78–9, 87–8, 102, 104–7, 110, 112, 116–25, 127, 132, 143, 149, 151–5, 157, 165, 168, 170, 172–6, 178
　　"The Voice in the Night" 24, 99–101, 104, 107, 115, 170, 172, 175, 178–9
　　The Voice of the Ocean xxviii, 104–6, 145, 148–50, 152–5
Honda, Ishiro 178–9
hope xxi–xxvi, 17, 63, 105, 118, 119, 132, 160, 168, 180
Horkheimer, Max, and T.W. Adorno 11
horror xiv–xvii, xxiv, xxvi, 1–4, 13, 17–18, 25, 32, 66, 115, 128, 174, 179–80
Howard, Robert E. xv, xix– xxi, 31, 55–6, 62, 85, 145
humanism xxi–xxiii, xxvii–xxviii, 105, 137, 141, 168. *See also* ab-human
Hurley, Kelly 22, 31, 42, 64, 79
hybridity 22, 41, 43, 160, 165, 176. *See also* ab-human, mutation

idealism 1, 13, 17–18, 28, 145
ideology xix–xx, 4, 6, 8, 13, 29, 31, 34, 54, 125, 145, 178
imperialism xxvii, 8, 12–13, 14–15, 27–8, 31, 51, 54, 56, 60, 62, 85, 125
indeterminacy xxii, 6
India 52–8
Ireland 51–2, 110, 115, 132

James, M.R. xv, xvi, 49
Jameson, Fredric xxii, xxiv–xxv, 9, 13, 82
Jews 32, 57–8
Joshi, S.T. xiv, xvii–xviii, 1, 32, 173

Kant, Immanuel 3, 128
Kelvin, William Thomson and First Baron 2, 9–10, 83, 138–41, 163
Kernahan, Coulson 73, 79, 89, 102, 106, 180

Killingsworth, M. Jimmie 147
Kipling, Rudyard 51, 54
knowledge xxi, xxvii, 1, 3, 5, 7–8, 10–12, 14, 16–17, 19, 23, 39, 82, 86, 100, 111, 118–19, 122, 125, 128, 142, 159–65, 169
Koenig, Herman Charles xvi, 47, 168, 172
Kolakowski, Leszek 6–7, 11
Kuttner, Henry xxviii, 172, 175–7

labor xviii–xxiii, xxvi, 1–2, 15, 23–9, 31, 41, 42, 49, 67, 149, 159
landscape xxiv, xxvii, 21, 35, 43, 81–8, 107, 110, 116, 118, 120–2, 124, 161, 173, 179
language xxviii, 2, 12–13, 17–18, 35–40, 43–5, 47–50, 57–8, 66, 69, 117, 121, 153, 157–8, 161–2, 165, 174
Le Guin, Ursula K. 14, 29, 81
Lefebvre, Martin 82
Leiber, Fritz xvi, 172–3
Lem, Stanisław 82–3, 87, 154
Lenzer, Gertrud 7–8, 12
Lewis, C.S. xiv, xix
liberalism xx, 27–8
Long, Frank Belknap xv, 144
Lovecraft, H.P. xv–xvii, xix–xxi, 1–3, 6, 17–21, 23, 25–6, 28–9, 31–3, 35, 37, 42–3, 47–9, 51, 59, 62, 64–5, 79, 86–7, 96, 106, 108, 117, 128, 134, 144–5, 148, 164, 168, 171–2, 176
Lyell, Charles 2, 127, 138–9
Lynch, Kevin 82

Macdonald, George xiv, xix, 139
Machen, Arthur xiv–xviii, xix–xx, 1, 5, 17–19, 28, 85–6
mapping xxvii, 5, 81–6, 89, 110, 116, 122–3. *See also* cognitive mapping, decognitive mapping
Marx, Karl 8, 14–16, 131
Marxism xx, 3–4, 14–16, 130–1
masculinity 40, 55, 57, 64, 77–9. *See also* gender
Masefield, John 90

materialism xx–xxii, 1–2, 6, 13, 15, 17–23, 25–9, 33, 46, 49, 54, 68, 83–4, 92, 94, 97, 109, 131, 137, 149, 154–6, 173
Melville, Herman 26, 91, 108
Mencken, Henry Louis (H.L.) 17, 20
merchant navy xiv, xx, 27, 36, 62, 64–5, 90, 145
messianic time xxvii, 129–31, 141–3, 163–4, 166
metaphysics xvii, xx, xxvi, 7, 12, 14, 20, 45–7, 103, 106, 129, 136–7, 145–6, 149–50, 153, 173
Michelson, Albert A. 8–10
Miéville, China xvii, xxviii, 1, 3–4, 12, 14, 22–3, 33, 35, 42, 86, 90, 108, 116, 128, 168, 176
Milner, Andrew 6
modernism xxvi, 4, 8, 49, 145, 154. *See also* pulp modernism
monster. *See* ab-human, cryptogams, swine-things, Watchers, weed men
Moorcock, Michael 14, 29, 43, 49, 84–5, 173–5
Moore, Alan 180
Moore, Catherine L. xv, xvi, xxviii, 33, 172, 175–7
morality xxvi, 5–7, 13–19, 21–2, 60, 66, 68–9, 83–7, 92–3, 100, 109, 125, 129, 151, 165. *See also* anethical, ethics
Morris, William xiv, xix, 14–16, 29, 35, 44, 83–5, 139, 158, 174
Moskowitz, Sam xxiii, 40, 58, 61, 64–6, 74, 90, 93, 170, 173
Murphy, Timothy S. 2, 14, 49, 84
mutation 20, 24, 87, 160, 165, 168, 172, 176, 179. *See also* ab-human

narrative xiv, xxiii–xxiv, xxvi–xxvii, 4, 12–13, 16, 18, 20, 26, 47, 49, 58, 79, 81–4, 86–7, 89, 91, 95, 99, 101–2, 106–7, 116, 117–18, 125–6, 128, 129–30, 132–4, 137, 139–40, 143, 144–5, 148, 158, 164, 167, 176
Nesbit, Edith 29, 52

Newell, Jonathan 51, 100
Nietzsche, Friedrich xvi–xvii, xx, xxv, 6–7, 15–17, 19–21, 83, 151–2, 155
nihilism xxi–xxii, xxviii, 33, 92, 168–9, 176
Noakes, Richard 137
nominalism 6, 161–2, 165

objectivity xxi–xxiii, 16, 125, 162
occultism 5, 20, 113, 170–1
ontology xx, xxii, xxiv, 11–12, 22–4, 26

Pater, Walter 69, 72
phenomenology xx, 23–6, 28, 151
philosophy xiv, xxi, xxvi, 1–2, 5–8, 12, 14–17, 23, 28–9, 33, 69, 72, 141
physical culture xix, xxiii, 40, 60, 64
physics 5, 7–10, 19
Plato xv, xxiv
pluralism 6, 16–17
Poe, Edgar Allan xviii, 18–20, 107, 135, 146–7
poetry 18–19, 25, 28, 31–2, 51, 64–6, 71, 90, 104, 132, 135, 139, 144–56, 157
politics xvii, xx, 1–2, 8, 14–15, 28–9, 31, 33–4, 51, 60, 67, 86, 131, 141
Popper, Karl 11
positivism xxvi, 5–13, 16, 18–19, 123, 140, 142
Pound, Ezra 28, 145
poverty xvii–xx, 20, 33
prophet 129, 137, 141–2, 153, 160, 163
psychoanalysis 13, 117
publishing business xviii, xix, 9, 45, 58, 74, 79, 91, 101, 107, 170–1
pulp magazines xv, 4, 6, 56–7, 172. *See also Weird Tales* (magazine)
pulp modernism 49, 145

quantum theory 10–11, 19, 176

Rabinowitz, Paula 49
race xvii, 31–3, 51, 64, 171
racism xvii, 29, 31–3, 39, 51–2, 57–8, 61, 171–2

rationalism xxiv, xxvii–xxviii, 2–5, 14, 17–18, 53, 86, 93, 97, 115, 118, 139–42, 168, 174
realism, literary xv, xxvii, 24, 26, 27, 36, 42, 44, 67, 73, 81, 89–90, 145
reason xxi, 5, 7–8, 12, 18, 53, 119, 128, 140–1, 152, 163, 166
redemption xxiii, xxvii, 13–14, 17, 22, 83–7, 106, 109, 123, 125–6, 128, 129, 142, 149, 163, 166–7. *See also* eucatastrophe
reincarnation 25, 78, 106, 118, 149, 151, 153, 155, 157, 166–7
relativity 10–11, 19
religion xviii, 14, 20, 36, 47, 51, 53–4, 92, 106, 125, 130, 138, 150–2, 160, 173, 179
Revelstroke, Simon 179–80
Rieder, John 125
Roberts, Adam 145
Robertson, Andy 47–8, 180
Robertson, Benjamin J. 128, 132, 162, 167, 176

sailors xiv, xx, xxiii, 20, 23–8, 37, 39–41, 57, 60–2, 76–7, 90–4, 96–104, 107–9, 146, 176
Sapir, Edward 12
Sargasso Sea xxiv, xxvii, 73–4, 89, 101–3, 106–9, 110–11, 171, 176
Sawyer, Andy 44, 49, 132, 134, 165
science 1, 4–9, 11–13, 18, 20, 21, 25, 83, 106, 110, 117, 137–9, 162, 163
science fiction xiv–xv, xix, xxiv, xxvi–xxviii, 1–6, 8–9, 13, 15, 18, 29, 44, 48, 50, 81–3, 85–7, 118, 123, 125, 128, 129, 137, 159, 172–4
scientific romance xiv, 6, 15, 18, 128, 137, 139, 141, 173
Scrope, George Poulett 127
seascape xxiv, 82–3, 86, 89
Serres, Michel 8
sexuality xxvii, 33, 57, 79, 171. *See also* gender
Shaviro, Steven 4–5
Shelley, Mary 81, 83
Shiel, Matthew Phipps (M.P.) xiv–xvii, xix–xx

Shklovsky, Viktor 49
Sinclair, Iain 51, 114, 179–80
Smith, Clark Ashton xiv–xvi, xix–xx, 86, 144, 148, 172, 174
sociology xiv, 7–9, 11
Sorensen, Leif 49
Space. *See* cartography, geography, landscape, mapping, topography
Spencer, Herbert 8–9
Spinoza, Benedictus de (Baruch) xvi, 13–14, 16, 23, 83, 151–3, 155
spiritualism 25, 110, 137, 151. *See also* Theosophy
St. Paul 101, 129–30
Stableford, Brian 111, 135–6, 157
Stapledon, Olaf xix, 148–9, 173
Stevens, Wallace 154
Stevenson, Robert Louis xv, 17, 139
Stoker, Bram xv, 17, 139
Stoddard, James 25, 42, 45–8
Strugatsky, Arkady and Boris 82–3, 87, 177
subjectivity xx, xxii, xxviii, 4–5, 15, 27–8, 73–4, 116–17, 162, 166
supernatural xv, 3, 14, 17, 20, 52, 60–1, 91, 132, 134, 137
Suvin, Darko xxiv, 3–4, 6, 9, 13, 82
swine-things 24, 51–2, 112–15, 133, 135–6, 143, 164, 180

technocracy 9, 33
technology 9, 11, 89, 117–18, 162, 174, 177
temporality xxvii, 25, 47, 113, 117, 127–8, 131–4, 137–9, 147–8, 151, 155, 157, 164–6
television 33, 178–9
Thacker, Eugene 20
Theosophy 106, 135, 137, 151
thermodynamics 2, 22, 138, 156, 163, 165
time. *See* abyssal time, future, history, messianic time, temporality, untimely
Tolkien, J.R.R. xiv, xix, 13–14, 35, 83–5, 125, 174

topography 82, 95, 107, 111, 121
Twain, Mark 37, 75

United States xvii, xviii, 6, 51–2, 60, 67–9, 87, 144
universality xxiv, xxvi, 4–7, 9–11, 13–19, 83, 125, 153, 165
untimely xxv, xxvii, 34, 79, 87
Ussher, James 137–8
utopia xxiii–xxiv, xxviii, 6, 9, 86, 103, 141

Valentine, Mark 120
Valentinus 105–6
VanderMeer, Jeff xvii, xxviii, 86–7, 128, 174–5
Verne, Jules xiv, xix, 6, 8–9, 82, 89, 108, 139
vitalism 122, 155, 161
Von Mädler, Johann Heinrich 135

Wallen, Martin 108
Watchers 112, 120–1, 123, 161–2, 175
weed men 62, 106, 108–9, 176
weird fiction xiv–xv, xvii–xx, xxvi, 1–8, 13–14, 16–29, 31, 33–4, 40, 42, 47–9, 81, 85–7, 95, 98–9, 127–8, 129, 131, 144–5, 151, 159, 167–9, 176
    New Weird 86, Old Weird xvii, xx, 31, 33, 85–6
Weird Tales (magazine) xv, 173
Wells, H.G. 6, 9, 82, 111, 134, 139–42, 159
    The Time Machine xiv, 9, 82, 111–13, 115, 134–5, 138–42, 153, 159, 164, 166, 168, 176
Wheatley, Dennis 170–2
Whitman, Walt 147, 153–4, 156
Whorf, Benjamin Lee 12
Wilson, Edmund 48
women 29, 33, 42, 64–70, 76–7, 163. *See also* femininity

Ypres, battle of xix, 170, 175. *See also* First World War, the

www.ingramcontent.com/pod-product-compliance
Lightning Source LLC
Chambersburg PA
CBHW052111300426
44116CB00010B/1617